Science and the Self

Mary Midgley is one of the most important moral philosophers working today. Over the last thirty years, her writings have informed debates concerning animals, the environment and evolutionary theory. The invited essays in this volume offer critical reflections upon Midgley's work and further developments of her ideas. The contributors include many of the leading commentators on her work, including distinguished figures from the disciplines of philosophy, biology, and ethology. The range of topics includes the moral status of animals, the concept of wickedness, science and mythology, Midgley's relationship to modern moral philosophy, and her relationship with Iris Murdoch. It also includes the first full bibliography of Midgley's writings. The volume is the first major study of its kind and brings together contributions from the many disciplines that Midgley's work has influenced. It provides a clear account of the themes and significance of her work and its implications for ongoing debates about our understanding of our place within the world.

Ian James Kidd is assistant professor at the Department of Philosophy at the University of Nottingham. His work ranges over epistemology, philosophy of medicine, philosophy of religion, and philosophy of science, and includes a number of papers on the authority of science, intellectual virtues, and the nature of a religious life. He was formerly an Addison Wheeler Fellow at the Department of Philosophy at Durham University.

Liz McKinnell is a Teaching Fellow in Philosophy at the University of Durham. She works on areas in applied ethics and political philosophy, including environmental ethics, the moral status of animals and intergenerational justice. She has published on moral obligations to the dead, and on connections between environmental ethics and the philosophy of cognition and biology.

Routledge Studies in Contemporary Philosophy

Science and the Self

Animals, Evolution, and Ethics: Essays
in Honour of Mary Midgley

**Edited by Ian James Kidd
and Liz McKinnell**

Routledge
Taylor & Francis Group

NEW YORK AND LONDON

First published 2016
by Routledge
711 Third Avenue, New York, NY 10017

and by Routledge
2 Park Square, Milton Park, Abingdon, Oxon OX14 4RN

*Routledge is an imprint of the Taylor & Francis Group,
an informa business*

Library of Congress Cataloging-in-Publication Data
Science and the self : animals, evolution, and ethics : essays in honour of
   Mary Midgley / edited by Ian James Kidd and Liz McKinnell. — 1 [edition].
      pages cm. — (Routledge studies in contemporary philosophy ; 70)
   Includes bibliographical references and index.
   1. Philosophy, English—20th century.   2. Philosophy, British—
20th century.   3. Midgley, Mary, 1919–   4. Animals (Philosophy)
5. Human beings.   6. Ethics.   I. Midgley, Mary, 1919– honouree.
II. Kidd, Ian James, 1983– editor.
   B1615.S335 2015
   192—dc23
   2015015870

ISBN: 978-1-138-89838-7 (hbk)
ISBN: 978-1-315-70846-1 (ebk)

Typeset in Sabon
by Apex CoVantage, LLC

MIX
Paper from
responsible sources
FSC   FSC® C013056
www.fsc.org

Printed and bound in Great Britain by
TJ International Ltd, Padstow, Cornwall

For Mary Midgley, naturally

Contents

PART III
Minds, Human and Animal

PART IV
Science and Evolution

PART V
Women and the World

Foreword

For over 60 years, Mary Midgley has worked to lay out an understandable explanation of our place in nature, our place within the greater natural order of things. She has continually stressed the fact that we are creatures of opposites, capable of love, compassion and 'goodness' on the one hand, anger, violence and evil on the other. We are capable of wickedness, which she defines as the absence of good—that is positive qualities such as generosity, compassion and courage. Her view of human nature is sensible and down to earth. She has pointed out that our lives are messy, our values, fears, memories and dreams all mixed together. We are both rational and irrational. We came be highly sophisticated, yet naïve to the point of absurdity. It is so important, she insists, that we recognize all these aspects of our complex selves.

I first became a devotee of Midgley when I read her 1978 book *Beast and Man*. In it she emphasized that 'We are not like animals, we *are* animals [my italics]'—a concept that was still derided by many scientists and philosophers alike. She insisted that an acknowledgement of our kinship with animals should not be considered in any way a 'dent to our pride or status [as human beings]'. This resonated with me as I had been so fiercely criticized, in the 1960s, for writing that we humans are not the only beings on the planet with personalities, minds capable of thinking, and knowing emotions such as joy and sadness, fear and anger. Mary Midgley and I both believed that we humans are part of and not separated from the rest of the animal kingdom. She believed that the behavior of non-human animals was not simply determined by a set of rigid responses to various stimuli. She shared my horror of the reductionist attitude of ethology in the sixties—It was this mentality that allowed research scientists to subject animals to horribly painful experimentation. Indeed, even today there are people who excuse cruelty with the remark 'It's only an animal'.

It was because our beliefs were so similar that Mary Midgley and I arranged to meet. She agreed to come and spend a night with us at my family home in Bournemouth, England. I was eager to learn more about her philosophy and views, and I think she was keen to learn more about chimpanzees, our closest relatives. After all, their behavior, so like our own in so many ways, was providing convincing support for all she believed about our human relationship with other animals. Our discussions were stimulating and rewarding, I think, to both of us. They certainly were to me.

Midgley argues quite fiercely against the 'selfish gene' explanation of behavior, and believes that we do what we do for reasons other than blind obedience to our genes. She sees no reason to deny the value of religion, which might be, she says, one of the ways in which we try to make sense of our lives. Moreover, it does seem, she points out, that there is some sort of tendency, something we might call, somewhat vaguely, a 'life force" that shows a tendency towards the formation of order. She bewails the fact that science and religion have become so polarized. And I remember telling her that my mother, and my mentor Dr. Louis Leakey, saw no conflict between a belief in God, or some kind of Life Force, and a belief in science and evolution.

One of the reasons why I was, from the first, so impressed by her books was not just because of the issues she discussed but because, unlike many philosophers—and many scientists—her writing is not only elegant, but beautifully free of jargon. She can discuss a most complex and profound topic in such a way that her argument is immediately understandable. I hate having to read a sentence three times to get at its meaning. When I read Midgley, one reading is perfectly sufficient. This means, of course, that her books are accessible to the general public as well as academic readers.

Science and the Self: Animals, Ethics, and Evolution: Essays in Honour of Mary Midgley is an important volume as it includes such a diverse array of contributors and covers the main areas that have always interested Mary Midgley: our relationship with animals, ethics, the environment, reductionism in science, religion and evolution, and feminism. It is a fitting tribute to a woman with tireless energy who is still working, still writing, still willing to get involved in debates. I for one salute a truly significant and logical voice that is striving to help us understand who we are and how we should view ourselves in the great scheme of things.

Jane Goodall, Ph.D., DBE
Founder, the Jane Goodall Institute, and
UN Messenger of Peace

Acknowledgements

The Editors are grateful to Mary Midgley for her inspiration, encouragement, and patience and to the contributors for their chapters and cooperation. We are also grateful to the team at Routledge for taking on the volume and for helping us to see it through to completion. Ian's research was funded by an Addison Wheeler Fellowship.

Introduction

Ian James Kidd and Liz McKinnell

IN PRAISE OF MARY MIDGLEY

This volume is written in honour of the British philosopher Mary Midgley. It is difficult to give a neat summary of the content and significance of her work. Many modern academic philosophers are encouraged, in various ways, to concentrate their thinking upon an 'area of specialisation' which they can make their own. It may be a very small area, admitting only of very technical study, intelligible and interesting only to a small community of fellow specialists. Such work has its place, but ought not to be bought at the expense of the 'big picture'—of the capacity to perceive and understand the ways that these specific areas of activity, experience, and concern relate to one another. Midgley is a rare exception to such narrow specialisation, and that is one reason why her work is so distinctive and important, and why we have put together this volume to celebrate and critically engage with it. Indeed, to do justice to her work, our diverse contributors include philosophers, biologists, an animal welfare scientist, a science writer and a polymath.

An efficient way to show the breadth of Midgley's writing is simply to list the topics on which she has written—animals, ecology, ethics, evolution, farming, feminism, the Gaia hypothesis, human nature, science, moral reason, myth and metaphor, personal identity, rationality, wickedness, and the practice and purpose of philosophy, among others. Such interests are reflected in the titles and subtitles of her books, such as *Beast and Man: The Roots of Human Nature*, *Animals and Why They Matter*, *Wickedness*, and *Science as Salvation*. But what is important is not simply that Midgley writes on lots of topics—for any journalist or blogger can do that— but rather that she relates all these specific topics to one another within a broader vision of our place within the world. Animals matter to us, but much of our treatment of them is grotesque; we behave wickedly to beasts as well as to our human peers. Our science matters to us, as a source of knowledge, utility, and prestige, but much of our thinking about it is confused and obscured by scientistic myths. And so on—reflecting the point that local problems are never just local problems. Topics that might seem disparate are complexly related. Ideas that seem at home in one academic discipline have roots that spread into others. Concerns that might seem the preserve of one group of experts might need the energies and insights of many others. Underlying these points is, of course, the hope that, by taking a broad view of our situation, we might be able to find more effective ways of improving it.

A good starting point for this sort of humane philosophical project is the fact that we find ourselves, 'always already', deeply and powerfully related to other things, creatures, places, and ideas. A striking feature of Midgley's writings, reflected in the chapters collected here, is her persistent call for careful sensitivity to the fact that our lives are deeply embedded in, and related to, other creatures, places, and ideas. We are related to the human and non-human animals with whom we share our world—parents, children, colleagues, strangers, birds and beasts—whether in relations of love, care, and dependence, or fear, coldness, and exploitation. We are related to our natural and social environment, messily tangled together as they are, including the far-off wild places we may never set foot in, or the gardens, cities, and places in which we live and work. We are also related, finally, to wider structures of concepts, ideas, and dogmas that, although often implicit and unrecognised, actively organise our experience, thinking, and valuing—a mishmash of scientific, ethical, and imaginative resources that clash, converge, and compel us to organise our lives in different ways. Midgley urges us to attend to these many relations, not just in isolation, but as collective aspects of a wider structure of life. The big picture matters—for without it, we remain blind to the assumptions, expectations, and prejudices that rumble away in the background. If we want to think clearly and act rightly, we can do nothing less.

The call for alertness to the web of relations and inherited ideas that provide the background to our thinking also informs Midgley's conception of the nature of philosophy. Many of the practitioners of that discipline still like to regard their activity as one of cool, detached reflection—looking down from afar on an isolated realm of which they are not a part, appraising but not engaging those busily engaged in its everyday activities. Even if few explicitly avow this ideal, it is still one that influenced the recent history of academic philosophy, and might still play a role today. If it is an ideal on the wane, it is because philosophers increasingly appreciate the fact that engaging with 'big issues' requires us to attend carefully to the work of other fellow enquirers—animal welfare scientists, farmers, environmentalists, and the like. Certainly large areas of philosophy nowadays do actively engage with others, forswearing armchair theorising for fieldwork, case studies, and other opportunities to empirically enrich philosophy by putting it in touch with people, beasts, and ecologies. Such developments were prefigured by Midgley, for since *Beast and Man*—perhaps her most important book—she has engaged with primatologists, ethologists, biologists, psychologists, environmentalists, and others who can ensure that philosophising is rooted in, and responsive to, the real world. If philosophers want to think clearly about our attitudes to animals or to environments or to science, then they ought to take seriously the deliverances of those people—scientists, scholars, activists—whose day-to-work is devoted to understanding them.

An important step towards this vision of philosophy is to rethink some of the attitudes and values that have, over the last century or so, become associated with it. Central among them is the idea that philosophy is an aggressive, agonistic activity in which clever and egotistic pugilists compete in fractious displays of cleverness. Midgley has noted that her own university experience included very little of this competitive cleverness and has opined that it was due to the unusual demographics of Oxford at the time. Most of the men were off to war, leaving behind women and a few men who were, either morally or temperamentally, opposed to the resolution of disagreement by competition. Those women of course included several other luminary figures of twentieth-century British philosophy, such as Elizabeth Anscombe, Philippa Foot, and Iris Murdoch. It is striking that the literary and philosophical writings of these four women are characterised by the sensitivity to the complexities of human relations—of how we actually think, feel, and act towards others.

A sensitivity to others ought to be naturally allied to a determined willingness to engage with attitudes, beliefs, and doctrines that would upset or impugn such sensitivity. Some people are naturally eager to learn from, rather than simply lecture to, others and, being on the side of the angels, we need not worry about them. But of course many people are far less eager, often lapsing into being 'closed off' to ideas, values, and ways of thinking and feeling. Since such people can very easily upset the party, one should be willing to engage in the business of challenging them. Not every slight deserves a scrap, of course, and wisdom dictates that one chooses one's battles. In Midgley's case, her chosen targets are those people—scientists, usually, but often others—who make exaggerated and inflated claims about the nature, scope, and value of science, or, more simply, who proffer *scientism*.

Anyone who reads Midgley will recognise straightaway that she deeply respects the modern sciences and the people who do it—what she is critical of are false ideas about what science is, how it developed, what it can do for us, and how it might fit into the modern world. From the early 1990s, we find a developing account of the role that 'myths' or 'imaginative visions' play in our thinking, including many that are shaped by various broad doctrines that have co-opted certain scientific theories. One myth is that of science as an isolated discipline able to absorb and discharge the purposes once assigned to philosophy, religions, and the arts—of inspiring and guiding our conduct as moral and spiritual beings. Another is the 'atomistic' vision of human beings as isolated, competitive creatures—'solitary selves', governed by rationally determined selfish impulses. No doubt the lives of some people are like this, but not the lives of all people. It is a mark of careful thinking to keep everything in its proper place and not to inflate local predilections into universal truths.

Even if few people really believe such claims, there are still some who evidently do, and those few sometimes have the power or platform to propagandise on behalf of their narrow visions. Midgley observes that these myths, alongside several others, play a role in academic and popular debate on hoary old topics such as science and religion, biotechnology, environmental protection, transhumanism, and other 'big issues'. Even if few really believe them, still they are there, like magnets, dragging our thinking about how to organise our lives and social policies in strange directions. A distraction plays a role in debate, just as much as an argument or a piece of evidence. This being so, one humble but important role for a philosopher is, says Midgley, to try to identify and to expose these myths—clearing the ground, as it were, of rubbish and rubble. That is an important job, to be sure, but not one that everyone is interested to take up. It is therefore worth saying something about Midgley's life and work.

LIFE AND WORK

What follows can be only a brief biographical sketch. Some salient details have been picked out, but will inevitably give a partial and selective account. We recommend that anyone interested in Midgley's life and work should read her memoir *The Owl of Minerva*. For an excellent discussion of Midgley's friendships and philosophical relationships with Anscombe, Foot and Murdoch, we recommend Benjamin Lipscomb's chapter in this volume.

Mary Midgley was born in 1919 to Lesley and Tom Scrutton. Her father was a curate in Dulwich at the time of her birth, before he and the family moved to Cambridge where he took up the role of chaplain at King's College Cambridge. When Midgley was five years old, they moved again to Greenford in Middlesex, where she recalls spending much of her time in the large rectory garden with her brother Hugh, playing with the family dog, building dens and forts, fishing in ponds and streams and playing hide-and-seek. From a very early age onwards, Midgley appears to have been drawn more to the outdoor world, with its propensity to feed and develop curiosity, and to play and artistic endeavours, than she was to the religious way of life that one might expect from a child of the church. It does not seem extravagant to suppose that this early experience has had a profound influence on Midgley's thought: she is comfortable with religious and spiritual views of the world, as she was comfortable with her liberal Anglican background, but is not personally drawn to organised religious structures or creeds, preferring to look to our common lives and our relationships with the animals and ecosystems that surround us.

When she was twelve years old, Midgley moved away to Downe House School, near Newbury, where she further developed her passions for history, poetry, classics and drama. A marvellous photograph in *The Owl of Minerva* shows the young Midgley as the elder brother in John Milton's *Comus*, which (if appearances are reliable) she played with a masculine swagger reminiscent of *The Three Musketeers*. Drama and poetry both provide ways of accessing new imaginative visions and looking at the world from fresh perspectives. In her reading of classics, she discovered how this aspect of life can connect with rational thought. It was her reading of Plato's dialogues that provided an insight that would inform all of her later thinking: 'I was startled at how the arresting imaginative vision, vividly shown in the dramatic setting of the dialogues and in the various myths and metaphors, grew directly out of the sober reasoning and in turn contributed to reshape it. . . . Thought and feeling did not seem to be at odds here. They were collaborating in real harmony.' (OM 62)

After a very brief spell in Vienna, cut short by the terrifying developments in the spring of 1938, Midgley started reading Classics at Somerville College Oxford. Midgley's fellow students included Elizabeth Anscombe, Philippa Foot, Iris Murdoch and Mary Warnock. It seems remarkable that such a crop of impressive philosophers—each in her own way providing formidable challenges to previous ways of thinking about philosophy, all doing much of their work in moral philosophy, and all female—could have come from the same place at the same time. A number of factors might go some way towards explaining this fact. The first was the Second World War. This meant, firstly, that many young men deferred their studies until after the war, allowing female voices to come to the fore with less interruption: 'I do think that a lot of good female thinking is wasted because it simply doesn't get heard. Perhaps women ought to shout louder, but of course there is still the question of whether men are going to listen' (OM, 123–4). This may have been particularly helped by the fact that many of the remaining men at Oxford, as conscientious objectors, were less inclined to regard combat as a model for intellectual debate.

A second effect of the war was a stark awareness of the effects of political ideologies on life and death, and on the day-to-day experience of living. In *The Owl of Minerva*, Midgley talks about the prominent role that politics played in student life. This may have interacted with a second prominent influence on the philosophical culture of Oxford in the late 1930s: the popularity of logical positivism. It seems sorely inadequate to dismiss certain conceptual questions as meaningless when these include questions about moral and political concepts so urgently in need of discussion.

In 1942, Midgley graduated with a first-class degree. For many philosophers, we might expect a smooth trajectory into academia from this point, punctuated with a steady list of publications. However, Midgley's first book, *Beast and Man*, was not published until 1978, when she was already in her fifties. In the intervening period, Midgley worked in the Ministry of Production, taught Classics to schoolchildren, did two years of graduate study, taught philosophy at Reading for four terms, and—not insignificantly—got married and had three children. She married Geoffrey Midgley, a fellow philosopher, and moved to join him in Newcastle, where he taught.

During the early years of her three sons' lives, Midgley began to involve herself in radio and television broadcasts, as well as in reviewing books and writing articles for newspapers and magazines, including for a range of high-brow journals, such as *The Listener* and *The Twentieth Century*. In the mid-1960s, when the boys were getting a bit older, Midgley started teaching half-time at Newcastle University, which had recently become formally independent from the University of Durham. By 1970, her contract was changed to full-time. During this and the ensuing period, Midgley's interest in animals really took off. She read voraciously about animal biology and behaviour, and this gave rise in 1978 to *Beast and Man*, which was immediately well received. From this followed an impressive record of publications (listed in an appendix to this volume).

As Midgley's writing career took off, she took advantage of an offer of early retirement, allowing her more time to work on her publications and to establish herself as a prominent public intellectual. Midgley herself notes that she is fortunate that her career has been able to take the shape that it has, allowing her to combine an impressive career as a philosopher with the demands of parenthood. This pattern is far less achievable in the present academic climate, in which job insecurity and the demand to publish creates pressures on younger thinkers at precisely the stages in their lives when they might have other priorities. Midgley's capacity not only to combine these aspects of life, but to make them beneficial to each other, demonstrates the value of considering philosophers as human beings, and not as writing machines. We might learn similar lessons from Geoffrey Midgley, who, despite publishing little, had an indelible influence on many of his students, as recognised in the many obituaries following his death in 1997. The couple appear to have been joyfully compatible, sharing interests, humour and not least a humane approach to the study and teaching of philosophy.

Since Geoffrey's death, Midgley has continued to publish at an impressive rate, publishing dozens of articles for periodicals, including *The Guardian*, *New Scientist*, and *Philosophy Now*, as well as giving many interviews for newspapers and radio. Combined with her steady stream of books and talks at high-profile venues such as the Hay-on-Wye Festival, Midgley has become one of the leading 'popular intellectuals' of the day. Certainly few other contemporary philosophers do as well as she in showing people how philosophy can be brought profitably to bear on topics of everyday concern and interest. Fewer still can match her energy—her latest book, *Are You an Illusion?* was published just last year, when Mary was ninety-three. It is for this commitment that Midgley was honoured with the distinguished Edinburgh Medal at the Edinburgh International Science Festival in April 2015, an event featuring several contributors to this volume, including her lifelong friends, Jane Heal and Mary Warnock.

THEMES AND SIGNIFICANCE

It is difficult to write a systematic survey of the themes of Midgley's work, since science, literature, ethics, politics, the history of philosophy and many other themes are interwoven throughout her writing. Another ever-present theme is metaphilosophy: what are the aims and scope of philosophy, and which methods should philosophers employ? It is here that we will try to begin.

There are two (often opposing) tendencies in philosophy: one to connect, to draw likenesses, metaphors and parallels; the other to dissect, to find differences and to challenge entrenched connections and associations. We need to do both of these things. If our only interest is in the project of building connections and drawing likenesses, we may be relying too much on faulty conceptual structures, and the whole architectural project may crumble. If we focus entirely on seeking differences and challenging connections, we will clear away some of the clutter, but we may be left with bare ground from which nothing can grow.

These tendencies are often at odds with one another: firstly, the fear of drawing parallels can invoke a kind of conceptual paralysis which prevents us from building constructive accounts. As Midgley notes, the myths and images, and our capacity to 'live by' them, depend upon a host of connections and parallels, and without such things we can say and do very little. When we are taught to be excessively wary of connections, we live in fear of metaphors and stories, in case they lead us astray. This can make any kind of conviction, philosophical or otherwise, difficult to maintain, since we are constantly in fear of being bewitched. As Alasdair MacIntyre put it, 'Deprive children of stories and you leave them as unscripted, anxious stutterers in their actions as in their words' (MacIntyre 1981, 201). This is true not only of children, but of adults too, including adult philosophers.

By contrast, if we look too much to similarities and resemblances, we may overlook important differences that impact not only upon our theories, but also upon our lives. An uncritical acceptance of similarity that glosses over distinctions can provide us with sets of concepts that are not fit for their applications. We may end up claiming, for example, that a dolphin is a person, without noticing that our concept of 'personhood' doesn't even accommodate many groups of people terribly well. The destructive force of philosophy must therefore be employed with a fine chisel, rather than a sledgehammer, and its constructive force must be used equally carefully, with constant checks that the raw material is still up to scratch.

Midgley is aware of both of these dangerous tendencies, and this has been reflected throughout her work, although perhaps she has had to wield her hammer and chisel more often than her trowel and mortar. She is also aware of the fact that going wrong in either of these ways can have real impacts on the lives of people, animals and the environments that they inhabit, influencing practical activities in all fields of life, particularly (at least in terms of Midgley's focus) in science and politics. This concern with the relevance of philosophy to the very practical fixes that we find ourselves in is always a dominant theme of her work and makes it important reading both in philosophy and in other disciplines. We hope that the content of this volume reflects the breadth of this significance.

In terms of her destructive projects, one of Midgley's central targets is a particular form of scientistic materialism characterised by mechanism and atomism and informed (however unwittingly) by a dualistic world view. This approach has come under attack in her work on animals, human nature, the mind and our relationship with the natural environment. In each of these areas, Midgley maintains, common and specialist understandings have been blinkered by an approach that aims to reduce things to their constituent parts and overlooks the richness and diversity of life. Perhaps this conception has reached its height of excess in the view, which Midgley attacks in her latest work *Are You an Illusion?*, that even the self that experiences this richness is nothing but an elaborate illusion brought about by the activity of the brain. The whole, in this case life as we experience it, is, she maintains, no less real than the parts: 'A microscope is a wonderful machine, but that does not make what is seen through it any more real than the things outside' (SS, 29).

While many scientific enquiries, as well as inquiries in the philosophy of mind influenced by the sciences, have been moving further toward materialism and reductionism, the study of ethics and politics has proceeded in a way that is very much removed from the biological, physical and material. Midgley attacks the idea of a view of ethics that has no regard for the nature of human beings as embodied animals with particular features and habits. Thus, the 'self' of biology is often misconstrued as an illusory entity entirely determined by material factors, while the 'self' of ethics is strangely immune from the biology of human animals. It seems no wonder, according to these opposing yet connected pictures, that many see an unbridgeable gulf between fact and value. It is also unsurprising that there have been corresponding disciplinary splits in the sciences between 'hard sciences' dealing with what is material and 'soft sciences' addressing aspects of our social lives, mirroring those in philosophy between the metaphysical or descriptive and the normative or prescriptive.

Here we see how Midgley's constructive aspect comes in to play. Much of her critical project is targeted at ways of seeing the world which build unhelpful and untenable walls between areas of thought. Once this critical task has begun, we start to see the possibility of making connections that previously seemed beyond our reach. Thus, Midgley's work on animals makes links between ethology, biology, ethics and politics. This aspect of Midgley's approach is probably most evident in her work on Gaia theory, which critiques a predominant view of the relationship between organisms and environment on both ethical and scientific grounds, and her proposal of Lovelock's vision as an alternative is intended as a corrective not just to a scientific picture, but also to an ethical one.

Critics of Midgley can (and do) claim that this approach is based on a basic error—that scientific method and discovery has no deep relationship with the ethical, and that any ethical criticism of metaphors and imagery employed in the sciences is at best superficial and at worst a hindrance to the proper work of science. In a materialist age, normative critiques of scientistic world views are sometimes regarded as a kind of superstition or anti-naturalism. This criticism is fundamentally misplaced: Midgley is a thoroughgoing naturalist. Her philosophy does not posit strange or mysterious entities like fairies at the bottom of the garden, but familiar ones like communities, societies, relationships, mutual dependence and vulnerability. Hers is also a thoroughly naturalistic view in that it does not exempt the philosopher or the scientist from the naturalistic stance that they take toward to their subject matter. Like their objects of study, the methods, prejudices and conceptual tools of the investigators are contingent and immersed in a particular environment. Rather than suggesting that ours is a 'view from nowhere', we must acknowledge and interrogate our place in the world that we are investigating, and this includes the ways in which predominant myths and metaphors shape our thought. It is the denial of this imperative that should properly be understood as running contrary to naturalism, since such a denial regards the eyes of the philosophers or scientists as akin to the eyes of the gods that many of them renounce.

Thus, as previously noted, Midgley's work should not be regarded as falling under a catalogue of distinct themes or disciplines, but rather as an overarching critique on predominant ways of seeing the world, which is destructive only insofar as it allows new conceptions and connections to be built.

CONTENT AND STRUCTURE OF THE VOLUME

This volume has fourteen chapters organised into four parts. Part one is devoted 'Animals and Environments'. In chapter one, the philosopher David E. Cooper addresses the 'realism' that characterises Midgley's writings on our ethical relations to animals. Careful ethnographic attention to how concrete communities relate to animals shows a complicated diversity of attitudes, with care, love and affection messily bound up with indifference, exploitation and hatred. Some species are prized, protected and even sacralised, while others are caged, hunted or excluded from moral concern altogether. Cooper criticises many mainstream animal ethical theories for lacking a properly realistic appreciation of the diversity and messiness of our attitudes towards animals. Few people could seriously pretend to be indifferent to the differences between species, a fact that, right or not, does shape how we think and feel about animals. Better, then, argues Cooper, to step back from these prevailing ways of thinking about animals—wild and domesticated, local and distant—and instead firmly root realistic moral thinking in our actual attitudes and arrangements.

The concern with the place of animals in our moral thinking is continued by Stephen R. L. Clark, a long-time philosophical champion of animals, in his contribution, 'Animals, Real and Virtual'. Starting from Midgley's observation that animals often function as 'symbols of wickedness', Clark asks whether such ethical notions are really useful. The main worry is that the qualities that animals are recruited to symbolise, whether virtues like courage or vices like greed, are quite different when they are manifested by human beings. It is the privilege of humans to reason about their ethical conduct and so, argues Clark, we ought to take care when making use of animals in our stories, fables and moral tales. Certainly animal imagery can play a useful role in indicating different possibilities for human conduct and character, a fact reflected in a long history stretching from Aesop to Uncle Remus. The better moral to take from this fact is, suggests Clark, that humans are essentially narrative creatures—we imagine and develop and share stories that explore virtual worlds, different from, but perhaps preferable to the world we currently inhabit. Animals can be invoked to explore these virtual worlds, as can other non-human agents, such as demons and aliens—and, if so, animals can inform our moral thinking, even when that thinking is not directed at them, but rather at ourselves.

Gregory McElwain continues to develop these moral themes by considering Midgley's idea of the 'mixed community', described in her 1983 book *Animals and Why They Matter*. That idea began in a critique of several dominant trends in moral thinking about animals, including its abstract, rationalistic character, and the misapplication to animals of normative concepts, like *rights* and *duty*, to which they apply badly. Midgley argued that the proper corrective is not to abandon reason and embrace an irrational, 'subjectivist' ethics—which would to be exchange one excess for another. Instead, our moral thinking ought to be rebalanced, with emotion and reason properly interwoven in our thought, as they are, so often, in our life. Even if animals do not have rights or duties or obligations, they are the objects of our love, delight, pleasure and sympathy—or at least, until some contingent prejudice or pressures succeed in nullifying those natural affective responses. The mixed community is therefore doubly mixed—it is a mixture of attitudes, feelings and concerns, but also a mixture of creatures, often very different from one another, but all bound up in a single moral and ecological community. In this community, human beings retain their exceptional status, but as reflective stewards, able to identify and to care for—or to corrupt—the communities of which they are members.

The final chapter in part one is by the animal behaviour researcher Françoise Wemelsfelder, who addresses the positive question of how our moral thinking about animals can be enriched by closer engagement with current research in the sciences. Central to Midgley's writings on animal ethics is the complaint that we need new and better ways to think about 'beasts'—an 'earthy realism' that takes seriously the richness and complexity of animals and of our relations to them. A natural place for such earthy realism to begin is, of course, those scientific disciplines that are directly concerned with the lives of animals and of human beings whose lives are still led in intimate association with them. Wemelsfelder offers two rich candidates, the first being social anthropology, in which one finds calls for a 're-animation' of prevailing intellectual frameworks for thinking about the ways that 'people, creatures, and landscapes dwell together'. The second is animal welfare science, a discipline in which the putatively 'abstract' methods of science are sensitively directed to identifying effective ways to ensure the welfare of animals. Both of these examples show how at least certain areas of our established intellectual traditions are actively seeking ways to better understand the lives of living creatures, both human and non-human, in ways sensitive to the earthly realities of those lives. In Wemelsfelder's discussion, we see clearly how science, reason, feeling and ethics can come together in a way that Midgley has been calling for.

The title of part two, 'Human Nature', may be misleading if it is taken to refer to some fixed nature or essence that human beings enjoy that marks them off from the 'beasts'. Certainly this is not how Midgley would use it, given that a central message of her early classic, *Beast and Man*, was that the 'roots of human nature' lie in our animal history. Humans *are* animals, albeit ones that are special in certain ways, and it is a useful and important exercise in philosophical anthropology to explore fully the implications of this fact. Nowadays, of course, many philosophers do just this, but back in the 1970s, when Midgley wrote the book, the claim was either marginalised or dramatized—as it was by E. O. Wilson, for whom evolutionary biology was, at long last, ready to take over ethics. The chapter by Raymond Tallis contextualises *Beast and Man* and appraises its enduring philosophical significance. Like much of her work, it was a corrective to a neglect of the importance of biology to our thinking about human beings. Nowadays, says Tallis, things have gone too far the other way—we are faced with 'biologism': too often, one finds large and complex areas of enquiry sudden prefixed with 'neuro-' or 'evolutionary' and declared done and dusted, and we go from paying too little attention to biology to paying it far too much. Balance is needed. Tallis carefully explores the different ways that ostensibly unique human capacities are deeply rooted in our evolutionary history and status as natural creatures—we *are* animals—but, he argues, there is still a gap between us and them.

Mary Warnock is equally interested in the implications for the idea of morality of certain conceptions of human nature. It is certainly true that human beings have very much in common, but not wholly clear that we have enough in common with one another to 'make possible a kind of common morality', even at the general level of broad conceptions of what it means to be a good, or even just decent, human being. Warnock argues that a consensus morality is possible, just as long as it is placed within certain limits. Our natures include much useful moral material, including evolved feelings of sympathy and concern and a deep need for security and stability—much, that is, which can be organised by articulate moral theory. Unfortunately, our natures are raw and not all good—we have impulses to vice as well as virtue—and so we must pay careful attention to the ways that our natures are expressed through our practices, traditions, and cultures. Although our moral vocabulary—of rights and duties, say—aspires to universality, our moral practices are shaped by cultural traditions that are far more particular. 'Human rights', for instance, may indeed belong to all human beings by virtue of our humanity, but unavailable to many people due to contingent prejudices and obstacles. If so, suggests Warnock, then the plausible aspiration to a consensus morality that is sustained by certain aspects of our natures is, alas, being obstructed by contingent features of our cultural traditions.

Part three addresses a specific aspect of the question of the relationship of humans to non-human animals—namely, the question of *minds*. Much of the scientific and philosophical literature on animals has explored the question of whether animals are minded creatures—conscious, self-aware, sentient—and, if so, to what extent. This question has a double significance: first, a creature's cognitive or psychological status has moral import—if 'brutes' are simply organic automata, then, reasoned Descartes, we can treat them as we will; second, to be a conscious, sentient, minded creature is to enjoy a special sort of metaphysical distinction, of a sort important to those who want to know just how we fit into the wider order of nature.

Rupert Sheldrake therefore challenges a familiar dogma of the philosophy of mind, namely that our minds are, as it is often put, 'in our heads'—or, better, identical with our brains. Such materialist conceptions of the nature of mind have encouraged philosophers, psychologists and others to proffer the 'Astonishing Hypothesis'—that the vast grandeur of our cognitive life is, astonishingly, a product of an assemblage of nerve cells. Midgley has long been suspicious of such materialistic treatments of consciousness, perceiving in them philosophical confusion wedded to scientistic excess—suspicions fully rehearsed in her most recent book, *Are You An Illusion?* Sheldrake's strategy is to fortify those suspicions by approaching the question of the nature of consciousness by focusing on a specific form of experience—visual experience, *seeing*—and using it to introduce a conception of the mind as extended. Sheldrake offers a body of evidence to suggest that both human beings and many animals have a capacity to determine when they are the object of another's' visual experience even when we have no conventional sensory means of doing so—or, that we can tell when we are being stared at—that, although of obvious evolutionary advantage, can be explained only if we take seriously a richer conception of the nature of the mind.

The richer conception that Sheldrake gestures at runs contrary to what many consider the dominant philosophical doctrine of *naturalism*. One thing that this slippery term reflects is the conviction that psychological concepts—such as 'belief'—are 'theoretical' terms, to be deployed in the prediction of the thought and behaviour of other. Jane Heal takes issue with this claim in her chapter, arguing that it represents a form of what Midgley calls 'muddled thinking' that unfortunately tends to lead us to making grandiose conclusions. There is a danger that we slide from certain sensible claims about our status as evolved, fallible creatures into much wider pronouncements about minds, brains and value, if not reality itself. Again, we hear Midgley's insistence that we ought to take seriously the fact that we *are* animals—but to keep our heads and avoid zealously inflating this into grander claims. Ian Ground echoes this call for carefulness in our thinking by considering a contemporary debate about the differences between ourselves and non-human animals. A promising focus for that debate is the idea that the distinguishing feature is our capacity for *meta-cognition*—roughly, that we can represent our psychological states to ourselves in language, in a way that other animals cannot. If we can think about what we think, then we can, at the least, continue to make progress on the question of how, if at all, we are distinct from non-human animals. Clearly the relationship of 'beast and man' retains the empirical and philosophical complexities that Midgley called attention to all those years ago, but we also have before us various paths, even if they are scattered with obstacles.

A latent theme of parts one and two is the important role played by science in our philosophical thinking about our relations to other creatures and to the environments we and they inhabit. Unfortunately, it is clear that science requires careful handling. The old positivist hopes that the results of scientific enquiry would briskly and efficiently answer any and all questions about life, the universe and everything are still not wholly behind us. No sensible person denies the importance of science, but over the last few decades, Midgley has increasingly worried about a cultural tendency to inflate the role and significance of science beyond all sensible reckoning. The titles of books such as *Science as Salvation* and *Evolution as a Religion* reflect a deep worry that public and academic understanding of science too often lapses into *scientism*. Unfortunately that term is rather slippery, and so it is difficult to specify precisely what it is that critics worry about. Ian James Kidd tries to resolve some of those uncertainties by offering a fairly systematic account of Midgley's conception and critique of scientism. Central here is the role that *myths*—or 'imaginative visions'—play in guiding our estimations of the significance of science in our life: whether we trust it, put our hope in it, fear its power, look to it for salvation, or see in it the sum of all things. Unfortunately, those myths often emerge spontaneously and are not always subject to reasoned debate and decision. Midgley argues that philosophers, among others, can help to critically appraise the 'myths we live by'—the title of her 2004 book—and so ensure that we do not do science an injustice by adopting false conceptions of what it is and what it can do for us.

The chapter by Andrew Brown continues the theme of scientism by examining one of the most contentious episodes in Midgley's career, namely, her relationship with the writings of Richard Dawkins. It is well-known that the interest of several philosophers in *The Selfish Gene* prompted Midgley to write a fiery article, 'Gene-Juggling', which marked the beginning of a long and acrimonious dispute. Few could deny that the tone was, as Brown puts it, 'brutal and needlessly unfair', but the question is whether the original criticisms were fair. Certainly the sorts of concerns raised are familiar to the philosophy of biology—the role of metaphor in biological explanation; the nature of 'the gene'; the import of biological ideas into moral and social theory—and Brown presents these issues and asks how Midgley's criticisms fare in light of more contemporary work.

Simon Conway Morris accepts Midgley's critique of scientism and the dogmatic optimism of those who hope or expect that all of our problems will be resolved by scientific labours. Science is good, but not that good, and certainly not by itself. It is on the topic of naturalism, however, that Conway Morris is less persuaded, for he worries that even the modest form of naturalism defended by Midgley is incapable of providing closure on certain topics of deep, indeed profound, human concern. Like other contributors to this volume, Conway Morris identifies consciousness as one area in which stricter forms of naturalism begin to falter, but he also adds another—namely, *evil*. The idea that our moral sensibilities partly reflect our status as evolved, embodied creatures is not new to either Midgley or moral philosophy, but Conway Morris argues that the claim that evil is an inevitable, if ugly, feature of our evolutionary development deserves further reflection. Although the results of such reflection are as yet unclear, the worrisome thought that evil may be more than a particularly striking instance of the problems inherent in social life adds a grimmer aspect to Midgley's naturalism. If our natures can bring forth evil and wickedness, sitting alongside goodness and virtue, then we become more interesting, but also more worrying creatures.

One thing that is worrying and often evil about human beings is their propensity to prejudiced ways of thinking, feeling and acting towards others. Historically, the victims of such prejudices are legion—animals, aboriginal peoples, nature and, of course, women. Many commentators identify a 'logic of domination' at work in our societies, reflected in the sorts of tendencies that Midgley opposes, including narrowly rationalistic and instrumental ways of valuing places, people, and creatures. Part four of the volume therefore addresses the relation of Midgley's thought to feminist philosophy and to the work of several of her distinguished peers. The chapter by Liz McKinnell discusses a theme that, though central to Midgley's thinking, is perhaps less appreciated than her work in, say, animal ethics or scientism—the theme of *feminism*. McKinnell argues that feminism flows into Midgley's thinking in several ways. One is the urge to pay attention to the historical development of our concepts and values, where sexist biases and prejudices of course have been dominant. Another is the hostility to narrowly instrumentalist attitudes that reduce creatures and environments to aggregates of 'functions' to be coldly appraised and manipulated. Indeed, such themes converge—prejudicial modes of thought are often necessary to motivate and justify exploitative practices. If so, suggests McKinnell, then 'feminist' concerns are intimately integrated with more general philosophical concerns, such that one need not be, in Midgley's phrase, a 'full-time feminist' in order to work to nullify gendered biases and prejudices.

The centrality of feminism to Midgley's thinking is further developed in the final chapter of the volume, by Benjamin Lipscombe, which offers a 'group biography' of Midgley and three of her most distinguished peers. These are the philosophers Elizabeth Anscombe and Philippa Foot and the philosopher-novelist Iris Murdoch, who surely class as one of the most influential group of women philosophers in the history of the subject (a fact due, of course, not only to their own distinction, but to the gendered biases in that history). Lipscombe starts from the observation that Midgley is much less influential within professional philosophy than these others, and asks why this is so, not least given the parallels between her work and theirs. All opposed the strict separation of 'facts' and 'values'. All called for closer attention to human nature, messy at that might be. And all were, albeit in different ways, opposed to some of the main currents of the prevailing British moral philosophical climate. In the process, Lipscombe ventures several insightful remarks about rival conceptions of the nature of philosophy—of what it is, could be, and should become—and concludes that Midgley had more to teach her friends and peers than they realised.

We—the editors and contributors—all share the sense that the life and work of Mary Midgley continues to teach us, about animals, ethics and evolution, and in the process shows us how to think clearly, deeply and widely about the world and our place in it.

REFERENCES

MacIntyre, Alasdair (1981) *After Virtue: A Study in Moral Theory*, 1st ed. (London: Duckworth).

References to Midgley's writings are to *The Owl of Minerva* (OM) and *Science as Salvation* (SS).

Part I
Animals and Environments

1 Animals, Attitudes and Moral Theories

David E. Cooper

REALISM AND THEORY

For over more than thirty years, an enduring quality of Mary Midgley's writing on attitudes towards non-human animals has been its realism, a recognition of actual beliefs and feelings that is missing from more abstract treatises on animal ethics. One thinks, for example, of her insistence that, before levelling accusations of 'speciesism', we recognize 'a deep emotional tendency . . . to attend first to those around us who are like those who brought us up' (1983: 106). One thinks, too, of the many places where she draws attention to the complexity of people's attitudes to animals, to 'incongruities' and 'paradoxes' among these attitudes. 'For as long as animals have been domesticated', she remarks, 'humans have looked at them with a kind of squint', seeing them now as 'things', now as 'something more or less like people' (2008: 22; see also 1985: 57). She is critical, as well, of generalizations that display ignorance of large differences in attitudes between whole cultures or societies. These include cultures in which totemic animals are held sacred and nomadic ones in which people form special bonds with horses, reindeer or camels (1983: 110). A further aspect of her realism is recognition of the many and complex 'barriers' that we have 'erected against concern for animals'. These range from intellectual fashions and prejudices, like Behaviourist psychology, to 'spasms of technological euphoria' that encourage the mutation of farm animals into 'agricultural products' (2008: 21).

It is a kind of realism, finally, that also informs Midgley's reservations about the value of broad moral 'notions like equality, rights and even justice' in addressing our treatment of animals. For these notions have their primary use when directing attention to some 'limited, chosen group', within which 'unfair privilege' or arbitrary discrimination is identified (1983: 82–3).

The question I discuss in this chapter is whether Midgley's admirable realism doesn't invite a harsher judgement on moral theorising than her own reservations about talk of equality and the like indicate. Is her realism about the motley of attitudes found among both individuals and societies consistent with maintaining, as she did in *Beast and Man*, that it is through moral 'rules and principles' that we may 'guide ourselves through the jungle' (1980: 169)? If not, then we need to consider the possibility that moral theorising is unhelpful, or worse, in the attempt to cultivate authentic concern for animals. Could it be that reliance on argumentation of the sort found in moral theories is one of those 'barriers . . . against concern for animals' that we have erected?

As my phrasing of these questions no doubt conveys, by a moral theory I mean something more specific than thinking about how to relate to and treat animals. I have in mind theories that Tzachi Zamir calls 'two-stage' theories, ones that first try to determine the 'moral status' of animals and then draw conclusions from this for our conduct towards them. Common to such theories is the thought that animals should be treated in certain ways '*because* they possess moral status'. He is right to observe that 'virtually all work in animal ethics attempts to establish or reform the "moral status" of nonhuman animals' (Zamir 2007: 16). For central to nearly all the many theories that invoke principles enjoining such-and-such treatment of animals are claims about moral status, 'considerability' or 'entitlement'.

Here are a couple of examples. One author's answer to the question 'why is it wrong to cause pigeons gratuitous harm' is that this is because 'pigeons . . . have *moral status*' and hence 'have *moral rights*' (DeGrazia 2002: 37). Again, Martha Nussbaum—having proclaimed a need for 'theories of justice' so that we may 'get the best out of our ethical intuitions'— argues that since animals, like human beings, have 'valuable' powers and 'capabilities', they possess 'dignity' and are 'worthy of respect'. This, she says, is why it is wrong to subject animals to intensive farming methods and other technologies (Nussbaum 2007: 31–4).

Before turning to the question of the limitations of moral theories in this sense, it will be helpful to elaborate on Midgley's reference to the motley of attitudes towards animals that men and women and whole societies have taken.

ATTITUDES AND WAYS OF LIFE

Midgley herself describes certain figures whose attitudes towards animals form a complex and perhaps incongruous mix. She imagines, for instance, someone who is considerate to his pets, active in wildlife conservation, but who has no 'scruples about hurting experimental animals, or eating factory-farmed meat, or even hunting' (1983: 17).

Let's consider, in more detail, the testimony of a man who was acutely aware in himself of the 'paradox' of a 'fondness of animals' combined with the bloodthirstiness of the hunter. Gavin Maxwell is famous for a trilogy of books, beginning with *A Ring of Bright Water*, that recount his years spent on a remote stretch of the west coast of Scotland. 'Fondness' is too facile a term to describe his love of the otters he adopted and the wild animals—deer, geese and others—that lived in the area. Yet this love is juxtaposed with far more aggressive feelings. The death of an otter left him as 'desolate as one who has lost an only child': but Maxwell then goes off duck-shooting. On one occasion, he undertakes a drive of 200 miles to take an injured gull to a vet and, soon after, enthusiastically joins in a day's hare-coursing. It is not just love for otters and deer that Maxwell experiences: he admires and respects them, for their 'nobility', 'steadfastness' and 'dignity', and he feels himself to be in 'intimate communication' with them, his 'neighbours', and to stand to them in a relation of 'trust'. These are not, however, attitudes he extends to the rats that he poisons with warfarin, or the sharks that he once ferociously hunted for profit.

Midgley, we noted, draws our attention not only to the complex attitudes of individual men and women, but to the variety of attitudes found across cultures. Consider, for instance, some of the attitudes that anthropologists attribute to many hunter-gatherer societies (see Brody 2001; Hurn 2012). A striking feature of these societies is the network of rules and customs that serve to regulate the hunting of animals. These determine who can hunt, when and where, and which animals can be hunted and in what numbers. Such customs belong to traditions that shape and constantly affirm attitudes towards different kinds of animal. Especially important are rituals, like the Native American sun dance, of respect for certain animals. These may take the form of thanking the animals for their willingness to be killed in the expectation that this will encourage a future supply. Further regulations serve to prohibit the killing of certain animals, at least in certain contexts. These may be totemic animals deemed to be sacred ancestors of the hunter-gatherer clan.

Several anthropologists emphasize the 'fluidity' or 'porousness' of the boundaries between human beings and animals that are drawn in societies where survival depends on constant intercourse and empathy with the lives of animals. One important skill of shamans is to cross these boundaries and to mediate between human and non-human animals. It is because of this porousness that, in many hunter-gatherer societies, people identify themselves with animals, maintain that people may transform into animals and vice versa, and treat certain animals, notably dogs, as companions who may be afforded funeral rites. It's been suggested that porousness reflects, in turn, the crucial adaptive capacity of *Homo sapiens* to attribute 'human-like minds' to animals (Mithen 1999: 204).

Attitudes towards animals are, of course, no less complex in agricultural societies. One has only to think of the elaborate and culturally diverse rules governing which animals may be eaten. But the examples of hunter-gatherer communities and of an individual like Gavin Maxwell are sufficient at least to suggest certain general truths about these attitudes.

They suggest, for a start, that attitudes—compassion and respect or callousness and indifference—are not free-standing, but interwoven with beliefs and practices. Especially significant are practices informed by beliefs about the relationship between humans and animals. The beliefs, for instance, that some animals are tribal ancestors, or that some animals are willing quarries, or that companion animals satisfy genuine human needs, or that wild animals were not created to be put under human control. The examples also suggest that concepts like respect for an animal, or its dignity, do not float free, but are situated or embedded within networks of beliefs and practices. Maxwell's respect for the red deer owed to the way in which, as he put it, he shared 'his world' with these 'neighbours'. It was not a respect he could intelligibly have extended to all creatures. Likewise, the dignity he discerned in otters was a quality peculiar to them and certain other creatures, not a universal quality of animals. Similar remarks could be made about the respect shown by hunter-gatherers to certain animals: it is a respect that presupposes an intercourse with, and dependence on, them that is missing in the case of many other creatures. It is a respect, moreover, that is expressed through appropriate practices, like that of Algonquian hunters who place the bones of slain bears in trees (Brody 2001: 256).

The examples suggest, too, that the tensions or incongruities among attitudes that philosophers and sociologists identify are, sometimes at least, more in the mind of these detached observers than in the lives of the people being observed. Maxwell refers to the 'paradox' in the combination of his love of animals and his 'bloodthirsty' hunting instinct, but he describes it as a 'pleasing paradox' with which he is happy to live. Indeed, it is clear that he does not really regard it as a paradox at all: it only appears so to people who don't live close to and engage with wild animals. And it would be rash to assume that apparent incongruities in the treatment of animals—considerate protection of some, ruthless extermination of others; worshipping a creature in one context, shooting it in another—demonstrate arbitrariness and inconsistency in a culture's attitudes. Closer inspection is likely to reveal that such discriminations make sense within the wider economy of the culture's beliefs and practices.

Put in the most general terms, what my examples suggest is that attitudes to animals, like the concepts which inform them, are situated within a form of life. Abstract them from a web of beliefs and practices, and they become idle. It is important here to emphasize a distinction between real or effective attitudes and what psychologists call 'non-attitudes' or 'vacuous' ones (see Herzog 2010: 240). These are attitudes that people voice—perhaps out of political correctness, convention, or simply because it is the sort of thing 'one says'—but that do not engage with or inform their actions. They float free, without an anchor in people's lives. This is a distinction to bear in mind now that I turn to the issue of the value or otherwise of moral theories when reflecting upon ethical concern for animals.

EXPLANATIONS AND ABSTRACTIONS

Accounts of the moral status of animals are usually yoked to general explanations of why people have tended to fail to recognize this status. Much work in animal ethics goes into exposing the reasons for this failure, in order that the proper moral status of animals will then become clear. Typically, these general explanations invoke dualisms or dichotomies that, it is argued, have obstructed recognition of moral status. The beliefs that only human beings have souls, that they alone are rational, that only they are made in the image of God, and the like have served historically to deny to animals the moral status attributed to humans. They have stood in the way, allegedly, of the appreciation, crucial to recognition of animals' moral status, that human beings are one species of animal among others.

But these general explanations are much too general. Once the motley of actual attitudes to animals is attended to, it is clear that dichotomies like those mentioned, even where they exist, do not by themselves dictate attitudes and practices towards animals. For example, people in some hunter-gatherer societies 'say that humans and animals exist in separate domains', but the further beliefs that shamans can sometimes 'cross this divide' and 'negotiate' with animals clearly influence what is held to be proper treatment of creatures (Brody 2001: 289). Again, for Buddhists, human beings are unique in that they alone are capable of enlightenment and liberation. Coupled, however, with the belief that humans may be reborn as animals, and vice versa, the implications for how animals are regarded are different from those drawn in religions where there is no such belief.

In many cultures, as also in the minds of many individuals, crude 'human versus animal' dichotomies or dualisms are not to be found. In some cultures, animals too have souls, or have the form of gods, or speak with men and women. The implications for how the animals are then regarded and treated are highly variable, as indeed are those of the wider belief that human and animals lives are on a continuum, that humans are a species of animal. This belief is perfectly compatible with holding that humans are such a superior species of animal that moral concern should be reserved for them, or with maintaining—in a Social Darwinist spirit—that between species there can be no moral relationship, only a struggle for survival and domination.

These simple observations make historical nonsense of a story often told by theorists about the moral status of animals. According to this 'expanding circle' narrative, moral concern is originally confined to a limited class of human beings and then inflates concentrically to ever larger classes until it encompasses humanity at large. Only then can the circle of concern expand so as to include animals. But clearly, neither for individuals nor for whole cultures does moral concern for animals post-date one for human beings at large. Maxwell, for instance, saw himself as having obligations towards his otters and dogs, arising from a relationship of trust, that he did not have to the mass of humanity. In many societies, a family's obligations to the animals—dogs, pigs and others—who live with it outweigh those to human strangers (see Serpell 1986). Many communities, observes Midgley, are 'multi-species ones' whose motley of complex attitudes cannot be captured in a diagram of 'concentric circles' of moral concern (1983: 111).

Moral theorists are liable to respond by saying that the idea of the expanding circle should not be taken historically. Like that of the social contract, it is to be read as an 'as if' story, a heuristically useful reconstruction of the rational development of moral concern. The story supposedly reveals how logical consistency requires that an initial moral concern for, say, members of one's family must extend—once relevant similarities with wider groups are perceived—to human beings at large and eventually to animals as well. Admittedly, the story is then no longer a chapter in an upbeat narrative of human progress, but its philosophical merits are not thereby impugned.

However, it is a bad 'as if' story, and for the same reason that, according to many critics, the social contract story is: it is overly abstract. The story is guilty of a number of pretences, each to the effect that the direction of moral concern may be determined in abstraction from actual human practices. There is the pretence, first, that the consistency or otherwise with past attitudes of a new instance of this concern is always settled in advance, as if the established attitudes inexorably laid down the tracks along which future ones must run. This means, in effect, that an established moral concern for certain beings must extend to all beings that are relevantly similar to these. Crucially, however, perceptions and criteria of relevant similarity are situated and enmeshed in webs of beliefs and practices. The hunter-gatherer who extends to wolves the respect he already has for bears isn't simply noting some general similarity between the two creatures—their intelligence, say—but bringing wolves into the same sphere of practice that bears already occupy. It is possible, and indeed quite common, for people to recognize a general similarity between humans and animals, or between some animals and other animals—such as susceptibility to pain—yet not to concede that this is relevant to an extension of moral regard. This is not due to a failure of logical consistency, but to structures of feelings towards and forms of engagement with animals that do not allow for the similarity to be perceived as relevant.

A second and related pretence is that the notions that figure prominently in theories of moral status—dignity, respect, moral considerability, rights, intrinsic value and so on—have any effective purchase and resonance in abstraction from actual practices. Utterances in documents like the Earth Charter to the effect that 'every form of life has value regardless of its worth to human beings' would surely have been unintelligible to most older cultures, including ones in which there were moral duties to certain animals—totemic ones, say. Such utterances would have been unintelligible for the same reason that the following pronouncement would now be for most of us: 'All objects in the world, including plastic cups and grains of sand, have dignity/intrinsic value/moral considerability'. They are not utterances or claims that can engage with real life, emotion and practice.

That, today, claims about the dignity or moral rights of all animals are not dismissed as meaningless does not show that we have become enlightened, that reason has at last compelled us to admit that dignity and rights are

possessed by all creatures. It may simply show that a moral rhetoric of justice has become familiar and entrenched, even though its terms—as Midgley
points out in the case of 'rights'—'cannot be salvaged for any clear, unam-
biguous use' in the discussion of why animals matter (1983: 63). It is an
exaggeration, perhaps, to declare that 'justice is an artefact of custom' (Gray
2003: 103), but there is no doubt that, unhinged from laws, conventions
and traditions, the language of justice and moral status comes to sound idle,
hollow. Fish have 'intrinsic value . . . irrespective of [any] utility' to human
beings: so announces the Preamble to the Millennium Ecosystems Assessment Report of 2005, whose discussion of water toxicity then proceeds to
focus almost exclusively on its unfortunate effects upon *people*—preventing
them, for example, from swimming and boating in lakes. Despite the ele-
vated language of its Preamble, the Report has been accused, therefore, of
representing fish simply as 'commodities' (Stibbe 2012: 93). There is a ritual-
istic flavour to many such declarations of the moral status of animals. 'Yes',
people happily agree, 'of course animals have rights, dignity and value', but
then they pass on, the implications for practice of what they agree upon left
entirely opaque. The rhetoric registers 'non-attitudes' of the kind referred to
earlier rather than live, effective convictions.

MORAL THEORIES AND MORAL CONCERN

Moral status theories, then, are too general and abstract—too tangen-
tial to the practices and ways of life in which moral notions are actually
deployed—to contribute to the cultivation and exercise of moral concern
for animals. Some critics would go further: these theories are among 'the
barriers against moral concern', to recall Midgley's phrase. These theories,
the charge goes, encourage distracting debates and obsessions, and in other
ways contribute to obscuring what is required if effective moral concern is
to extend to the animals most in need of it in the modern world.

A prominent champion of 'virtue ethics' concludes that we 'can dismiss the question of the moral status of animals without a qualm', not
least because of the 'overly theoretic stance' that the question presupposes
(Hursthouse 2006: 140, 146). One unfortunate aspect of this stance is an
obsession with the relative rankings of humans and different kinds of animals in terms of their status. Questions that are senseless outside of particular cultural contexts—whether the life of a vegetative human being has more
or less value than that of a healthy dog; whether fish are sufficiently 'subjects
of a life' to have rights—are regularly addressed in philosophy journals. In
focussing on such issues, moral theorists in fact play into the hands of those
who have vested interests in the exploitation of animals. Factory farmers
and animal experimenters, for example, are more than happy to have public
debate bogged down in questions about the relative status to be accorded to
this or that kind of animal. Chickens or salmon, some scientist can always

be found to say, don't enjoy the degree of feeling or intelligence to qualify for high status.

It is not only factory farmers and animal experimenters who benefit from an excessive focus on issues of moral status. The 'overly theoretic stance' threatens, more generally, to be indulgent to people for their maltreatment of animals. The emphasis of the moral theorist is upon lack of moral concern for animals as a cognitive failure, for which lack of knowledge or a defect in practical reason is responsible. Someone who mistreats turkeys either does not know what turkeys are like or fails to draw the right conclusion about their moral status. Either he doesn't recognize that they are intelligent, sensate creatures, or he fails to draw the required moral conclusion from their similarity in these respects with human beings. Tzachi Zamir surely provides the proper response to this when recalling his and his friends' bungled, bloody killing of a turkey years before.

> What we lacked was not an acknowledgment of some basic equality between people or animals. Nor was it our speciesism that was at fault. We were simply the standard stone-hearted products of a society for which the living animal is merely a transition phase on the way to becoming food (Zamir 2007: 136).

Implied in this confession is an array of 'barriers against moral concern' that are more extensive and operative than the failures of understanding, consistency and practical reason on which moral theorists dwell. Zamir and his friends, like the rest of us who live in developed countries, are 'products' of a hedonistic, consumerist, technophiliac environment in which most people are indifferent to the harsh lives and deaths of the billions of creatures that feed them. Few of these people proclaim the dualisms, prejudices and denials of animals' moral status on which moral theorists concentrate. They are more likely to be 'silent about animals. Not against, just silent' (quoted in Patterson 2002: 155). These are the words of an American Jewish doctor when reflecting on the relationship between industrial farming and the Holocaust. They are quoted in a book whose title is taken from a short story by Isaac Bashevis Singer, in which he famously refers to 'the eternal Treblinka' that is the condition of the animals that live and die in industrial farms (Singer 2011: 271).

Here is not the place for a detailed consideration of an analogy that has prompted heated exchanges, protests and even legal actions. But there is no need to endorse the analogy *tout court* in order to accept that, as with the Holocaust, so with Singer's 'eternal Treblinka': it is a combination of willed ignorance, indifference, conformism and the pursuit of personal comforts and pleasures that clears the way for those capable of callousness and brutality to proceed with their work unhindered. It is a combination, of course, that can easily exist alongside love, kindness and sympathy towards particular people or particular animals—family, friends, pets, birds in the garden, elephants. It can do this because, to recall the Jewish doctor's words, people are not 'against' the animals they eat and otherwise use, any more than most Germans were 'against' Jews. In both cases, it is a combination of attitudes more effective, and more deadly, than the 'theoretic stance' of those who, on some ground or other, deny moral status to certain people or animals.

'HEART' AND SPONTANEITY

Zamir spoke of the 'stone-heartedness' of people, including his earlier self, for whom turkeys and many other animals are only 'phases' in an industrial food process. He is not the only one to imply that the main barrier against moral concern for these animals has more to do with closure of the heart than with defective knowledge or logic. 'I was hoping not to have to enunciate principles . . . open your heart and listen to what your heart says', urges Esther Costello—the vehicle for J. M. Coetzee's views in his book *The Lives of Animals* (1999: 37). On the cover of a recent issue of *Animal Times* (2, 2014), Paul McCartney wears an 'Eat No Fish' T-shirt and invites readers 'to let 'em into your heart'.

A merit of this rhetoric of the heart is to help redress an underlying assumption of theories of moral status. The assumption is made explicit by Bernard Williams: when it comes to 'ethical relations' with animals, 'the *only* question there can be [is] how they should be *treated*' by us (1993: 118, my italics). This might be true if the only thing that is relevant to ethical relations to animals is their moral status: for status—the possession of rights, say—is typically assigned to beings in the context of determining their treatment. But it isn't true, and someone with a moral perspective on relations with animals will ask plenty of questions besides Williams's 'only' one. Do the lives of animals hold moral lessons for us? Can human lives be bettered through engagement with animals? Do some animals themselves display moral understanding? Is an assumed human 'kingship over other creatures' a sure sign, as Montaigne thought, of the vices of 'presumption' and 'arrogance'? (Montaigne 1991: 487). What feelings are appropriate towards animals of this or that species? Except on the peculiarly narrow conception of ethical relations presupposed by moral theories, the domain of these relations to animals is rich and many-sided. (Notice that I have switched from 'moral' to 'ethical'. It is a legitimate worry whether questions about relations to and concern for animals, once detached from the framework of moral theories, are ones about morality, an institution, as Williams (1993) persuasively argued, that tends to be defined in terms of obligations, rules, principles and status. 'Ethical', arguably, is free from these associations, hence the term usually preferred by 'virtue ethicists'.)

Attention to cultivation of the heart is not so much deflected, but actively discouraged, by moral theories. It is 'reason—not sentiment, not emotion— [that] compels us to recognize . . . [animals'] equal right to be treated with respect', urges one champion of such a theory (Regan 1985: 24). The fear, it seems, is that introducing matters of the heart will obscure the logical arguments for assigning moral status to animals. But argumentation, as Cora Diamond in her reflections on Coetzee's book suggests, may be 'a way we make unavailable to ourselves . . . a sense of what animal life is', and at any rate renders the cultivation of such a sense immaterial (Diamond 2008: 53). It is no good for the moral theorist to reply that he or she holds that animals, like humans, are sentient, intelligent or 'subjects of a life'. For it is not such sweeping claims about animals, but a sense of, an empathy with, the lives—and struggles for life—of particular animals, that inspires effective moral concern. Another commentator on Coetzee's book, the primatologist Barbara Smuts, describes how it is through engagement in 'personal relationships' with animals that an 'opening [of] the heart' to animals is made possible, as indeed is a recognition of them as 'persons' in a richer sense than the thin ones—'subjects of rights', say—advanced by moral theorists (in Coetzee 1999: 120).

If close attention to and personal engagement with the lives of animals is one way to cultivate and open the heart, another is to reflect on what is wrong with people who exploit and harm animals. Reflection suggests that vices of the emotions—ranging from indifference to a love of violence—are what is wrong with them, not lack of knowledge or reason. It helps to open the heart to certain animals to appreciate that those whom we recognise as oppressing them are people whose hearts are closed, whose feelings are distorted. This is why it is important when, for example, Rosalind Hursthouse identifies the 'vain-glory' of fox-hunters and their 'self-indulgent . . . impious, cruel and callous' pleasures (Hursthouse 2000: 162). It is unlikely, of course, that the fox-hunting enthusiast will see himself in this light. But the people who do are thereby encouraged to open themselves up to an experience of animals less distorted by vices of the heart.

Coetzee's heroine gives a public lecture called 'The Poets and the Animals', whose aim is to bring to the audience's attention a kind of poetry—Ted Hughes is mentioned—that is 'the record of an engagement' with particular animals, that communicates an 'attentiveness to animals' (Coetzee 1999: 51–2). This, she thinks, will be more effective than the language of 'the whole animal rights business' in combatting the 'contempt' that many people feel for the animals they eat and otherwise exploit. She is not the only writer to propose that poetry makes animals present to the moral imagination in a way that professional moral philosophy cannot. One author, for example, persuasively argues for the merits of the Japanese *haiku* tradition, in which many of the poems refer to animals. These record, with 'empathy and positive regard', 'actual encounters' with individual animals 'living according to their natures'. They are poems that inspire a 'reconnection' with animals and a sense of their 'importance', and they do this 'with no need for recourse to abstractions such as "the intrinsic value of nature"' (Stibbe 2012: 148, 162). The little verses of Issa, Bashō and many others show, one might say, what the language of moral theories unsuccessfully endeavours to state.

These tributes to the role of poetry in dismantling barriers against ethical concern for animals indicate, importantly, that cultivating a sense of animal lives, and opening the heart to them, does not issue in yet one more moral theory to add to the rest. If attentive regard and empathy for these lives prompts compassion and concern, this is not as the outcome of argumentation. Here there is no 'two-stage' movement from a premise about the moral status of an animal to a judgement on how it should be treated. The compassionate person, whose heart is open, seeks no justification for his response. Indeed, as Alasdair MacIntyre remarks in connection with generous behaviour, 'to offer or even request such a justification is itself a sign of defective virtue' (1999: 158). Once a good person is alert to, mindful of, the cruelty of a practice, he or she sees at once that this is not something to be party to. To propose that the practice is wrong *because* it violates the rights or moral dignity of a creature is to go an argument too far (see Hursthouse 2006: 143).

This could be put by saying that the responses to animals of a person attentive to their lives are 'spontaneous'. Spontaneity is a virtue especially associated with Daoism, and it is interesting that, for the Daoist sages Zhuangzi and Liezi, compassionate regard for animals is a mark of a person who perceives them for what they are and whose feelings are 'flowing, unforced, uncontrived'. The contrast here is with people who govern their actions by reference to 'rules and principles'—to considerations of moral status, one might say. The tendency to do this is a sure sign of people's loss of spontaneous virtue and, thereby, of the *dao*, the Way (see Cooper 2014a and b). The sages look back with nostalgia to a time before this loss, when 'people lived together with the birds and the beasts'.

The Daoist sages held out little hope that there could be a return to these happier times and would have held out even less if they were witness to a world in which billions of animals pass through an 'eternal Treblinka'. But they would have recognized that it is possible for some human beings to live in a better relationship to animals. They would have recognized, too, that the incentive to do so is unlikely to be provided by moral theories and other distractions from the cultivation of spontaneous concern and openness of the heart.

REFERENCES

Brody, H., *The Other Side of Eden: Hunter-Gatherers, Farmers, and the Shaping of the World* (London: Faber & Faber, 2001).

Coetzee, J.M., *The Lives of Animals* (Princeton, NJ: Princeton University Press, 1999).

Cooper, D.E., 'Birds, Beasts and the *Dao*', *The Philosopher's Magazine*, 65 (2014a): 84–90.

Cooper, D.E., 'Daoism, Nature, and Humanity', *Philosophical Traditions: Royal Institute of Philosophy Supplement* 74 (2014b): 95–108.

DeGrazia, D., *Animal Rights* (Oxford: Oxford University Press, 2002).

Diamond, C., 'The Difficulty of Reality and the Difficulty of Philosophy', in S. Cavell, C. Diamond, J. McDowell, I. Hacking, and C. Wolfe (eds.), *Philosophy and Animal Life*, New York: Columbia University Press, 2008), 43–90.

Gray, J., *Straw Dogs: Thoughts on Humans and Other Animals* (London: Granta, 2003).

Herzog, H. *Some We Love, Some We Hate, Some We Eat: Why It's So Hard to Think Straight About Animals* (New York: HarperCollins, 2010).

Hurn, S., *Humans and Other Animals: Cross-Cultural Perspectives on Human-Animal Interactions* (London: Pluto, 2012).

Hursthouse, R., *Ethics, Humans and Other Animals* (London: Routledge, 2000).

Hursthouse, R., 'Applying Virtue Ethics to Our Treatment of Other Animals', in J. Welchman (ed.), *The Practice of Virtue: Classic and Contemporary Readings in Virtue Ethics* (Indianapolis IN: Hackett, 2006), 136–55.

MacIntyre, A., *Dependent Rational Animals: Why Human Beings Need the Virtues* (Chicago: Open Court, 1999).

Maxwell, G., *The Ring of Bright Water Trilogy* (London: Penguin, 2001).

Midgley, M. *Beast and Man: The Roots of Human Nature* (London: Methuen, 1980).

Midgley, M., *Animals and Why They Matter* (London: Penguin, 1983).

Midgley, M. 'Persons and Non-Persons', in P. Singer (ed.), *In Defence of Animals* (Oxford: Blackwell, 1985), 52–62.

Midgley, M., 'Why Farm Animals Matter', in M. Dawkins and R. Bonney (eds.), *The Future of Animal Farming: Renewing the Ancient Contract* (Oxford: Blackwell, 2008), 21–32.

Mithen, S., 'The Hunter-gatherer Prehistory of Human-animal Interactions', *Anthrozoos* 12 (1999): 195–204.

Montaigne, M., *The Complete Essays*, trans. M. Screech (London: Penguin, 1991).

Nussbaum, M. 'The Moral Status of Animals', in L. Kalof and A. Fitzgerald (eds.), *The Animals Reader: The Essential Classic and Contemporary Writings* (Oxford: Berg, 2007), 30–36.

Patterson, C., *Eternal Treblinka: Our Treatment of Animals and the Holocaust* (New York: Lantern, 2002).

Regan, T., 'The Case for Animal Rights', in P. Singer (ed.), *In Defence of Animals* (Oxford: Blackwell, 1985), 13–26.

Serpell, J., *In the Company of Animals: Study of Human/Animal Relationships* (Oxford: Blackwell, 1986).

Singer, I., *Collected Stories* (London: Penguin, 2011).

Stibbe, A., *Animals Erased: Discourse, Ecology and Reconnection with the Natural World* (Middletown CT: Wesleyan University Press, 2012).

Williams, B., *Ethics and the Limits of Philosophy* (London: Fontana, 1993).

Zamir, T., *Ethics and the Beast: A Speciesist Argument for Animal Liberation* (Princeton NJ: Princeton University Press, 2007).

2 Animals Real and Virtual

Stephen R.L. Clark

One of Midgley's principal themes has been that 'the use of [non-human] animals as symbols of wickedness has done ethics no good'.[1] Our most serious sins are rarely a matter of giving way to 'animal inclinations', and saintliness or heroism or ordinarily decent conduct are not found only amongst 'intellectuals'. 'Intellectuals', indeed, may find it especially easy to rationalize their own bad conduct. Nor has the use of animals as 'symbols of wickedness' done *animals* any good: at best they need to be disciplined and tamed, and may suffer still worse penalties at our hands. How non-human animals are or should be treated is a larger topic; here I shall address only the former question—are 'the beast within' or 'the beast as bad example' useful ethical notions? Epictetus thought they were:

> When do we act like sheep? When we act for the sake of the belly, or of our sex-organs, or at random, or in a filthy fashion, or without due consideration. When we act pugnaciously and injuriously and angrily and rudely, to what level have we degenerated? To the level of wild beasts, solitary carnivores.[2]

Modern self-help books often say much the same. Steve Peters, describing our 'lower, emotional self' as 'the Chimp', urges athletes to identify themselves with 'the Human', and so evade the perils both of laziness and of aggressive competition.[3] These images may be drastically unfair to actual non-human animals, yet still have something to contribute to our own self-knowledge and self-discipline. Moralists who employ them may also reject their application to actual non-human animals, rather as Socrates, in Plato's *Phaedrus*, rejects the literal interpretation of Greek myths in favour of asking whether he is himself 'a more complex creature and more puffed up with pride than Typhon'.[4]

We need not believe that there actually is, in the 'real world', any monster much like Typhon, nor trouble to identify his mythical description with a volcanic eruption.[5] It is enough for us to acknowledge our *own* 'Typhonic' nature. We may similarly distinguish—even ancient moralists have distinguished—the *actual* nature of wolves or sheep from their symbolic significance. Even symbolically they may stand as well for 'virtues' as for 'vices': dogs remember their masters over many years of absence, and pigs display courage in defence of their young as well as undisciplined appetite.[6] Those human failings that can be called *theriodes* or *nosematodes* are not strictly *moral* failings at all, but faults in nature: like the woman who was said to cut open pregnant women and eat the children[7]—hardly what any non-human animal would do, or even be thought to do. Phobias and irrational compulsions require *medical* rather than moral intervention, and calling them *theriodes* implies neither that this is how all non-human animals or even all *wild* animals behave, nor that *ethical* failures depend on giving in to merely 'animal' impulses. The 'further barbarians', Aristotle supposes, may be naturally '*alogistoi*' and '*monon te aisthesei zontes*' (living without deliberating; responding only to immediate perception)[8], and may therefore be living 'like animals'. For that very reason they cannot be reckoned 'wicked', any more than any other animal. At most, they are missing specifically *human* possibilities, both of vice and virtue.

Non-human animals, it is widely agreed, don't need to *reason* their way to conclusions: instead they respond to their immediate situation in ways refined by evolutionary selection over many million generations. Those responses can be rationalized, as they routinely were by the same Stoic philosophers who denied that 'animals' had reason. Hunting dogs could be seen, *as it were*, to reason syllogistically: 'either my quarry went this way, or this way, or this way. But neither this way, nor this way. Therefore this way'.[9] But this was only our way of seeing what was happening: the dogs themselves, the Stoics thought, had no grasp of syllogistic form, nor any way of questioning their premises. Our own impulsive action, our 'leaping to conclusions', on the basis of inadequate information or logical confusion, is faulty; theirs is not—but simply and entirely what dogs do to catch their prey.

How is it that we cannot—or at least we do not—rely, like other creatures, entirely on instinctual responses? As Plotinus pointed out, very many living creatures (both human and non-human) manage their lives quite well without recourse to 'reason'.[10] They may sometimes mistake their situation, and do entirely the wrong thing, but whatever it is they generally do is something that has worked very well before, and may continue to do so. Conversely, would-be intellectuals who insist on acting only for reasons that they themselves can see, and disregard their own and others' instinctual reactions, may find that they are making as great an error as the post-revolutionary lawyers criticised by Edmund Burke.[11] Despising or ignoring common feelings may seem an attractive strategy: surely it must be easy to devise some system that allows almost all of us to gain what we most enjoy for as little cost as possible? But 'what we enjoy' and 'what is a little cost' will still depend on how we, individually, feel, and it is far from clear that we are capable—as individuals—of weighing others' enjoyments equally with ours, or working out the complex consequences of any innovation. Ethicists who urge us all to ignore what they call 'the yuk factor' in favour of a supposedly more rational calculation of eventual gains are usually blind to their own dependence on what could be called 'the yum factor' (that is, their own immediate enjoyment of some particular outcomes). Ancient philosophers, whether or not they were theists, respected our given natures. Modern evolutionary theorists, though not perhaps consistently, also endorse the notion that common feelings record the general success of just the strategies they recommend. How wise are we to ignore the weight of generations? And why, in that case, is such deconstructive calculation ever offered as a strategy at all? How is it that the major moral theories most often offered as alternatives (Kantian or Utilitarian) both ignore our actual moral feelings (shame, indignation, disgust, loyalty, parental and filial affection), rather than (as even or especially Stoic philosophers did) building a wider loyalty and sense of justice on those natural beginnings?

As Berkeley insisted, 'if we were left, everyone to his own experience, [we] could know little either of the earth itself or of those things the Almighty has placed thereon: so swift is our progress from the womb to the grave'.[12] Even if we concede that there might be (and theists agree that there is) a genuinely impartial and omniscient intelligence, would it not be very strange to identify *that* intelligence entirely with our own? Consider Philo of Alexandria's warning:

> Even now in this life, we are the ruled rather than the rulers, known rather than knowing. Is my mind my own possession? That parent of false conjectures, that purveyor of delusion, the delirious, the fatuous, and in frenzy or senility proved to be the very negation of mind.[13]

Popular advice to children, students, citizens that they should learn 'to think for themselves' may sometimes be really bad advice! Would we happily advise them all to *calculate* for themselves, or rather to consult accountants, or to *self-diagnose*, rather than consult a medic? At least the accountant and the medic may have some record of achievement—though their crafts too may turn out unreliable. At least they can be held responsible for any errors. And even amateur calculation or self-diagnosis may be a safer enterprise than 'thinking' (that is, most often, daydreaming or reciting half-remembered stories). Even or especially the Very Clever, or those who think that they are Very Clever, should perhaps be warned away from relying on their own 'reasoning' about what is or should be. Notoriously, the Very Clever are very apt to rationalize their own desires. Conversely, thinking too hard about our situation, even if we avoid outright delusion, may leave us with no ground to stand upon. That, after all, was the usual result of Socrates' interrogations[14]: finding that we cannot *think* our way through problems about what is right, or what Right is, we may either freeze or relapse again on everyday convictions, customs, so far successful strategies, not because these convictions are correct, or proven to be correct, but because we have no other guide to rely upon.

On this account, we may call our decisions 'rational' and others' merely 'emotional'. This is, indeed, exactly what many experimental scientists say when challenged to defend, for example, their use of animals. Their opponents, they suggest, are moved only by deeply rooted feelings of disgust or sympathy which lead them to imagine 'feelings' in laboratory preparations that do not exist, or do not 'really' matter. The same experimental scientists may also appeal to images, say, of suffering children whose pains might possibly be relieved through further experimentation. Sympathy for human children is reckoned 'rational', while sympathy with monkeys, dogs or mice is merely 'sentimental'. Sometimes this theory is defended by insisting that only language-users can be said to think or feel (despite the unwanted implication that aphasic infants might be used as well). Sometimes the appeal is rather to a 'species-solidarity' that sits very ill with modern accounts of what 'a species' is (namely, a set of interbreeding populations with no necessary essential nature).

Most often the appeal relapses simply upon common judgement, that 'we' mind less about monkeys, dogs or mice than about human children. 'Reason', then, is only a set of strategies for achieving what 'we' mind about—and it might in the future be discarded. At least there is no opposition between 'reason' and 'emotion': emotion, as David Hume declared, is what sets our goals for us, and 'reason' is its slave.[15]

Other creatures manage well enough without having to think through the consequences of their actions, or what it would be like to be the object of those actions rather than their agent. Wolves do not often fight other wolves to the death, but do not need to have rationalized this behaviour. Their 'reasoning'—if they reason—will be of a kind that Hume could recognise: adjusting their behaviour to the particular movements of their prey and partners. Other creatures may even adapt to radically changed circumstances, where their older ways are no longer so effective, but do not need to 'think about' the changes, or invent new strategies from scratch: the many million years of evolution have recorded *different* strategies to be evoked by differing circumstance.

> *Hieracium umbellatum* [leafy hawkweed], for example, occurs at the Swedish west coast in two different ecotypes. One ecotype is a bushy plant with broad leaves and expanded inflorescences growing on rocky cliffs at the sea. The other is a prostrate plant with narrow leaves and small inflorescences, that grows on sand dunes. As the rocky cliffs and the sand dunes alternate along the coast, so does *Hieracium umbellatum* giving rise alternatively to its corresponding ecotypes. The plants keep their habitat-specific appearance under standardized experimental conditions. If, however, plants from one habitat were moved to the other type of habitat, they changed their appearance and adapted to the new environment. These experiments demonstrate the profound selective advantage of different genotypes in different habitats. Furthermore,

they show, that a given genotype has enough flexibility to produce phenotypes, that are optimally adapted to the actual environmental conditions through modification.[16]

We may correspondingly imagine that a prolific species suddenly faced by a radical change of circumstance may change its way of life accordingly. If our hominid ancestors, for example, were compelled to move out from the African forest to grasslands (or on a less approved hypothesis, the seashore), they would not have needed any rational insight to succeed: indeed, without the bare physical possibility of surviving any rational insight into what a radically *other* species might attempt would have been wholly useless. Creatures, in brief, may fall back on forgotten possibilities that are still encoded in their DNA, without any need to *imagine* novelties, or work out from scratch what novel strategies were needed in this new world.

But even if 'reason' wasn't strictly *needed* for our ancestors to survive, any more than ants, corvids, beavers or rats require an intellect, it may still be that an evolutionary accident, perhaps propelled by entirely different needs, resulted in an intellectual capacity to consider novelties, to wonder what others felt and thought, to begin to identify with something larger or longer-lived than either the present moment or an individual life. Perhaps we were telling each other stories long before we had to leave the woods, or before we began the long trek round the coastline up from East Africa into the Levant and on to Europe, Asia and Australia. Some of those stories—to judge from later days—were hardly more than gossip, to keep us well acquainted with our immediate others.[17] Others—again to judge from later days—were fantasies about other lands, about other forms of life and about the perennial questions: where do we go when we're dead, and why is it dark at night?

In this context, the use of animal imagery to indicate different *human* possibilities has a long history, and considerable merit. Other creatures (perhaps) may shift from one set of behaviours and their associated feelings to another according to the season or the situation. We may choose to perform these shifts ourselves, allowing the emergence of many different personalities within a single person. 'Some of us', in Midgley's words, 'have to hold a meeting every time we want to do something only slightly difficult, in order to find the self [that is, the personality] who is capable of undertaking it'.[18] Animal fables, from Aesop to Uncle Remus to the latest children's fantasy, are ways of representing these differing selves. Precisely by conceiving these subordinate impulses and prejudgements under the image of 'animals', we can learn to distinguish them from our true and abiding selves. 'Knowing that I have a naturally bad temper does not make me lose it'[19]: knowing that this 'temper', this violent 'wolfish' or 'leonine' presence, is not simply me, enables me to stand aside from it.

That evolutionary story, that our ancestors were saved, in part, because they were story-telling animals, is not one we can document or demonstrate.

Considered as a palaeological hypothesis, it merely joins the array of similarly indemonstrable tales. But my aim here is different, to explain or at least to indicate why human beings so often think they are more than animals, or more at least than the animals they encounter. Non-human animals, as far as we can tell, inhabit simply the world as it is for them[20]. According to the ancient story, we human beings encounter, or can at least imagine, the world as it is in itself. That declaration places us alongside the gods themselves, and indicates why 'the world', on that ancient story, is only for gods and humans—since it is only gods and humans that can even envisage that single encompassing World.

The moral may be a good one—but not one that I shall explore here-now. Maybe, after all, we are deluded, and as little likely to be able to conceive, still less imagine or perceive, the single World (if such a single encompassing reality exists), as a termite can conceive the African plains where she inhabits her mounds. It is enough to notice that we have *imagined* a larger world or set of worlds than any we encounter by direct perception or even through the stories of our neighbours' past encounters. We all live in a larger realm than sense, and even what we do perceive by sense is influenced and contaminated by the larger story. 'Animals' as we conceive them are all realists, at least within their limits: they need not dream, nor imagine ghosts, nor even—on every occasion—recognise what we consider continuing entities. A dog may savage the very child, a chimpanzee may kill and eat the baboon he has hitherto been playing with, not recognising the very same thing under differing guises. Nor are they troubled by any returning spirit.

I repeat that this is how—perhaps mistakenly—we conceive non-human animals, as living indeed very much like Aristotle's savages, merely by perception. Human beings—including those fabled savages—are always living with stories. Our forebears live amongst us, and we expect ourselves to live beyond our deaths. We see the very same creatures always returning, both in the heavens (where we project more stories) and on the seasonal earth. We imagine subtle or tremendous changes in the everyday, and are not too startled if they take on a more material form (a form, that is, that affects us bodily).

We imagine what it would be like on the other side of oceans, or high up in the heavens. We also imagine what it would be like ourselves to be somewhat different—and perhaps our ancestors were aided in this by actual encounters with different hominid species, whom we now recall as elves, or giants, or goblins.[21] In imagining that we might be different, choices are placed before us that no animal less concerned with stories need conceive. We might ourselves be ogres, elves or angels—and may also worry that the very next human tribe that we encounter might have made that choice, to step away from the familiar and instinctual rules.

So after all there is a split within the human spirit: it may be misleading to divide ourselves into the Chimp and the Human, or to suggest that there are monsters both within and outside ourselves. But we are citizens, as it were, of more than an *earthly* nation, because we also inhabit the fertile realm of story, as no other animal of our present acquaintance does. The older story (with which I have some sympathy at least) is that we are made citizens of the real, the original, world from which we have fallen into the fragmented, partial worlds of sensual experience. The distinction that Plotinus drew between our ordinary selves and the indwelling immortal soul was not straightforwardly Cartesian: it is not a simple distinction between an unthinking body and an immaterial thinker. His distinction is between the psychophysical unity of our ordinary corporeal selves, the assembly of disparate and sometimes competing impulses that can be represented through animal fables, and Carl Jung's 'timeless, imperishable stone', distinguished from 'the sum of [his] emotions'.[22] The error of later moral theorists was to equate that 'stone', that immortal '*nous*', with an abstract, systematizing intellect, progressively detached from piety, disgust and affection. *Nous* is better understood as a loving appreciation of our shared reality.

But even if that grand design is a delusion, we have a wider realm than any other animal, simply because we can multiply delusions! Our well-being as human storytelling beings may require—as any other creature's well-being requires—that we have 'enough' to eat and drink, fair shelter and good company. What Aristotle saw was that we also sought good reasons for what we did, and that our welfare chiefly lay in making the better choices, in choosing among the possible roles to play.[23] We therefore needed to cultivate such characters as would facilitate those choices, so as to live agreeably to our distinctive nature. His goal—as that of most philosophers till recently—was to understand and enjoy the world entire. Forsaking that higher vision, and remembering only that we all live by stories, our goal may be to tell and inhabit an inclusive story, finding a place in it for all the creatures human, non-human, para-human we encounter.

This may certainly seem as unlikely and grandiloquent a vision as the older hope that we are to be called up to the courts of heaven. The stories that we too often tell are ones that emphasise how different and how dangerous are the creatures, human and non-human, with whom we share even the sensual world. Science-fiction writers, embarked upon the creation of a distinctive story-telling genre, have often rather imagined how things might go very wrong than sought to show how well. Those imaginings of apocalypse, of course, have so far played some part in saving us from apocalypse. They have also helped to envisage what worlds might 'float', as it were, on another's blood.[24] It is on this point that Midgley is a little unfair, in saying that science fiction writers mostly depict aliens 'just as scientists with green antennae', emphasising a form of intellect that would be at home at MIT.[25] On the contrary, SF aliens—though they may (hopefully) have reached some similar conclusions about the natural history of the universe—have usually been grounded in differing conceptions of identity and honour. They have been the elves and ogres of our older visions—as have, of course, many earthly nations in our conception of them. And the goal that SF writers have mostly set before us is simply how we may reconcile those different visions without falling into the trap of tyranny. Most often, indeed, the reconciliation and the victory go to the ties of personal affection, not to the sort of intellects that H. G. Wells imagined: 'intellects vast and cool and unsympathetic, regard[ing] this earth with envious eyes'.[26]

Both the fear of 'unsympathetic intellects' and the hope for personal affection as a binding force for all the myriad possibilities may be unfounded. It may be as absurd to expect that creatures of another ancestry and habit than our own should ever be bound by personal affections and ancestral pieties as that they should find us sexually attractive (even supposing that sexual attraction is a universal theme). It may be rather less absurd to fear that alien intelligences might consider our world as desirable real estate—simply because that is indeed how we ourselves have usually treated others. Perhaps we may console ourselves with the thought that biologically rooted intellects must at least have some space in their lives for social attachments of a sort that can be universally extended—as we ourselves sometimes manage to extend them even to monkeys, dogs or dolphins. Which may in turn explain why one recurring theme is that we biologically grounded beings may find ourselves in the end at odds with purely mechanical intelligence, embodiments of the sort of intellects that we most fear: cold, calculating and unwearying.[27] That sort of story has at least this comfort: precisely by imagining such demons we may be reconciled to the fertile variety of the *biological*, and to all the creatures (human, non-human, para-human) with whom we share both the 'real' and the 'virtual' world. Alternatively, we may hope that our Platonic predecessors were correct, and that there is an immortal element common to all sapient creatures, an element that gives us access to a universal truth.

So in conclusion: we are—and maybe every intelligent species is also bound to be—a storytelling species, and inhabit both the 'real' or sensual world, and the 'virtual' or imaginary. In that virtual world are all the lands and creatures we imagine and remember, compose and resurrect. In telling stories about them and their relationships we may slowly identify those aspects of ourselves that need most care and compassion: the monsters and unsympathetic intellects that we know we might become.

Man is a lumpe where all beasts kneaded bee,
Wisdom makes him an Arke where all agree.[28]

NOTES

1. Midgley 2002: 33 and 2005: 56.
2. Epictetus, *Discourses* 2.9.2.
3. Peters 2012
4. *Phaedrus* 229b4–230a6.
5. Greene 1992: 46–72
6. Stephens 2014.

7. *Nicomachean Ethics* 7.1148b19–21
8. *Nicomachean Ethics* 7.1149a9–11. The idea that there are 'savages' far away, entirely devoid of loyalty or forethought, is of course a dangerous fantasy: such savages, it would not be absurd to think, had better—in their interests as well as in their civilized neighbours' interests—be enslaved. See Clark 1985 and 2003. That there are 'savage' elements within our very own person is not so fantastic.
9. Chrysippus, according to Sextus Empiricus *Outlines of Pyrrhonism* 1.69, in Long and Sedley 1987, vol.1, 216 [36E].
10. *Ennead* I.4 [46].2, 35–43.
11. Burke 1975: 321.
12. Berkeley 1955: 14.
13. Philo of Alexandria, 'On Cherubim' 114f, *Collected Works*, tr. F.H. Colson, G.H. Whitaker et al. (Loeb Classical Library, Heinemann: London 1929–62), vol.2, p.77.
14. Plato *Meno* 80a: Socrates, it is said, *numbs* his victims, like an electric eel, or reduces them to helpless silence.
15. Hume 2003 [1739–40]): 295 (2.3.3): 'reason is, and ought only to be the slave of the passions, and can never pretend to any other office than to serve and obey them'.
16. https://s10.lite.msu.edu/res/msu/botonl/b_online/e37/37b.htm (accessed 18th October 2014), after Göte 1922, (http://people.wku.edu/charles.smith/biogeog/TURE1922.htm).
17. See Dunbar 1997.
18. Midgley 1984: 123.
19. Midgley 2002: 4 and 2005: 24.
20. See *Ennead* VI.6 [34] .17, 42, as interpreted by R. Ferwerda *La Signification des Images et des Métaphores dans la Pensée de Plotin* (Groningen: J.B.Wolters, 1965) p.33: 'l'intelligence possède la sphere totale; l'animal lui est postérieur et ne possède que la sphere de l'animal'.
21. See Clark 2009.
22. Jung 1967: 59.
23. *Nicomachean Ethics* 1.1097a7–12
24. Lewis 1952 [1938]: 121: ' "Your thought must be at the mercy of your blood," said the old *sorn* [one of the three sorts of 'rational animal' inhabiting Lewis's imaginary Mars]. "For you cannot compare it with thought that floats on a different blood" '.
25. Midgley 1996: 115 and 2005:140.
26. Wells 1898.
27. For example, Benford 1984, and its sequels.
28. John Donne, *Complete Poetry and Selected Prose*, ed. John Hayward (Nonesuch Press: London 1929 ['To Edward Herbert' 1610]), p.163. See Clark 1997 and 2012.

REFERENCES

Berkeley, George, 'Sermon on Immortality' (1708), in A.A. Luce (ed.), *Works*, vol. 7 (Edinburgh: Thomas Nelson, 1955), 9–15.
Burke, Edmund, *On Government, Politics and Society* (Glasgow: Fontana, 1975).
Clark, Stephen R.L., 'Animals', in Charles Taliaferro, Victoria S. Harrison, and Steward Goetz (eds.), *The Routledge Companion to Theism* (London: Routledge, 2012), 528–40.

Clark, Stephen R.L., *Animals and their Moral Standing* (London: Routledge, 1997).

Clark, Stephen R.L., 'Elves, Hobbits, Trolls and Talking Beasts', in Celia Deane-Drummond and David Clough (eds.), *Creaturely Theology* (London: SCM Press, 2009), 151–67.

Clark, Stephen R.L., 'Slaves and Citizens,' *Philosophy* 60 (1985): 27–46.

Clark, Stephen R.L., 'Slaves, Servility and Noble Deeds', *Philosophical Inquiry* 25(3–4) (2003): 165–76.

Donne, John, *Complete Poetry and Selected Prose*, ed. John Hayward (London: Nonesuch Press, 1929).

Dunbar, Robin, *Grooming, Gossip, and the Evolution of Language* (Cambridge, Mass.: Harvard University Press, 1997).

Greene, Mott T., *Natural Knowledge in Pre-classical Antiquity* (Baltimore: Johns Hopkins University Press, 1992).

Gregory Benford, *Across the Sea of Suns* (London: Macdonald, 1984).

Hume, David, *Treatise of Human Nature* [1739–40] (New York: Dover, 2003).

Jung, C.G., *Memories, Dreams, Reflections*, ed. A. Jaffé, trans. R. and C. Winston (London: Fontana, 1967).

Lewis, C.S., *Out of the Silent Planet* [1938] (London: Pan Books, 1952).

Long, A.A., and D.N. Sedley (eds.), *The Hellenistic Philosophers* (Cambridge: Cambridge University Press, 1987).

Midgley, Mary, *Beast and Man: The Roots of Human Nature* (Routledge: London, 2002).

Midgley, Mary, *The Essential Mary Midgley*, ed., David Midgley (Routledge: London 2005).

Midgley, Mary, *Utopias, Dolphins and Computers: Problems in Philosophical Plumbing* (Abingdon: Routledge, 1996).

Midgley, Mary, *Wickedness: A Philosophical Essay* (London: Routledge and Kegan Paul, 1984).

Peters, Steve, *The Chimp Paradox: The Mind Management Programme to Help You Achieve Success, Confidence and Happiness* (London: Ebury, 2012).

Philo of Alexandria, 'On Cherubim', in *Collected Works*, vol. 2, trans. F.H. Colson, G.H. Whitaker et al. (London: Loeb Classical Library, Heinemann, 1929–62).

Stephens, William O., 'Epictetus on Beastly Vices and Animal Virtues', in Dane R. Gordon and David B. Suits (eds.), *Epictetus: His Continuing Influence and Contemporary Relevance* (Rochester, NY: Rochester Institute of Technology Press, 2014), 205–238.

Turesson, Göte, 'The Species and the Variety as Ecological Units', *Hereditas* 3 (1922): 100–13.

Wells, H.G., *The War of the Worlds* (London: Heinemann, 1898).

3 The Mixed Community

Gregory S. McElwain

Mary Midgley opens her first book, *Beast and Man*, with the oft-quoted line: 'We are not just rather like animals; we *are* animals' (BM xxxiii).[1] This simple yet vital premise is central to her work and has important implications for our moral thinking. We are embodied social animals navigating a morally complex world fraught with conflicting values and claims. We also share a social and ecological context with a multitude of non-human animals. For Midgley, this context and connection with animals and the natural world is often overlooked and neglected, though it should ultimately hold an important place in our discussions of ethics and animals. The concept of 'the mixed community', which Midgley elucidates in her 1983 book, *Animals and Why They Matter*, is an especially valuable description of this context and connection with animals. The modest focus of this essay is to draw out the meaning of this rich concept and highlight its value and relevance to animal ethics.

MORAL CONCERN, REASON, AND EMOTION

In order to understand Midgley's conception of the mixed community, we must first take a brief look at her critique of animal ethics discourse in the early 1980s. When Midgley wrote *Animals and Why They Matter*, animal ethics had emerged as a burgeoning new field of philosophy, and animals were receiving more attention in ethical theory. This attention ranged from inclusion to dismissal of animals from the 'lifeboat' of our moral concern, represented most notably by theorists such as Peter Singer (1977) and R. G. Frey (1980) respectively, though animals were still regularly ignored or overlooked in general. Midgley joined this philosophical conversation, as she often does, to set a few things straight, and to help us *think* more clearly about animals in our moral deliberations. As such, much of *Animals and Why They Matter* is relatively 'destructive'—as she puts it—with the purpose of critiquing and dismantling inconsistent, incoherent, and misguided thinking about animals. In what follows, I will briefly characterize this critique before going on to focus on the more constructive elements of the mixed community concept.

In her systematic critique of rationalism in moral philosophy, Midgley targets misconceptions in theoretical and practical thought on the 'animal question'. This critique is primarily directed toward those who oppose or dismiss animal ethics, either relatively or absolutely. *Absolute dismissal* is the attitude—exemplified for instance by Descartes and Spinoza, among others—that rejects animal claims outright: as creatures both metaphysically and functionally equivalent to machines, animals command no special moral importance, either theoretically or practically. This position is most often assumed, and arguments for it are rarely made—it is simply taken to be *obvious* that animals do not matter. *Relative dismissal* positions, instead, 'merely give [animals] a very low priority', and animals are more of a distraction that 'must come at the end of the queue, after all human needs have been met' (A 13). This is where much of the Western philosophical tradition has found itself—not booting animals out of the moral lifeboat absolutely, but rather relegating them to the lower end of the moral spectrum. Ultimately, Midgley argues that these positions neglect the care, compassion, and relations that we are capable of and often do extend toward others, including other species (see Cooper, this volume).

The question of animals in the Western philosophical tradition has a long and colorful past that generally leans toward human exceptionalism. Though certain thinkers such as Voltaire and Jeremy Bentham offered oppositional views to the dominant streams of human exaltation over animals, reason came to be trumpeted as the banner under which moral considerability was granted. And since animals were not considered rational, their moral worth was dismissed: animals simply did not matter. Reason, much like the soul, gradually became the mark of moral agents (and perhaps moral patients as well), which inevitably lent to the extreme Cartesian position of animals as mere automata or machines (for additional background on the Western perception of animals in classical, late antique, and modern philosophy see Clark (2011) and Garrett (2011)). Midgley understands this excessive glorification of reason as a carryover from the Enlightenment project to elevate reason and science over 'irrational prejudices'. This emphasis certainly served an important purpose at the time, but exaggerations such as this should be reevaluated or even disposed of when they are no longer helpful or begin to do harm. She takes aim at this 'hyper-rationalism', and argues that it must be challenged due to the subjugated status it has placed on animals (and, in many cases, certain humans).

A further element in Midgley's critique is her examination of abstract, rationalist categories of morality—duty, rights, equality, justice, and contract thinking, among others—and their efficacy in dealing with animals. An exhaustive summary of this critique is beyond the scope of this essay, though its main features are clear enough. Midgley demonstrates the inconsistencies in these approaches and how they can be misleading in their usage. These categories, often stemming from technical legal contexts, are generally focused on one particularly narrow area of morality and cannot be seen to cover the whole, as they are often represented or assumed to do. Her further tactic here is to show that there are usually additional assumptions that lie behind the intellectual gymnastics required to construct such narrow and restrictive grounds for moral worth. She highlights the complexity that is left out of these formulations, including the assumptions of worth and value that are sometimes implicit in the positions themselves. In the end, it is better to rephrase our discussions of morality because the current parameters are too limiting to be useful:

> Whenever the spotlight picks out a particular moral area like this [rights] as central, things outside it tend to glide unnoticed into the shadows and be forgotten. Terminology, developed for central purposes, becomes unable to express them clearly. In such cases, philosophy must not just record and follow the usage of current theories. It must also be their critic (A 63).

Reliance on these rationalist categories of morality distracts from rather than enriches animal discourse, and 'notions like equality, rights and even justice tend to imprison our attention in the area which has now become familiar' (A 83).

This critique of hyper-rationalism should not, however, be taken as anti-rationalism. For Midgley, reason is crucial to moral thinking and should not be jettisoned. She is critical of those who one-sidedly exaggerate the primacy of reason to the neglect of other important variables in human life and morality, including emotions. Emotions for Midgley are comprised of a 'whole range of our feelings, motives, and sympathies' that support and invigorate our moral faculties and contribute to 'well-grounded belief on important subjects': they are, in other words, 'the power-house which keeps the whole lot going' (A 35). Our moral concerns and what we care about are very naturally accompanied by feelings—of alarm, disgust, love, joy, worry, and so on—and reflect our sense of the seriousness of the cases, deeply connecting us to what matters in our lives. However, this does not mean, as certain Emotivist theories claim, that morality is nothing but an expression of our emotions. 'The Emotivist's mistake', she explains, 'is in supposing that it [morality] requires nothing else; in trying to detach such feelings from the thoughts that properly belong to them' (A 35). Though emotion can be an ugly 'buzz word', it need not be, and is not for Midgley, for whom the 'real fault must lie not in the presence of feeling, but in the absence of thought, or in the unsuitability of feeling to thought' (A 35). Rationalists tend to reject feelings as reactive physical states, rather than embrace the interwoven nature of reason and emotion. For Midgley, these two areas work together in a complementary way as part of the same process.

THE MIXED COMMUNITY CONCEPT

While Midgley's critique runs throughout the book, a more constructive portion is spurred by her examination of species and the species-barrier, arguing that both those who marginalize and those who exaggerate the latter are equally off the mark. These positions are represented by those levelling the charge of 'speciesism' and behaviourist scepticism respectively, each of whom she confronts. In response to those who cast human exceptionalism as speciesism, she argues that the species-barrier is real and significant, and awareness of it is ultimately essential to properly understanding and respecting each species and each individual animal. To do otherwise is to engage in a form of 'patronizing thinking' which flattens out the integrity and distinctions of different animals. Discriminating and distinguishing between animals is not then prejudicial, but rather an important necessity in appreciating value. For Midgley, this homogenization of beings and bodies is characteristic of rationalist thought, which tends to overlook that 'we are not just disembodied intellects, but beings of particular kinds' (A 99). Moreover, the drive toward levelled interspecies egalitarianism tends to downplay the important place of the intraspecies bonds and our relationships as social beings. The challenge and concern of morality is to constantly evaluate and engage this tension between special bonds and justice more broadly to others without eliminating much of what really matters to us in the process.

The species-barrier then is real, important, and should not be marginalized. But nor should it be exaggerated, and Midgley's discussion of why this is the case is where she develops the core of the mixed community concept. The species-barrier, however real and important, is also semi-permeable, allowing for animals of various species, including humans, to impressively interact and live together. 'All human communities have involved animals', she observes, and it is 'one of the special powers and graces of our species not to ignore others, but to draw in, domesticate and live with a great variety of other creatures. No other animal does so on anything like so large a scale' (A 111 and 112). Such domestication was achieved largely because animals were able to 'form individual bonds with those who tamed them', by understanding social signals, learning to obey particular persons, and so on. Taming was possible, continues Midgley, 'not only because the people taming them were social beings, but because they themselves were so as well' (A 112). This shared sociality and connection between humans and other animals is the foundation that makes the mixed community a historical fixture.

Though animals may not be 'persons' in the strictest sense of the word, as members of the mixed community, they are certainly fellow subjects, not objects (see P for Midgley's exploration of the concept of personhood). Our intersubjectivity, sympathy, empathy, and shared sociality with animals all highlight 'a direct capacity in man for attending to, and to some extent understanding, the moods and reactions of other species' (A 114). Our positive relations (which she focuses on) confirm this, but so do our negative ones—for instance, cruelty indicates a belief in sentience and pain in others, since 'there is very little comfort in working off ill-temper on a cushion' (A 114). Cruelty toward animals, then, involves an implicit acceptance, not a denial, of their consciousness: for belief in animal sentience is 'essential . . . for exploiting them successfully'—in fact, 'exploitation *requires* sympathy' (A 114 and 116). Abuse and cruelty to animals then is an unfortunate result of the very real human ability to understand the 'inner' as well as the 'outer' states of animals—something which behaviourism dismisses as impossible—coupled with the tendency to devalue or disregard these states.

This ability to understand animals, for Midgley, rebuts the behaviourist insistence that the 'subjective' feelings of animals are 'quite hidden from us, cannot concern us and may well not even exist' (A 115). We can, however, talk of the subjective states of animals very much for the same reasons that we can do so in humans—a range of observable behavioural patterns that can be recognized, noticeable similarity between nervous systems, and a history of successful interactions built on this recognition of subjectivity. This capacity for reading human and animal subjectivity is not always perfectly accurate, and sometimes it fails completely, but the imperfection of this capacity is not a strong enough reason to reject the ability to say anything positive about animals. Here the charge of 'anthropomorphism' is quickly made if any attribution of human emotions is transferred onto animals. If things are understood in the context of the mixed community, however, anthropomorphism is only wrong when it *improperly* describes the emotion or feeling; otherwise it is completely appropriate to refer to corresponding emotions between humans and animals in this language. Midgley wishes to remove the stigma of anthropomorphic language altogether as a red herring:

> This attack assumes that human language is invented in the first place not only *by* humans, but exclusively *about* humans—to describe them and them alone. Any use of it to describe any other being would then be an 'extension'—a leap out into the unknown. But if language has, from the start, arisen in a mixed human-animal community and has been adapted to describe all beings whose moods etc. might be of general importance and interest, then that is the proper use of the concepts from the start, and no leap is needed (A 124).

Anthropomorphizing language, then, is a defensible way to refer to animal behaviour on many occasions and appropriate in light of human-animal coevolution.

In this context, in which our very language is reflective of our coexistence with animals, most of us are imprinted by interspecies sociality from a young age, and those who do not receive it seek it out. We crave animal contact from our youth because 'animals, like song and dance, are an innate taste' (A 118). Bonds with animals work alongside our bonds with people as part of a full human life—and such loving sociality, with both humans *and* animals, is what gives rise to the mixed community. Midgley paints a lively image of this mixed-species world:

> Accordingly, the species-barrier, imposing though it may look, is rather like one of those tall wire fences whose impressiveness is confined to their upper reaches. To an adult in formal dress, engaged in his official statesmanly interactions, the fence is an insuperable barrier. Down below, where it is full of holes, it presents no obstacle at all. The young of *Homo sapiens*, like those of the other species present, scurry through it all the time. Since all human beings start life as children, this has the quite important consequence that hardly any of us, at heart, sees the social world as an exclusively human one (A 118).

In this world, love for animals does not replace love for humans, but it also does not distract from that love. Rather, it strengthens it, and she likens love to a special substance that need not be hindered by the species-barrier: the one 'does not need to block another', says Midgley, 'because love, like compassion, is not a rare fluid to be economized, but a capacity which grows by use' (A 119).

The curious human trait of 'neoteny' refers to the various ways that we can 'prolong certain infantile characteristics into maturity, develop them and continue to profit by them as adults', encouraging an 'eager reaching-out to surrounding life and to every striking aspect of the physical world' (A 119). Midgley explores how the child inside of us undergirds 'the capacity for widely extended sympathy, for social horizons not limited to one's familiar group, is certainly part of this childish spontaneity' (A 120). This expanded sympathy through our neotenous characteristics is a trait that aids interspecies interaction:

> It is also the window through which interest in creatures of other species enters our lives, both in childhood and—if we do not firmly close the window—in later life as well. It is one aspect of that openness to new impressions, that relative freedom from constraining innate programmes, which makes us culturally malleable and enables us, through pseudo-speciation, to accept and build such varied ways of life (A 120–1).

Moreover, this helps us in understanding our broader connection and kinship with the natural world. 'It carries with it, too', she expands, 'that still wider curiosity, that capacity for interest in other, inanimate surrounding objects—plants and stones, stars, rocks and water—which extends our horizon beyond the social into the ecological, and makes us true citizens of the world' (A 120). This reflects our roots alongside other species in the natural world and is part of the reason that we are drawn to and feel connected with nature:

> Evolutionarily speaking, then, it is likely that a species such as ours would find itself equipped for the position which some Old Testament texts give it, of steward and guardian, under God, placed over a range of creatures which he is in principle able to care for and understand, rather than in the one often imagined in science fiction, of an invader exploiting an entirely alien planet (A 122).

Such stewardship, it should be noted, is more representative of our special abilities than a mandate or license for simple human exceptionalism.

In wrapping up her conversation on the mixed community, Midgley once again illustrates the complexity and interconnection of our moral concepts and discourse. Here she identifies feelings of exceptionalism and superiority not only in human-animal relationships, but also in the colonial mentality of domination. This logic of domination is indicative of the interwoven oppressions of 'inferior' cultures and other species. Many who object to interspecies sympathy, empathy, care, and communication do not do so because of behaviourist scepticism or similar arguments, but because these things are undesirable to them and are equated with 'primitives' and children. These 'civilized' adults 'recommend indifference to animals—and indeed to all non-human nature—as a condition of emotional maturity' (A 122). 'Advanced' European civilization is thought to have moved beyond preoccupation with animals. She summarily challenges this, stating that 'emotional maturity is not necessarily achieved by limiting one's emotional commitments, nor by rejecting interests held in common with children. Increasing callousness is, on the whole, rather a bad sign for it. Children and 'primitives' need not always be wrong' (A 122). In addressing the colonial mindset, Midgley highlights the interconnected systems of domination that have led to exploitation and subordination of animals, along with women, children, nature, and indigenous cultures, which ecofeminist literature has since accentuated (see McKinnell, this volume, and Warren (1990), for instance. See also Donovan and Adams (2007) for a collection focused on animals). Such dominating attitudes are explored in varying degrees in *Animals and Why They Matter*, illustrating her overriding position that animal discourse is connected to our broader discussion of morality, all of which must be regularly interrogated. This all, for Midgley, matters morally and is routinely overlooked.

THE MIXED COMMUNITY AND THE WIDER WORLD

In much of her work, Midgley argues that values are organic and have to make sense in the context of our lives on this planet. Individuals cannot be abstracted apart from the wholes which they are part of, both socially and naturally, mixed and ecological. Elsewhere, in *Evolution as a Religion*, she similarly expresses this in an organic metaphor:

> Of course, human beings are distinct individuals. But they are also tiny, integral parts of this planet—framed by it, owing everything to it, and adapted to a certain place among its creatures. Each can indeed change its life, but does not originally invent it. Each receives life in a family (as a petal does in a flower), in a country (as the flower does on the tree), and in the biosphere (as the tree does in the forest). Our environment gives us nearly everything we have (ER 169–170).

She expands this organic metaphor with a more detailed look at the relationship between the parts and the wider whole:

> If, on the other hand, we use a biological or 'organic' model, we can talk also of a variety of asymmetrical relations found within a whole. Leaves relate not only to other leaves, but to fruit, twigs, branches, and the whole tree. People appear not only as individuals, but as members of their groups, families, tribes, species, ecosystems and biosphere, and have moral relations, as parts, to these various wholes (ER 178).

This is a helpful way of understanding the self in relation to others at the individual, social, and ecological levels in the mixed community. Any effort to explain our moral universe in terms that neglect these connections and relations—and their correlative emotions, sympathy, empathy, care, and compassion—simply is not comprehensive enough to understand the variety of claims and obligations that we have to others, including animals and nature. This holistic relationality stresses the interplay of parts and wholes and, importantly, does not exaggerate either to a fault.

Relational thinking should not, as can happen, over-exaggerate the principle of nearness or proximity, which can be used to dramatically limit one's moral boundaries and even serve as a form as egoism (A 21). This said, Midgley does not dismiss *nearness*, but embraces the concept in the context of the mixed community because of its value and argues that 'the proper way to treat it is to recognize nearness as a perfectly real and important factor in our psychology, and therefore in our morality, but to refuse to treat it as the sole or supreme one' (A 21). Once again, the answer is not in the extremes, but in a balanced appraisal of the values at play. Nearness is a major factor in our moral relations, from self to family to friends, pets, and so on, but there are other claims that can often outweigh those nearest to us. 'The moral universe', she writes, 'is not just a system of concentric circles, in which inner claims must always prevail over outer ones' (A 22–3).

No system of concentric circles or carefully detailed prescriptions can adequately help us fully understand and decide on difficult moral dilemmas.

Those moral theories that aim to identify a 'simple formula' with which one can assess competing priority claims 'make the job look simple' and so 'can only deceive us' (A 30). We should work out maps or webs of dynamic, overlapping values and obligations, not to 'fix priorities', but as a mark of our recognition that 'relatively isolated claims' sometimes prevail—that our moral thinking ought to be adaptable and non-dogmatic (A 30). This runs counter to approaches that seek to pare down our moral concern, leaving us with a limited range of things to be concerned with in order to not spread out our obligations too thin. As Midgley puts it,

> [Compassion] does not need to be treated hydraulically in this way, as a rare and irreplaceable fluid, usable only for exceptionally impressive cases. It is a habit or power of the mind, which grows and develops with use. Such powers (as is obvious in cases like intelligence) are magic fluids which increase with pouring. Effective users do not economize on them (A 31).

What develops for Midgley is a comprehensive approach to a wide array of complementary and interrelated ethical issues. Discussion of animals runs quite seamlessly into issues of gender, social justice, ecology, family, and politics: they all are tied together as things that matter to us and are central to our lives. These are the issues that factor into our values and decisions, and they are intricately related in the unity of human nature, another important theme in her work. The mixed community is a way of understanding the significant place of animals in our lives. Animals are indeed one of the many important 'components' of our 'value systems'—to use the language of much of modern ethics—that we constantly weigh and prioritize as we sift through the hectic and confusing array of conflicts we encounter. In this pragmatic approach to the variability of value systems, the parts relate to each other, priorities and values shift, social and ecological settings change, and the rules are constantly rewritten. There are no easy answers, and it seems that no single ethical system can account for the diversity and unpredictability of moral issues that arise in these worlds. Those that claim to do so, Midgley says, ultimately mislead us.

We should not, then, simply plug animals into existing ethical systems that promise all the answers. We should see them in the complex context of our lives on this planet and how they are related to us, how they share this world with us. Ultimately, animals have always been part of human communities, and 'things' are not parts of communities. Though this wide-ranging community could seem a bit abstract, this conception is really more of a starting point, and this larger understanding of community can reduce down into smaller, concrete ones. We can then see ourselves as diverse, variegated, and mixed social and ecological communities that are intimately connected to the larger whole. There are broad ranges of relationships that we have with animals in this setting, and they do not necessarily stop at the traditional and often forced line between domestic and wild. Midgley would likely contend that varying contexts would make it difficult to discern this line even if we insisted upon it. Animals fall all along a domestic-wild spectrum based on context—dogs, feral cats, squirrels, deer, pigeons, elephants, snakes, chimpanzees, sheep, gerbils, whales, and so on. Differing relations and contexts determine where these animals land on the domestic-wild scale. The terms 'domestic' and 'wild' are not helpful as essential categories that preordain the moral status of animals, which tends to occur in polarizing approaches to animal ethics between individualists and ecological holists (see Callicott 1980 and 1988; Sagoff 1984; Hargrove 1992).

Midgley does focus on domestic animals in discussing the mixed community, but community, connection, empathy, and sympathy do not stop there. Her discussion of social and ecological claims in *Animals and Why They Matter* is helpful in understanding her distinctions. *Social claims* are those that we respond to in our social communities, claims on behalf of sentient members (she roughly equates 'sentience' to consciousness, acknowledging the complications therein). The claims of animals are not to be seen as the claims of machines or even the claims of equals, but as social claims of fellow community members. *Ecological claims* are those we respond to in our ecological communities, claims on behalf of non-sentient members. These include trees, forests, species, and the biosphere as a whole. We constantly weigh and prioritize these claims in our value systems, which is where we place 'what matters to us' in relation to everything else.

Social and ecological claims are both important and reflect our unique connection to the whole, which 'cannot be a matter of moral indifference to us' (A 91). Moreover, there is not always a sharp distinction between social and ecological claims, or between mixed and ecological communities: 'Our duties to swarms of very small or distant animals, or to whole species, seem to be partly of the ecological sort, resembling in many ways our duty to plants, but they can also have a social element of response to consciousness' (A 90). Rather, it is important to view both within a ranged value system of priorities and claims, in which the social and ecological sort are sometimes independent, sometimes continuous, and sometimes conflicting. Pragmatically navigating this moral terrain is more challenging than most ethical systems let on, and Midgley ensures that the complexity of these issues is not lost in animal discourse.

Midgley does not claim to have all of the answers—and she is adamant about that—but her thinking lends us practicality, relevance, complexity, and common sense when abstract and alienating conceptions of moral worth risk going off-course. It is not necessarily that these systems have nothing to offer. Instead, it is more so what they leave out—or were leaving out in the early 1980s—in exaggerating their particular categories of morality: important elements of human life and morality such as community, relations, care, emotions, sympathy, and empathy. She also offers us a better set of questions than the 'either/or' approaches of liberal individualism or ecological holism in dealing with animals. The individual and the whole each matter for Midgley: the one does not trump the other, and there is more complexity involved. Ultimately, animals should quite simply be prioritized because they are our fellow beings in the mixed community. They matter to us.

NOTE

1. References to Midgley's writings in the text are to *Animals and Why They Matter* (A), *Beast and Man* (BM), *Evolution as a Religion* (ER) and 'Persons and Non-persons' (P).

REFERENCES

Works by Midgley

A   *Animals and Why They Matter* (Athens, GA: University of Georgia Press, 1983).
BM   *Beast and Man: The Roots of Human Nature* (London: Routledge, 1995).
ER   *Evolution as a Religion: Strange Hopes and Stranger Fears* (London: Routledge, 2002).
P   'Persons and Non-persons' in *In Defence of Animals* (Oxford: Basil Blackwell, 1985): 52–62.

Works by Others

Callicott, J. Baird, 'Animal liberation and environmental ethics: Back together again', *Between the Species* 4 (1988): 163–69.
Clark, Stephen R. L., 'Animals in Classical and Late Antique Philosophy' in *The Oxford Handbook of Animal Ethics* (Oxford: Oxford University Press, 2011): 35–60.
Cooper in this volume.
Donovan, Josephine and Carol Adams (eds.), *The Feminist Care Tradition in Animal Ethics* (New York: Columbia University Press, 2007).
Frey, R.G., *Interests and Rights: The Case Against Animals* (Oxford: Clarendon Press, 1980).
Garrett, Aaron, 'Animals and Ethics in the History of Modern Philosophy' in *The Oxford Handbook of Animal Ethics* (Oxford: Oxford University Press, 2011): 61–87.
Hargrove, Eugene (ed.), *The Animal Rights/Environmental Ethics Debate: The Environmental Perspective* (Albany, NY: SUNY Press, 1992).
McKinnell in this volume.
Sagoff, Mark, 'Animal liberation and environmental ethics: Bad marriage, quick divorce', *Osgoode Hall Law Journal* 22 (1984): 297–307.
Singer, Peter, *Animal Liberation* (London: Granada, 1977).
Warren, Karen, 'The power and promise of ecological feminism', *Environmental Ethics* 12(2) (1990): 125–46.

4   How Pigs Talk
The Need for 'Earthy Realism'

Françoise Wemelsfelder

Mary Midgley's work stands up for life as people, animals and other organisms actually live it, in the face of abstract scientific and moral theorising[1]. She exposes the logical absurdities that arise when whole living beings cease to be at the centre of our thinking and are made subservient to a language of cause and effect. Such language does not have power to address the sensitivity, complexity and ambiguity—in short, sentience—of relationships in the world, but in pretending to do so is at risk of impoverishing our understanding of those relationships. Midgley calls for acknowledgement that our world is 'one world, but a big one', and for new 'conceptual plumbing' capable of reflecting this understanding. This chapter will address this call through discussion of two areas of work. One area is that of social anthropology, concerning relationships between indigenous people, animals and land. These relationships are perceived by indigenous people in ways that frequently differ from what Western (scientific) views can accept as 'real' and hence see as cultural or even mythological. Anthropologists, however, are increasingly critical of such contrasts. Tim Ingold, for example, argues that to do justice to the way people, creatures and landscapes dwell together, we need to 're-animate' western traditions of thought. The other area is that of animal welfare science, where, driven by concern for the well-being of captive animals, scientists endeavour to address animals as sentient creatures. However the Western mechanistic paradigm and the dread of anthropomorphism that it entails restrict the language that scientists are willing to use to qualify the experience of animals. Yet people sharing their daily lives with animals experience a richness of communication and valuing that calls for a more comprehensively expressive, experiential descriptive language. Relationships between living beings, it seems, are personal and communicative; a form of 'speaking together' goes on, regardless of whether or not there is perfect understanding. The challenge, as Midgley argues, is for academia to take such 'earthy realism' seriously and allow it to inform the shaping of human and non-human quality of life.

EARTHY REALISM: THE CHALLENGE OF
MULTIPLE PERSPECTIVES

Pigs are very earthy animals. With their tremendously strong noses, they dig the earth for hours on end, searching for roots, seeds, insects or fungi. When it is hot, they like to wallow in earthy mud pools, created with rainwater or water from a drinker; the mud keeps their skin cool and protects it from sunburn. Pigs love to communicate: they grunt and squeal and touch and sniff each other all the time. They are quite like dogs—sociable, affectionate, curious, loyal—walking towards you, grunting and inviting contact, boisterously wriggling if they recognise you. As human beings we can engage with this pig-world. Research shows that humans can understand the emotionally expressive body language of pigs (e.g., if they are scared, content or curious; Wemelsfelder et al. 2012), and also gauge the emotional meaning of their sounds when hearing these from a recording (Tallet et al. 2010). Pigs share important physiological features with human beings—similar internal organs, hairless skin, light eyes—and are therefore prime organ-donors whose heart-valves, skin-grafts, and retinas have saved many a person's life. Pigs in earth, pigs in us—just one example of how life interrelates in myriad ways, connecting through flows of matter, activity, need and communication.

Midgley's work puts this connectedness at the foreground and calls for an 'earthy realism' that acknowledges lived, 'on the ground' relationships as the epistemic ground on which academic activity must stand. Humans (including academics) are part of the vastly complex earth-system, and our languages and imaginations have evolved to make sense of things we experience and do. Midgley argues that such earthy entanglement is not a hindrance towards meaningful knowledge but a help, to be harnessed rather than suppressed. Her stance is not relativist, but pluralist, recognising that there are multitudes of valid perspectives on the world, generating flows of knowledge that are complex, ambiguous and open to change.[2] Midgley does not see this as a weakness, an undesirable subjectivity, but as a strength, an ability to be responsive and relevant to life as people, animals and other organisms actually live it.

By contrast, the received scientific conception of knowledge postulates only one valid perspective, the objective one, which perforce its privileged nature must detach from, dominate and shape any views held 'on the ground'. The latter are not regarded by science as true perspectives, not even partial ones, but are seen, relative to the objective viewpoint, as arbitrary opinion. More inclusive views of scientific objectivity have been put forward (e.g., Barad 2007), but the greater part of mainstream science continues to favour a privileged position. True objectivity, in modern life science, is associated with mechanistic causation, relying on abstract, technical language that models living beings as complex, functional, rule-bound systems. Such models are 'perspective-less' by design, unequipped to consider the perspectives of living beings, other than in objectified terms, as 'internal (i.e., invisible) mental states'. The scientist's own perspective is isolated *outside* mechanist knowledge systems, as the single authoritative reference point for interpreting these systems. One knowing subject—multitudes of blinded objects. The possibility of other subjects remains forever hypothetical; a scientist will find nothing in the biological system she studies that remotely resembles herself.

This epistemic rupture is mostly taught to scientists as the natural order of things—as how objectivity should work. However, the notions of objectivity and subjectivity have deeply layered histories, and the way in which they were understood and translated into research techniques has changed through the centuries (Daston and Galison 2010). What objectivity is taken to mean, is, as with other perspectives, contingent on local times and mores and open to reflection and innovation. Framing knowledge in mechanistic terms was well-suited to the seventeenth-century interests in human dominance over nature and industrial manufacturing, as, for example, evident in the writings of English philosopher Francis Bacon, who associated objective truth with human power and utility (Zagorin 1998). However, Midgley argues, themes of human dominance and power have run their course, and in light of the grave current threat to the health of planet earth, must be transformed. 'Like babies, we are tiny, vulnerable, dependent organisms, owing our lives to a tremendous whole' (2007: 8). Articulating that dependency is now a matter of survival and requires that we change the very 'conceptual plumbing' of knowledge—that we become sensitized to life around us, rather than perpetuating our domination.

For many western minds, the question is whether, if a privileged objective stance is abandoned, one can still speak of 'knowledge'. Can the development of 'knowledge' accommodate perspectives from the ground, or does it then disintegrate into opinion and prejudice? Can it accommodate more qualitative, individually expressive languages, yet find common understanding? I will contemplate these questions in light of two areas of academic work, which I think connect closely with key themes in Midgley's writing: first, social anthropology, then, animal welfare science.

EARTHY REALISM IN SOCIAL ANTHROPOLOGY

Social anthropology has in recent years seen a revived interest in the relationship of indigenous people with non-human life. Indigenous people often talk about animals, plants, land, and climate, in animate, personalised language, portraying these as communities of sentient beings, all with their own unique perspectives on the world. Western (scientific) attitudes find it difficult to accept such portrayals as real, and are inclined to view them as cultural, or even mythological, narratives. However, anthropology no longer tolerates attitudes which it views as essentially colonial ('primitive natives'), and so finds itself presented with the challenge of making sense of highly divergent perspectives, involving both the perspectives of indigenous people and the perspectives of the animals, plants and climatic forces that these people perceive (Kohn 2013).

To consider the possibility of a multi-perspective reality, anthropologists must, and do, question the privileged externalised status of the Western scientific knower. Students of anthropology are taught to think participatively and self-reflectively at all stages of inquiry; if the greatest sin for a biologist is to be personally visible as a researcher, for an anthropologist it is *not* to be visible as one. An anthropologist's reflection on her situation within a community she wishes to study provides context to any insight she offers, but, more deeply, conveys the relational dynamics of knowing. Clarifying how one's own perspective is situated makes it possible to engage with other situated perspectives out there: now there are multitudes of knowing subjects, rather than just one. However, that an investigator reflects critically on his perspective does not automatically mean that the dominance of this perspective, so deeply embedded in western language and thought, is reduced. A shift to relational knowing, as Midgley says, requires proper conceptual re-plumbing. Anthropologists speak of the need for 'de-centering' Western (or more generally, human) perspectives, and 'foregrounding' indigenous (or more generally, more-than-human), perspectives. A key term used in Western academia to designate new terrains of connectivity is 'ecological', and so the search is for a 'sacred ecology' (Berkes 1999), a 'sentient ecology' (Anderson 2000), or an 'ecology of selves' (Kohn 2013). Fikret Berkes, a pioneer in articulating the importance of 'Traditional Ecological Knowledge' in the Western world, characterises it as 'a "community-of-beings" world-view . . . incorporating people who *belong* to that land and who have a relationship of peaceful co-existence with other beings' (1999: 274; original emphasis). A key feature of such a world-view is that it is not just a 'body of knowledge', but a 'way of life', something you *do* (Berkes 1999: 8; original emphasis). The primacy of acting and moving in forging a 'community-of-beings' is crucial and requires that we change our baseline perspective from 'knowing about' to 'living with'.

One social anthropologist deeply engaged with creating an epistemology of 'living with' is Tim Ingold, whose writing persistently questions and deconstructs the ingrained objectivist slant of the English language, clarifying how such language traps us into a distancing, dominating mode of thought. We assume that such thought is neutral, unproblematically 'real', but, as Ingold shows, what in fact it achieves is the removal of life's dynamic connectivity from our immediate awareness. We do not live *on* the earth, but *in* it. Earth is not merely *below* us, but all *around* us—we are intrinsically connected to its fabric, tracing routes through it, at the same time as other life forms trace *their* routes, all routes merging into an ever-changing dynamic meshwork. 'This tangle', Ingold says, 'is the texture of the world.

In the animic ontology, beings do not simply occupy the world, they *inhabit* it . . . along the lines of their relationships' (2006: 14; original emphasis). People, sky, plants, wind, animals, water, rock, all move with, through, by and against each other, in a process of open-ended, communal inhabitation. The sky, for example, is not merely an object of perception, something we see 'out there'—as light; it is what we see *in* or *with*, just as we hear *with* sound—our lives are possible only in communion with such other life-forms. 'We must', elucidates Ingold, 'imagine ourselves in the first place as participants, each immersed with the whole of our being in the currents of the world-in-formation . . . Participation is not opposed to observation, but is a condition for it, just as light is a condition for seeing things, sound for hearing them, and feeling for touching them' (2011: 129). Thus we literally see and understand what is possible only through moving with the earth moving around us, and it is this intrinsic, indispensable intimacy that indigenous people acknowledge when speaking of other life forms in familial, personable terms (e.g., Kopenawa and Albert 2013). By contrast, modern Western thought depicts all such co-presences as 'environment'; a bland, simplified, anthropocentric turn of phrase that ignores the existence of other creatures pursuing and appreciating life on earth. To remedy this, and be a coherent knowledge practice, Ingold argues, science 'must be rebuilt on the foundation of openness rather than closure, engagement rather than detachment. Knowing must be reconnected with being, epistemology with ontology, thought with life. Thus has our rethinking of indigenous animism led us to propose the re-animation of our own, so-called "Western" tradition of thought' (2006: 19).

Midgley's work has persistently sought to build a platform for such re-animation from within Western thought. She frequently refers to the work of the scientist James Lovelock (2000), who proposed that the organisms and elements of earth all interconnect through tightly coupled feedback loops, forming a whole, self-regulating system that could be compared to a living cell. To convey this earthly animated unity, Lovelock, on the advice of his friend, the novelist William Golding, famously invoked the Greek earth-goddess Gaia. This characterisation immediately led to a better grasp of these ideas by the general public; scientists, however, received it with great suspicion. What was this talk of 'Gaia'—dodgy science, or just a harmless metaphor, and, if the latter, why use it? But as Midgley argues in her books *Science and Poetry* (2001) and *The Myths We Live By* (2004), all science involves imaginative language and the use of metaphors, and no metaphor is ever harmless. Every concept, image or idea affects how we engage with reality—for instance, regarding the brain as a computer—so let the pot (science) not tell the kettle (Gaia theory) that it is black. 'Was it necessary to use language that apparently personified the earth? It seems that it really was so. . . . What personification does is to attack the central, disastrous feature of the mechanistic paradigm—the conviction that the earth is inert and lifeless' (Midgley 2007: 8).

Indeed, that the earth is not inert and lifeless and that its inhabitants move, live and die together in tightly interwoven patterns, is increasingly supported by good, not dodgy, science. We now know, for example, that the introduction of wolves in a region affects all life forms in that region and can shift the course of rivers and that the digestive habits of whales can affect global warming (Monbiot 2013). To detect such patterns and judge their meaning for the health of the earth, we need an open-minded, sophisticated ecological science, a science that goes on searching for the right language, so that it can ask the pertinent questions and knows where and how to look. What is absolutely crucial in such an endeavour, as both Midgley and Ingold indicate, is that scientists are willing to move beyond a purely objectifying, mechanistic language. Western ecological language, talking of ecosystems, networks, patterns and feedback couplings, still essentially views nature as a collection of 'things', blindly linked through complex functional cause and effect chains. Such terms do not begin to cover what Ingold and other anthropologists mean by 'living with', the multi-perspectival connectivity at the heart of indigenous experience; they do not convey the dynamic, sentient engagement between creatures that underlies emerging ecological systems.

What we need is a language expressive of that engagement—a language of movement and meaning, which, as Ingold said, re-animates and empowers our thought. There are Western scholars who have explored and pioneered such an approach, such as David Abram (1997), Brian Goodwin (2007), Stephan Harding (2006), Maxine Sheets-Johnstone (2011), and Wendy Wheeler (2006). These authors, in different ways, emphasize the importance of allowing more qualitative, open-ended, poetically expressive terminologies into science, to be able to recognise, and do justice to, emergent meanings of life's movements. I do not, here, have the space to discuss this work in more detail, but in the next section I will continue the discussion focusing more closely on animals. It is likely easier for Western people to think of animals as fellow sentient creatures than to think this way of plants, or rocks[3], and animals therefore present a good case study for the questions raised.

EARTHY REALISM IN ANIMAL WELFARE SCIENCE

The human-animal relationship, and moral concern for animals, have long been at the heart of Midgley's thought. 'We are not just rather like animals; we *are* animals' (1995: xxxiii; original emphasis) is her starting point, and given that primary unity, her view is that a reductive approach to understanding animals serves neither humans nor animals—all are sentient creatures with unique perspectives.[4] Of course, the motives, desires, feelings and thoughts of different species vary and coincide in complex ways, and science can play an important role in disentangling and clarifying these ways. For that to be possible, however, scientists must be at ease with using richly expressive, experiential descriptive language for both humans and animals. For, as Midgley (1983) clarifies, to be able to make comparisons and articulate differences, the notion of there being such a thing as an animal's experience must be generically accepted in the first place. That is the key insight around which further understanding of animals ought to be built.

The question of whether or not animals are sentient, and what it means to say this, has a long history in animal science. In recent times, particularly since Donald Griffin's book *The Question of Animal Awareness* (1976), it has indeed become more acceptable to consider animal sentience a legitimate topic for scientific research (Duncan 2006). As Marian Dawkins (1990), a leading scientist in the field of animal welfare science, has argued, it makes sense to investigate the well-being and suffering of animals only if we are willing to grant those animals a perspective and talk about their needs and feelings. This stance has given rise to a thriving field of animal welfare science, in which scientists are encouraged to develop concepts and measures for investigating whether animals are feeling well, or are suffering, in the conditions in which they are kept.

However, this practice is confused and weakened by the insistence of many scientists, including Marian Dawkins, that all talk of animal awareness and feeling is, in principle, anthropomorphic. Anthropomorphism, in this context, is regarded as 'the almost universal human tendency to attribute human qualities to things that are not human' (Dawkins 2012: 19). Thus 'feeling' is first and foremost seen as a human quality, which animals, as 'things that are not human', may or may not have—any capacity for sentient awareness, and well-being and suffering, remains to be demonstrated. However, for scientists, that demonstration has to take place in mechanistic terms, which, as outlined earlier, are 'perspective-less' by design, unequipped to consider the perspectives of living beings other than in objectified terms (i.e., as 'internal mental states'). There is thus a deep conceptual tension running through the theoretical framing of animal welfare research, leaving it unresolved whether animals 'really feel' things, or, as complex functionally programmed systems, only behave 'as if' they do (Dawkins 2012).

This seems quite a conundrum—but the spectre of anthropomorphism is likely to always loiter in the shades of mechanistic knowledge construction (Wemelsfelder 2012). If, as outlined earlier, a scientist's perspective is the single authoritative reference point for interpreting information, then inevitably this perspective will be projected on to animal information—it is the only perspective going. This, not surprisingly, leaves scientists uneasy, not satisfied that their interpretation truly reflects the animal's feelings—how can they be sure it is the animal's, not their own reflection? Great importance is placed on the use of sophisticated controlled experimental testing conditions, but in such conditions too, the animal's experience remains elusive, as the following quote indicates: 'Of course, even if we can use measurable components of emotional responses to locate an animal's position in core affect space, we cannot be certain that they experience the *conscious* component too' (Mendl et al. 2010: 2896; original emphasis). Thus, mechanistically defining and measuring emotion does not get us closer to the actual experience of the animal whose emotions they are. If the animal's perspective is not explicitly accounted for, the human perspective dominates. So for scientists to lament the threat of anthropomorphism, and resort to more reductive measures, seems entirely counterproductive. What the situation calls for is not that scientists declare animal feelings private and unknowable, but that they open up the boundaries of objectivity, as Midgley advocates, and encourage the use of a richly expressive, experiential descriptive language. Then we may be better equipped to appreciate animals' perspectives and bring them into scientific research.

Interest in directly engaging with animal perspectives is indeed growing in different areas of academic inquiry, right across the spectrum of philosophy, social science, zoology and the humanities (e.g., Bekoff 2007; Haraway 2008; Bussolini 2013). In all such areas, there are efforts to develop relational concepts and methodologies and to explore what it takes to give animals a voice (Birke and Hockenhull 2012; Buller, 2014; Ogden et al. 2013; Wemelsfelder 2007). A first principle underlying such work must be that the whole sentient being is placed at the centre of our thought. Animals have psychological presence and integrity: there is *someone there*, an individual with an outlook on the world. Animals are not merely assembled systems; they are beings, subjects to whom things matter, and the way in which they engage with the world is expressive of that meaning, never just blind physical movement. Seeing animals this way, what we gain is not so much a 'knowing about' as a 'getting to know': a form of communication, becoming acquainted, an appreciation of 'being with' fellow creatures.

Midgley (1995) points out that scientists often must tacitly rely on such communication to know what their physical measures mean and to make them useful. However, scientists' reticence to discuss this openly prevents the development of a truly appropriate, sufficiently complex and expressive language for describing how animals act and feel. As philosophers Michael Bavidge and Ian Ground point out in their book *Can We Understand Animal Minds?* (1994: 163): 'We have to have the right kind of relation to one another, before we can begin to speak of knowledge'. The difficulty in creating such relations with animals, they argue, is that

> we do not feature in the lives of most animals. Hence we are never or only rarely the object of their expressive attention. . . . The real problem of other animal minds is . . . to find ways of interacting with our neighbour species, extending our capacity to recognise other creatures in their expressive presence in the world (pp. 163–164).

Indeed, it is true we do not feature much in animal lives; rather, they feature in ours, an imbalance imposing major restrictions on how we know animals. Whether they be animals grown for agricultural production, animals bred in zoos, or cherished companion animals, animals are subject to humans, who define the parameters of their existence and shape their means of expression. Unless animals have considerable freedom to roam, we rarely if ever witness how animals would naturally express themselves, and what it would mean to 'live with' these animals on spontaneous, equal footing. Again, human dominance is bound to restrict and commodify the language we use to portray animals in these situations (Dunayer 2001).

Interesting accounts do exist by people who were able to develop spontaneous, unforced relationships with wild animals—with garden birds, for example (Howard 1958)—and were thus, in Bavidge and Ground's words, genuinely 'the object of these animals' expressive attention'. Particularly well-known are accounts by animal ethologists such as Jane Goodall, Dian Fossey, Cynthia Moss and Barbara Smuts, who spent years living and working amidst primate and elephant communities and developed a mutual understanding and trust with individual animals that enabled them to evaluate these animals' experience and outlook on life in great depth, and with great compassion. Barbara Smuts, for instance, reflects how this transformed her view of animals:

> Although animals had always fascinated me, my time with baboons and chimps in Africa greatly enhanced my awareness of the individuality of each animal I encounter. Before Africa, if I were walking in the woods and came across a squirrel, I would enjoy its presence, but I would experience it as a member of a class, 'squirrel'. Now, I experience every squirrel I encounter as a small, fuzzy-tailed, person-like creature. Even though I usually don't know this squirrel from another, I know that if I tried, I would, and that once I did, this squirrel would reveal itself as an utterly unique being, different in temperament and behaviour from every other squirrel in the world. In addition, I am aware that if this squirrel had a chance to get to know me, he or she might relate to me differently than to any other person in the world (2001: 301).

Smuts goes on to describe how this perspective more generally changed her experience of the world around her:

> My awareness of the individuality of all beings, and of the capacity of at least some beings to respond to the individuality in me, transforms the world into a universe replete with opportunities to develop personal relationships of all kinds. Such relationships can be ephemeral, like those developed with the birds in whose territories we might picnic, or life-long, like those established with cats, dogs, and human friends (2001: 301).

Thus, animals can and do speak to those who take the time to get to know them. 'Speaking' in this context, of course, does not refer to human-like

verbal expression, but to the expressive personal communication and comprehension that is possible between sentient beings. Such communication
is direct, yet not guaranteed to be successful: communicating beings can
misunderstand each other, or fail to reach each other at all. Most species use
specialised sensory ranges, such as long-distance hearing or infrared vision,
that other species, including humans, may not be able to perceive. And even
if, through sophisticated technology, we could discern how animals express
themselves at these ranges, we may not interpret it right. We may be too
anthropomorphic, inadvertently projecting human meaning on to the communicative dynamics, or too 'bird-o-morphic', or 'dolphin-o-morphic', if
these are the animals we happen to know. Or we may fail to connect altogether if a species is too alien to us—a deep-sea crab, for instance.

But the important thing to understand here, as Midgley (1995) has persistently pointed out, is that none of such potential restrictions undermine
that animals are sentient beings, with whom it is, in principle, possible to
connect.[5] Anthropomorphism is a specific, secondary mistake of misjudging
another's expressions, a mistake that logically implies the primary acknowledgement that those others are expressive sentient beings. When meeting
people from a different culture for the first time, we may not understand
anything they say or do, but that would not cause us to deny that they
were sentient beings, or to assume that their experiences were private. We
would simply realise that time and effort must be spent to learn to communicate with them effectively. The extent to which this can be accomplished
is, in the end, an empirical question that can be pursued through prolonged
authentic engagement with animals, in personal interaction and in appropriate research. Perhaps it turns out not to be so difficult to connect with,
say, chameleons or penguins, or even deep-sea crabs, if we find the right
medium of communication. Humans and animals are far more likely to be
fundamentally interconnected than to exist in separate emotional realms
(Midgley 1995: 337–8).

There are many ways in which animals and their perspective can be
placed at the centre of research. Perhaps the most straightforward angle
is an anthropological one. Many areas of anthropology already focus on
narratives of participative engagement and could give animals their rightful
place in projects of 'multi-species ethnography' (Ogden et al. 2013). But for
animal welfare science, too, it is important to think how this can be done.
A range of whole-animal research approaches do exist, such as asking animals to express their preference when given a choice of options, asking them
to indicate how motivated they are to gain access to something, or an array
of learning tasks enabling animals to indicate how they evaluate their surroundings. Much has been learned from such tests; however, because they
tend to be framed in mechanistic terms, they are at risk of super-imposing
anthropocentric hypotheses and insufficiently question how the animals
themselves view these tests. The animals may well respond from a very different angle than intended by the researcher. To address this, close attention

must be paid to the expressive dynamics of exactly how animals engage with a test: how they enter it, interact with it, communicate with other animals and humans whilst performing it, and also how they behave after it has ended. Knowing this, we might assess more realistically what test outcomes mean from the animal's point of view, which may, or may not, coincide with the scientist's assumptions (Despret 2009).

It will not be easy to capture animals' complex flows of expressivity in a way that is genuinely animal-centred and is also workable for scientists. In the context of animal welfare science, one approach is to conceive whole-animal expressivity as a dynamic 'body language' (Wemelsfelder 2007 and 2012). The whole animal is expressive in a way that physical body parts or processes never are; it is not the ear positions, facial features or brain waves that carry meaning, it is the dynamic, ever fluid way in which the animal holds and moves with such features that is full of expressive, sentient detail. Animals can, for example, move around in ways that are curious, confident and relaxed, or wary, anxious and tense. By observing and describing such expressive qualities over time, we gain a closer understanding of how animals experience their surroundings, and how this may affect their well-being and quality of life. The question for scientists is, can this be done reliably? Our first studies of assessing animal body language were made with pigs; pigs are lively, curious, affectionate animals, whose expressivity is more easily discernable to untrained human observers than that of, say, sheep. Indeed, we found that participants showed good agreement in how they characterised the pigs' body language in different situations, even when their professions and attitudes differed (e.g., pig farming, veterinary care, animal protection). In addition, such characterisations corresponded well with physical measures of pig behaviour and stress physiology and played an important role in interpreting the relevance of these measures for the pigs' welfare. In subsequent years, similar results were found by various research groups for other species, including cows, sheep, goats, chickens, horses, donkeys, elephants and dogs. What these outcomes indicate is that taking animal perspectives seriously can indeed be a reliable and useful part of scientific investigation; pigs talk, and listening carefully makes for better, not worse, animal welfare science (Wemelsfelder and Mullan 2013).

That animals are sentient beings is now reflected in European law, and attitudes towards animals are slowly changing for the better across society. In animal welfare science, there is a growing emphasis on the positive aspects of animal welfare; well-being is no longer defined as merely the absence of stress and suffering, but is recognized to require that animals should have a 'good life', involving qualities such as comfort, play, opportunities to search for food and social relationships (Boissy et al. 2007). As part of this, the animal body-language research described above is enjoying growing acceptance and interest among animal welfare scientists. Carefully observing how animals express themselves can show us whether animals are actively, happily engaging with the world around them, or are depleted, not actually able to relate properly, appearing bored, aloof and irritable.

It is a traditional farming stockmanship skill to know animals as individuals and see from small shifts in their expression whether they are well or not. Farmers rarely complain about anthropomorphism; living with animals day-in and-day-out, they know that these animals have characters, thoughts and feelings. For farmers, the struggle is to make a living; they may well complain that farms are not luxury holiday camps for cows. However, generally they care and would make changes to improve their animals' welfare if this were practically feasible and economically viable. Recent studies in social geography and anthropology, and in animal welfare science, have begun to look more closely at human-animal relationships in rural communities, on farms, in fields and in homes, describing how individuals interact and converse with each other, whether they be humans, cows, birds, bees or dogs (Ellingsen et al. 2014, Jones 2014).

Such 'on the ground' work seems a promising way forward to find new concepts and expand and enrich our expressive language for characterising flows of communication between living beings. 'Flourishing', for example, is a lovely poetic word that does better justice to what creatures wish for in their lives than the prosaic scientific term 'positive welfare' (Harfeld 2013). Flourishing is readily seen as an aspiration for human communities, but communities are never just human. Humans, animals, plants, trees, rocks, sky, all want to flourish, and can only flourish together—that is the 'earthy realism' for which Midgley's work stands.

CONCLUSIONS

Remembering the questions at the start of this chapter, it does not appear the case at all that a multi-perspective, participative, earthly realism abandons all claims at knowledge and disintegrates into arbitrary opinion. Its basic stance is personal, yes, but not arbitrary; rather it is relational, sentient and expressive, generating flows of communication that interconnect perspectives, meanings and forms of life. Such communication is more than knowledge; it is the very foundation on which knowledge and common understanding become possible. Indigenous people recognize this, and Western academics are beginning to surmise it. Yet if allegations of anthropomorphism still haunt our recognition of animals as fellow sentient creatures, then how much harder will it be to see trees, rocks and sky this way? Relating more personally to trees and rocks is not necessarily to say that they are individuals in the way that humans and animals are (though many indigenous people do say so), but it is to say that they are not merely things. They too, take part in the ecology of 'living with', and, as such, speak to us, as all poets know. To listen, and to come down from our privileged human position, it is essential that we begin to bring together insights gained in very different areas of academic inquiry. We cannot afford to ignore Midgley's deep and urgent understanding that science and poetry must merge in facing the enormous moral dilemmas of our time.

NOTES

1. See also David E. Cooper's chapter in this volume.
2. See also Ian James Kidd's chapter in this volume.
3. Though recent research at the University of Florence suggests that plants are capable of flexible decision-making and communication, and hence may qualify as intelligent, social creatures (Baluška et al. 2006).
4. In their chapters for this volume, Ian Ground and Raymond Tallis also consider this theme in Midgley's work.
5. Reference can also be made here to Wittgenstein's argument that the fallibility of expressive criteria does not mean such criteria are not publicly observable (Hacker 1993).

REFERENCES

Abram, D., *The Spell of the Sensuous: Perception and Language in a More-than-human World* (New York: Vintage, 1997).

Anderson, D.G., *Identity and Ecology in Arctic Siberia* (Oxford: Oxford University Press, 2000).

Baluška, F., Mancuso, S. and Volkmann, D., *Communication in Plants: Neuronal Aspects of Plant Life* (Dordrecht: Springer, 2006).

Barad, K., *Meeting the Universe Halfway: Quantum Physics and the Entanglement of Matter and Meaning* (Durham, NC: Duke University Press, 2007).

Bavidge, M. and Ground, I., *Can We Understand Animal Minds?* (London: Bristol Classical Press, 1994).

Bekoff, M., *The Emotional Lives of Animals: A Leading Scientist Explores Animal Joy, Sorrow, and Empathy—and Why they Matter* (Novato, Calif.: New World Library, 2007).

Berkes, F., *Sacred Ecology* (New York: Taylor and Francis, 1999).

Birke, L. and Hockenhull, J. (eds.), *Crossing Boundaries: Investigating Human-animal Relationships* (Leiden: Brill, 2012).

Boissy, A., Manteuffel, G., Jensen, M.B., Moe, R.O., Spruijt, B., Keeling, L.J., Winckler, C., Forkman, B., Dimitrov, I., Langbein, J., Bakken, M., Veissier, I. and Aubert, A., 'Assessment of positive emotions in animals to improve their welfare'. *Physiology and Behavior* 92(3), 375–397, 2008.

Buller, H., 'Animal geographies II: Methods'. *Progress in Human Geography* 31, 2014. DOI: 10.1177/0309132514527401.

Bussolini, J., 'Recent French, Belgian and Italian work in the cognitive science of animals: Dominique Lestel, Vinciane Despret, Roberto Marchesini and Giorgio Celli'. *Social Science Information* 52(2), 187–209, 2013.

Daston, L. and Galiston, P., *Objectivity* (Brooklyn: Zone Books, 2010).

Dawkins, M.S., 'From an animal's point of view: Motivation, fitness, and animal-welfare'. *Behavioral and Brain Sciences* 13(1), 1–9, 1990.

Dawkins, M.S., *Why Animals Matter. Animal Consciousness, Animal Welfare, and Human Well-Being* (Oxford: Oxford University Press, 2012).

Despret, V., *Penser Comme un Rat*. (Versailles: Quae Editions, 2009).

Dunayer, J., *Animal Equality: Language and Liberation* (Derwood: Ryce, 2001).

Duncan, I.J.H., 'The changing concept of animal sentience'. *Applied Animal Behaviour Science* 100, 11–19, 2006.

Ellingsen, K., Coleman, G.J., Lund, V. and Mejdell, C.M., 'Using qualitative behaviour assessment to explore the link between stockperson behaviour and dairy calf behaviour'. *Applied Animal Behaviour Science* 153, 10–17, 2014.

Goodwin, B., *Nature's Due: Healing Our Fragmented Culture* (Edinburgh: Floris Books, 2007).

Griffin, D.R., *The Question of Animal Awareness: Evolutionary Continuity of Mental Experience* (New York: Rockefeller University Press, 1976).

Hacker, P.M., *Wittgenstein: Meaning and Mind. Part I, Essays* (Oxford: Blackwell, 1993).

Haraway, D., *When Species Meet* (Minneapolis : University of Minnesota Press, 2008).

Harding, S., *Animate Earth: Science, Intuition and Gaia* (Dartington: Green Books, 2006).

Harfeld, J.L., '*Telos* and the ethics of animal farming'. *Journal of Agricultural and Environmental Ethics* 26, 691–709, 2013.

Howard, L., *Birds as Individuals*, 6th ed. (London: Collins, 1958).

Ingold, T., 'Re-thinking the animate, re-animating thought'. *Ethnos* 71(1), 9–20, 2006.

Ingold, T., *Being Alive: Essays on Movement, Knowledge and Description* (London: Routledge, 2011).

Jones, O., "Who milks the cows at Maesgwyn?' The animality of UK rural landscapes in affective registers'. *Landscape Research* 38(4), 421–442, 2013.

Kohn, E., *How Forests Think. Toward an Anthropology Beyond the Human* (London: University of California Press, 2013).

Kopenawa, D. and Albert, B., *The Falling Skye: Words of a Yanomani Shaman* (Cambridge, Mass.: Harvard University press, 2013).

Lovelock, J., *Gaia: A New Look at Life on Earth* (Oxford: Oxford Paperbacks, 2000).

Mendl, M., Burman, O.H.P. and Paul, E.S., 'An integrative and functional framework for the study of animal emotion and mood'. *Proceedings of the Royal Society B* 277, 2895–904, 2010.

Midgley, M., *Animals and Why They Matter* (Athens, GA: University of Georgia Press, 1983).

Midgley, M., *Beast and Man*. Revised ed. (London: Routledge, 1995).

Midgley, M., *Science and Poetry* (London: Routledge, 2001).

Midgley, M., *The Myths We Live By* (London: Routledge, 2004).

Midgley, M., *Earthy Realism. The meaning of Gaia* (Exeter: Societas, 2007).

Monbiot, G., *Feral* (London: Allen Lane, 2013).

Ogden, L.A., Hall, B. and Tanita, K., 'Animals, plants, people, and things. A review of multispecies ethnography'. *Environment and Society: Advances in Research* 4, 5–24.

Sheets-Johnstone, M., 'The imaginative consciousness of movement: Linear quality, kinaesthesia, language and life'. In: Ingold, T. (ed.), *Redrawing Anthropology: Materials, Movements, Lines* (Farnham: Ashgate, 115–128, 2011).

Smuts, B., 'Encounters with animal minds'. *Journal of Consciousness Studies* 8, 293–309, 2001.

Tallet, C., Spinka, M., Maruscakova, I. and Simecek, P., 'Human perception of vocalizations of domestic piglets and modulation by experience with domestic pigs (Sus scrofa)'. *Journal of Comparative Psychology* 124(1), 81–91, 2010.

Wemelsfelder, F., 'How animals communicate quality of life: The qualitative assessment of animal behaviour'. *Animal Welfare* 16(S), 25–31, 2007.

Wemelsfelder, F., 'A science of friendly pigs: carving out a conceptual space for addressing animals as sentient beings'. In: Birke, L.I.A. and Hockenhull, J. (eds.), *Crossing Boundaries: Investigating Human-animal Relationships* (Leiden: Brill, 223–251, 2012).

Wemelsfelder, F. and Mullan, S., 'Applying ethological and health indicators to practical animal welfare assessment'. *OIE Scientific and Technical Review* 33(1), 111–20, 2014.

Wemelsfelder, F., Hunter, A.S., Paul, E.S. and Lawrence, A.B., 'Assessing pig body language: agreement and consistency between pig farmers, veterinarians, and animal activists'. *Journal of Animal Science* 90, 3652–65, 2012.

Wheeler, W., *The Whole Creature: Complexity, Biosemiotics and the Evolution of Culture* (London: Lawrence and Wishart, 2006).

Zagorin, P., *Francis Bacon* (Princeton: Princeton University Press, 1998).

Part II

Human Nature

5 *Beast and Man*
Thirty-Five Years On

Raymond Tallis

INTRODUCTION

Thirty-five years after it was published, Mary Midgley's *Beast and Man: The Roots of Human Nature* remains a landmark in British philosophy and one of the most significant recent attempts to make sense of human nature. The opening sentences set out Midgley's principles with characteristic lucidity:

> We are not just rather like animals; we are animals. Our differences from other species may be striking, but comparisons with them have always been, and must be, crucial to our view of ourselves (1979: xiii)

In many respects, *Beast and Man* was a corrective—in particular to the venerable philosophical tradition of separating the animal human body from the rational, spiritual human mind, person, or soul, and identifying humanity with the latter, while disregarding the former.

In the years since it was published, however, the balance has tilted the other way. Biologism, expressed in the crude simplifications of evolutionary psychology, genetic determinism, and the reduction of persons to their brains, has assumed a dominant position in the academic discussion of human nature, and this has been picked up and disseminated in the popular press. The invasion of the humanities by hybrid disciples with 'neuro-', 'evolutionary-', or 'neuro-evolutionary' prefixes (such as 'neuro-law', 'neuro-theology', 'evolutionary economics' and 'neuro-evolutionary aesthetics') is the most striking testimony to this shift in thought (see Tallis 2011).

For these reasons, *Beast and Man* is more relevant than ever. There is an additional reason: its style. Midgley's careful arguments are illuminated by a truly profound common sense—of the rare kind that enables someone to see what is in front of her nose—and expressed in prose that has a distinctive tone of voice present throughout her now considerable oeuvre. It is this that makes her case as much as the arguments she deploys—which is why I have quoted her verbatim extensively in this essay.

She herself has highlighted the importance of this neglected aspect of philosophical writing:

> Hume's or Plato's tone of voice comes through the centuries, sharp and unmistakable, filling in for the imagination a whole immense background of personal reaction that completes the sense of what they are literally saying, making all the differences between an isolated argument and a comprehensive view of life, between, in fact, a little philosopher and a great one (1979: 242)

If more contemporary philosophy were written as Midgley writes it, philosophers might assume more prominent role in the conversation that society has, or should be having, with itself.

MIDGELY'S CORRECTIVE

Midgley's thesis in *Beast and Man* is that the gap between man and other animals is not to be found where it is traditionally located and, what is more, that it is rather narrower than we are inclined to think. I shall come to this second point, where I dissent somewhat from her views, in the later part of my essay. For the present, I want to focus on the first part of the thesis. Re-thinking the relationship between man and non-human animals requires, she argues, that we shall set aside at least two widespread assumptions.

The first is the Cartesian notion that animals are machines:

> Actually only machines are machines. Nothing else is made by humans from parts and for purposes entirely supplied by themselves. Nothing else can therefore be understood simply by reading off those parts and purposes from the specifications. (1979: 2)

While the machine analogy may be adequate to explanations of insect behaviour, 'at any higher level it is an incubus' (1979: xvi): 'the motivation of the more advanced creatures is enormously more complex than the traditions suppose'.

This is often obscured by the fact that we tend to view animals—and see how they contrast with man—not as they are but as projections of our own fears and desires. For example, we have displaced our sense of our own ferocity by projecting it on to animals. Our bad behaviour is un-human 'beastliness', 'bestiality' or 'brutality'. The wolf is a symbol of our own predatory propensities. As John Gay put it, however, this is a case of pots and kettles:

> A Wolf eats a sheep but now and then;
> Ten thousands are devour'd by men'

'Beasts' Midgley concludes 'are neither incarnations of wickedness, nor sets of basic needs, nor crude mechanical toys, nor idiot children' (1979: 39).

Midgley suspects that resistance to acknowledging our animality arises because we fear negative implications for our freedom and dignity. Against this she argues that 'the notion that 'we have a nature', far from threatening the concept of freedom, is absolutely essential to it' (1979: xviii). This, of course, makes perfect sense. If we were entirely blank sheets, we would be open to infinite manipulation by the environment. What is more, we would have nothing to be free for, or about. A blank sheet would have no basis for choosing one path over another. Interestingly, this criticism applies with equal force to those who argue that our having no nature makes us some kind of limitlessly plastic slop. Actions, after all, 'are not just physical jerks, they signify, they count as something. But they cannot do so except against a background of expectation, of regular, definite alternatives' (1979: 296)

Midgley singles out for criticism Existentialist philosophy, in particular the brand associated with Jean-Paul Sartre. She cites his hugely influential essay 'Existentialism and Humanism', where he declares that

> there is no human nature . . . Man first of all exists, encounters himself, surges up in the world, and defines himself afterwards. If man as the Existentialist sees him is not definable, it is because to begin with he is nothing. He will not be anything until later, and then he will be what he makes himself (1958: 28)

Leaving aside the problem of getting a particular someone from a general nothing, Midgley reiterates that having a nature is not some kind of congenital disability, limiting our freedom, predestining us to a particular course in life. Like other animals, we have a nature; but this does not mean that we are 'just' animals:

> Man has his own nature, not that of any other species. He cannot, therefore, be degraded by comparison, if it is careful and honest, because it will bring out his peculiarities, it will show what is unique about him, as well as what is not (1979: xvii)

And the comparisons are, Midgley argues, necessary. 'Had we known no other animate life-form than our own, we should have been utterly mysterious to ourselves as a species' (1979: 18). She quotes primatologist Jane Goodall:

> It is only through real understanding of the ways in which chimpanzees and men show similarities of behaviour that we can reflect, with meaning, on the ways in which men and chimpanzees differ. And only then can we really begin to appreciate, in a biological and spiritual manner, the full extent of man's uniqueness (1971: 250–1, quoted in Midgley 1979: 227)

Characteristically, she illustrates this with a homely example: the discomfort we sometimes feel in being stared at. We can cast light on this by relating the idea of a 'personal space' that is invaded by the other's gaze to the wider ethological notion of a territory to be protected for obvious reasons connected with the pursuit of nutrition and the rearing of offspring.

Equally characteristically, she then points out that 'territorial invasion' is the beginning, not the end, of explanation. Territoriality is a complex concept, which has different manifestations in different species, particularly in the case of the species *H. sapiens*. Comparisons between us and other animals 'make sense only when they are put in the context of the entire character of the species concerned' (1979: 24). General dispositions allow considerable room 'for particular developments within them and bargains between them' (1979: 63). Slaughter in humans, for example, does not demonstrate that they are innately aggressive, if only because 'it is often linked with some of the most precious elements in human nature, namely, loyalty and friendship' (1979: 63) Human instincts, as in all higher animals, are 'open'. This commitment to a joined up approach to thinking about animal (and human) propensities and traits is evident throughout *Beast and Man*, which draws on a careful and extensive reading of a literature that examines actual animal behaviour in a natural setting rather than in the laboratory.

The radical behaviourist B. F. Skinner proclaimed that:

> The perceiving and knowing which arise from verbal contingencies [of reinforcements] are even more obviously the products of the environment [and that] abstract thinking is the product of a particular kind of environment not of a cognitive faculty (1971: 188–9)

Midgely responds by asking: 'Why can't a psychologist's parrot talk psychology'?' (1979: 21) Her response illustrates a general principle expressed in a beautiful aphorism: 'We do not just have to verify our hypotheses carefully but also to form them intelligently' (1979: 21).

Midgley addresses rival claims for the contributions of culture and nature to our upbringing and make-up by arguing that 'nature and culture are not opposites. We are naturally culture-building animals. But what we build into our culture has to satisfy our natural pattern of motives. (1979: 29) These motives are not to be reduced to mere drives or instincts simply construed, though human motives clearly have roots in biology.

The emphasis on culture is connected with her hostility to a simplifying biologism and, more broadly, to a reductive scientism. *Beast and Man* was in progress when, in 1976, Richard Dawkins published *The Selfish Gene*. Dawkins has subsequently been an important interlocutor in what has proved to be a dialogue of the deaf, though the deafness is not on Midgley's side.[1]

Dawkins advocated a gene-eyed Darwinitis, an inflamed form of Darwinian theory that aims to explain not only the origin of the organism *H. sapiens* but also the human person. It is a particularly striking example of the reductionism that has two aspects: the assumption that higher-level, macroscopic behaviour is explained by some lower-level constituent of the entity in question; and that for any explanation to be taken seriously (and to count as 'scientific') it must be rooted ultimately in physical science. This is widespread view is most clearly expressed by the physicist Steven Weinberg:

> The explanatory arrow points downwards from societies to people, to organs, to cells, to biochemistry, to chemistry, and ultimately to physics. (quoted in Shermer 2008)

The gap between the explanation—'it's all in the genes' (essentially molecules)—and the explanandum—the phenomena to be accounted for (our emotions, our social behaviour, our institutions)—is often concealed by ascribing higher-level features to the lower-level phenomenon. What I have elsewhere called 'explanation by transferred epithet' (Tallis 2004) is illustrated by the idea of 'the selfish gene' which, though meant metaphorically, even semi-humorously, does much of the explanatory work of trying to read humans out of genes.

Dawkins does not appear in *Beast and Man*, but E. O. Wilson's hugely ambitious *Sociobiology: The New Synthesis* is challenged robustly for its similarly gene-eyed view of all living creatures, including humanity. 'Love', Wilson asserts,

> joins hate; aggression, fear; expansiveness; withdrawal; and so on, in blends designed not to promote the happiness and survival of the individual, but to favour the maximum transmission of the controlling genes (1975: 4)

Midgley challenges this by pointing out that it is 'irrational to pick on any stage of the species's continuation as containing the point of the whole thing', adding that:

> Genes are not little men. We are describing a very complex process, all stages of which (and not only reproduction) have been refined by evolution to contribute to the whole. (1979: 93)

She also points out that, since genes do not make decisions or take advice, the moral lessons that Wilson bases on his biologism would be pointless if genes really were the ultimate drivers of our behaviour, the captains of our soul. Midgley also notes that Wilson 'scrupulously avoids any discussion of purpose, motive, mind, consciousness, feeling, intention, or any related notion, and omits them from his index' 1979: 113). This may be appropriate for an entomologist thinking about ants, as Wilson was for most of his career in science. Yet to talk about human behaviour without them 'leads to chaotic use of language in which these concepts appear in a ghostly and uncriticised form' (1979: 113).

The reductions of altruism to 'a mechanism by which DNA multiplies itself through a network of relatives' and spirituality to 'just one more Darwinian enabling device' (1979: 121)—views that are now mainstream in the world of evolutionary psychologists—are demolished wittily and courteously by Midgley, who points out that if this 'mechanism' were to work in our complex world, our 'calculation of consequences would have to be immeasurably more strongly developed, commoner and more efficient than it actually is in man, let alone in other species' (p.128). What is more, 'If the "aim" the steady, impartially determined advantage, were just surviving, amoebas would be the thing to be' Since an amoeba reproduces by division, 'its first members are in a sense still here in person. There's survival for you' (1979: 153).

Midgley contests the belief that survival is the only value (or the root of all values) and the connected idea of evolution necessarily moving towards increasing complexity in pursuit of increasingly efficient means of survival. In fact, improved survival and increased complexity may not go hand in hand (1979: 150). There is no obligation to 'climb the ladder'; and metaphors such as 'ruthless marches, relentless pressure, brutal cutthroat competition and all the rest of it' are just—well, *metaphors*, and not very good ones. The notion of 'ascent' terminating in the 'higher animals' is the result of 'a disastrous tangle between the ideas of time, height, and value' (1979: 159).

This underpins Midgley's challenge to the idea of man as occupying the top spot in the evolutionary tree. She offers an alternative notion of the tip of a branch in a bush whose foliage represents different ways in which living organisms become fit for different conditions. The worldview that places man at the top of the tree of life is connected with the Christian tradition (given metaphysical underpinning by Descartes' view of animals as mere things) of 'a positive duty for man to recognise his superiority over, and lack of indebtedness to, nature' (p.219). Creatures that are seen by us as inferior are, she says with typical acerbity, simply organisms that 'have failed the test of becoming more like us'. For this reason, we cannot appeal to evolution 'to furnish a test to resolve our clash of values' (1979: 165) and biology to underpin an objective ethics and address the challenge of moral relativism.

Long before the birth of 'neuro-ethics' Midgley pointed out why neurology cannot replace moral philosophy. This is because arguing over norms is not something carried out in 'the meat of any thinker's brain, but in language':

> It is the relation of proposed acts to certain standards, principles, and ideals that we accept as binding, not just on ourselves, but on anyone else who becomes involved with them . . . a moral problem is public (1979: 173)

And of course none of the organs of the body, not even the brain, is 'public' in the sense in which discourse is public. This has not influenced writers such as Patricia Churchland, who has tried to justify her homespun wisdom by appealing to brain science, with risible consequences (see Churchland 2014).

The longest chapter in *Beast and Man* is devoted to 'Speech and Other Excellences'. Midgley is sceptical of the notion of a single differentiating feature that captures what is distinctive about humanity. Echoing what she earlier said about machines, she argues against the assumption that 'things not made by man' (including man himself) 'will necessarily have an essence we can grasp and a simple characteristic excellence we can see the point of' (1979: 204). The broader capacity for conceptual thought might, however, qualify as a distinctive characteristic because it is 'a structural property, one affecting the whole organisation of the life of the species' (1979: 205). What is more, this is part of a cluster that includes reason, language, culture, self-consciousness, tool-using, productivity, laughter, a sense of the future' (1979: 206). For this reason, she argues, it is not possible to 'find a mark that distinguishes man from "the animals" without saying which animals.' Structural properties do not have to be exclusive, necessarily excellent, or yes-or-no matters, and she adds that '[h]uman beings are judged by their ideal performance, animals by their actual ones' (1979: 210).

Midgley concludes from her reflections on human language and primate communication that, rather than looking for a single distinguishing mark, we should expect 'a knot of general structural properties . . . language might form part of such a knot, instead of being an isolated miracle' (1979: 253). And this, she argues, is as true for the other distinguishing features such as rationality, which is not to be narrowly construed as measurable intelligence: it includes having the right priorities which are different from isolated impulses; cleverness, yes, but also integration rooted in a firm and effective priority system. Without the latter, it is possible for intelligence to be the servant of stupidity.

These principles provide the foundation for insightful discussions of self-control, aggression, conscience, and the virtues and vices, the purposes, linked to lasting character traits, that go into the making of individual human beings—developing Midgley's thesis that thinking about animal behaviour (in a manner that takes its rise from an unprejudiced examination of the actual data) might help us to see our own nature more clearly, in particular the complex relationships between emotions, thoughts, and reason—which 'does not develop as a neutral, computer-like, technological device, detached from all aims' (1979: 280).

There is much more to *Beast and Man* than I have discussed. Midgley has explored many of its themes in books published over the last three decades. Reductionism remains a particular bugbear, particularly in the form of gene-eyed Neo-Darwinism (the idea that we are 'lumbering robots' acting out the instructions written in our genes that manage to be self-centred despite having no self) or that ultimately we are just collections of atoms. The wider intellectual harm caused by misplaced atomistic thought is a major preoccupation of *Science and Poetry*. She is particularly exercised by the support that gene-eyed Darwinism seems to give excessive individualism and narrowly contractual social thinking: they seem to derive a false authority from the application of a quasi-evolutionary thought to human life. By denying that we are all part of each other and that even our self-interest is best served by looking far beyond the horizon of our short-term interests, social contract thinking and individualism threaten catastrophe on a planetary scale—another of her preoccupations.

Equally damaging is the denial of the reality of the self and its freedom on the basis of a biologism that reduces humans to the activity of one organ, the brain. In *Are You an Illusion?* She cites Francis Crick's famous, though daft, claim:

> You, your joys and sorrows, your memories and your ambitions, your sense of personal identity and your free-will, are in fact no more than the behaviour of a vast assembly of nerve cells and their attendant molecules (1994: 3, quoted in Midgley 2013: 5)

Among the arguments she deploys against this dissolution of the self is that it is self-contradictory. One has to have quite a bit of pretty sophisticated self to claim that one's self is an illusion.

Ultimately, her opposition to this kind of thinking is to oversimplifications resulting from focussing exclusively on isolated aspects of any phenomenon. Reductionist scientism—which sees animals as molecular machines, while ignoring the richness and connectedness of their lives, and contemplates human behaviour largely through the lens of an animal nature defined by the single goal of 'survival'—fails to recognise that science is rooted in human needs and draws on imaginative faculties that we deploy in other contexts. Nevertheless, while she is a scourge of scientism, she recognises (notably in *Science and Poetry*) that even atomism was once a liberating revolt against superstition and priestly authority.

The key message of *Beast and Man*, set out in the final chapter 'The Unity of Life', is that 'the traditional distinguishing marks of man—speech, rationality, culture—are not something opposed to our nature, but continuous with and growing out of it.' This reflects her desire to contribute to a true humanism which 'cannot only mean destroying God: its chief job is to understand and save man. But man can neither be understood nor saved alone' (1979: 363). We have to recognise our animal nature. And so we return to the opening sentence of her book and her fundamental thesis: 'We are not just rather like animals; we are animals'.

A CORRECTIVE NEEDING A CORRECTIVE?

As I said at the outset, *Beast and Man* was a corrective, both to the biologism that asserts that we are like animals understood in the simplest terms (so all our actions are directed at survival to maximise the replicative capacity of our genes, and to a false humanism, still imprisoned in religious modes of thought, that denies our animal nature and sees nature itself as entirely alien to us. Her subtitle, 'The Roots of Human Nature', indicates a direction for future thought about what it is to be a human being: determining, or at least clarifying, the extent to which natural roots are still present in the leaves of human culture, so that we can understand the latter through examining the former and, given the mighty gap between man and (the other) beasts, make a start on trying to understand how we came to be so different.

It is possible, however, that her corrective itself needs a corrective, particularly since the voices of biologism have become increasingly noisy in philosophical and adjacent thought (neurophilosophy, teleosemantics, evolutionary ethics and psychology being just a few examples), in academe more broadly, and in the popular imagination in the thirty-five or more years since *Beast and Man*. While *Beast and Man* is clearly opposed to simplifying biologism (not the least by acknowledging the complexity of both man and beasts), there are elements of this extraordinarily rich work that may suggest that the distance between ourselves and other species is narrower than I believe it is.

I ought to declare an interest. In a series of publications, I have criticised naturalistic accounts of humanity, based on a neural theory of human consciousness, computational theories of mind, and neo-Darwinian accounts of persons and the societies in which they pass their lives.[2] I have highlighted the gap between us and even our nearest primate kin, and emphasised that what is exceptional in us is not confined to a few 'excellences'. Though have found *Beast and Man* invaluable, I have a sneaking suspicion that Midgley underestimates the distance between the characters separated by the conjunction in the title of her book. I shall devote the remainder of my essay to this concern.

Let me begin with a particularly striking example. Midgley discusses an observation by Wolfgang Kohler (1957) of what he describes as spontaneous dancing in chimpanzees. 'Naturally', she says,

> this sort of thing is not just what goes on at the Bolshoi ballet. But it does something to indicate on what bush, growing out of what soil, ballet is a flower. (1979: 248)

This drastically compresses the distance between the biological roots and the cultural leaves. The highly formalised movements of the ballet, developed explicitly over several centuries, set down in books of instruction, the years of training in a school entered through competitive examinations, the valuation of virtuosity, the critical assessment of performances according to explicit criteria that are often argued over, the complex relationships between music, movement, and narrative, the role of the audience (connoisseurship, tickets, programmes) constitute a much greater gap than a bush-sized distance between primate soil and human flowers.

This example is a reminder of how much human behaviour is rooted in explicit institutions, argued-over values and norms, treasured and challenged traditions, rules (often visibly arbitrary) of countless games, and in different kinds of social relations (including those that arise out of a division of labour that does not correspond to anything in the animal kingdom). Human groupings—exemplified by a team of performers such as the Bolshoi ballet and the audiences that watch them—have little to do with the kinds of spatial aggregations seen in herds of grazing animals or hunting packs or even a few chimpanzees finding themselves spontaneously jigging in unison. They derive their principles of generation and organisation from an infinitely rich medium of signs, a semiosphere[3], in which we pass our lives.

The social lives and cooperative activities of humans arise out of a sea of meant and understood, interpreted and misinterpreted, meanings—comprehended, accepted, contested. They draw on spaces and times that go beyond the biosphere or the sphere of sense experience in which other organisms, even other higher primates, forge their destinies. Merlin Donald captures this succinctly when he says that in humans, '[t] he individual mind is essentially a node in a larger networked structure supported by external memory' (2005).

On account of our 'exographic storage mechanisms' which have an unlimited capacity, '[t]he externalisation of what is internal deepens the internal and this in turn deepens and extends the external' (2005: 737). We have been set on a course (over tens or perhaps hundreds of thousands of years) that enables us, uniquely, to be capable of indefinite, self-driven transformation and consequently to surpass ourselves without limit. Donald has set this out in his detailed discussion of 'the three major cognitive transformations by which the modern human mind emerged over several million years, starting with a complex of skills presumably resembling those of a chimpanzee' (2005:237). I have no space to discuss this here but I would strongly recommend reading Donald's work.

We could explore what we might call 'the human capacity for new capacities' in many different ways, but I would like to focus on just a few aspects. Let me begin with language. According to Midgley, '[c]onceptual thought formalizes and extends what instinct started' (1979: 41). This has some truth, but misses much out. Even the most commonplace linguistic exchange is at such a distance from (unreflective) instinct as to make the claim that it is a formalisation and extension of something instinctive dubious at best. Consider a seemingly straightforward example: what is in play when we decide when, where, and with what terms and in what tone of voice to greet another individual? Or the kind of items that we routinely establish as topics for conversation which are typically abstract, or presented under abstract categories, as well as absent. The incomplete development in other primates of the basic notion of reference is betrayed in their failure sufficiently to understand even the principles governing pointing for them to be able to use it declaratively (as opposed to imperatively) in the way that a ten-month-old infant will do reliably (see Tallis 2010).

Pointing is one of the basic means by which humans join their attention; and the trillion cognitive handshakes out of which the semiosphere in which we dwell is woven would not be possible without explicit joint attention. Pointing is absent or virtually so in chimpanzees in the wild. The evidence for chimpanzee pointing in captivity is equivocal. Even those who argue that captive chimpanzees do point (Leavens et al. 2005) concede that pointing is invariably imperative (close to Wundt's 'abbreviated reaching') rather than declarative. It is immediately related to a basic biological need rather than the sharing of attention—for the sheer pleasure of sharing or for later use. Recent careful studies have indicated a very poor grasp of communicative intent when pointing is used to assist chimpanzees to identify the box in which a food reward is hidden (see Zlatev et al. 2013). There seems little reason to revise the leading primatologist Tomasello's (1999) conclusion, based on extensive observation, that chimpanzees 'do not understand the communicative intentions of others'.

This gives us an insight into their radically different (or deficient) metaphysical world. This been investigated in some depth (see Povinelli 2003).[4] The sense of (material) objects having a continuous independent existence that transcends experience appears to be unique to humans and it is acquired very early. One consequence of the attenuated sense of the reality of objects is a failure to grasp the notion of the material world having intrinsic properties, such as weight, or being subject to laws and exhibiting causal relations (see Povinelli 2011 and Wolpert 2003).[5] These major cognitive differences between humans and other primates explain why there has been little or no technological advance in primate cultures over several million years.

The kinds of inquiries undertaken by human beings are also fundamentally different from the trial and error, or nose-following, or even the most 'open' (to use Midgley's phrase) instinct-driven searches, seen in other primates. Inquiry in humans is often led by explicit formulated possibility, by general ideas, or even theories. It may be too strong to argue that man is the species that invented doubt, but it is certainly the species that has cultivated it, driven by a sense of yet-to-be-arrived-at truths that may be at odds with what one believes, and an intuition of realities utterly different from appearances. (The very idea that material objects have an intrinsic existence, independent of experience and continuing in its absence, lies at the root of the intuition of a reality different from appearance). The quantification of the surrounding world, so central to human experience, is not matched in the differences between 'large and small', 'a lot and less', that animals can recognise. Numbers do not have an explicit, independent existence, and 'stuff' is not unitised.[6] The equivalence between 'one sheep' and 'one cow' is not part of the non-human primate world picture.

The planning that goes into a journey that will take me to a destination in order to do something specific as part of a larger plan is not seen in animals. Species that migrate do not plan in this way. One of the most striking examples of this is the way that we so order our affairs in order to advance our knowledge, understanding, or competence. The difference is evident at even a basic level: it is very rare to see animals rehearse actions in order to improve their competence, or to seek assistance from a teacher. This has been highlighted by Donald (2004), who emphasises the role of 'auto-cueing' in active memorising, practising and self-directed learning. Humans have special mimetic skills 'based on an abstract model . . . that allows any action of the body to be stopped, replayed and edited under conscious control' (Donald 2004: 46).

Animal learning is essentially based on *bumping into* rather than *seeking out* and information that is acquired is essentially for consumption on the spot. This difference highlights the capacity of humans to transcend the immediate environment—as is the deliberate acquisition of factual knowledge about items that are not present but may be salient to future well-being.

The storing of 'potentially useful facts' is also (and perhaps even more significantly) an aspect of an elaborated propositional knowledge *that* things are or that they might be. This is a mode of consciousness that is hardly developed if at all in other species (see Tallis 2005). The possibilities we entertain can be placed outside of ourselves and inspected critically, argued over and even tested.

The question of whether other species have beliefs—a fundamental aspect of human consciousness—or other propositional attitudes such as thoughts—has been extensively discussed by philosophers.[7] Even if we do not stack the cards against animals by making verbal expression the key criterion, it seems very unlikely that the kinds of networks to which individual human beliefs belong are developed in other species. Our beliefs, like thoughts, are located in what Wilfred Sellars called 'the logical space of reasons', in which permissible co-existence is governed by different rules (consistency, non-contradiction, entailment) from those which regulate co-existence in 'the space of nature'. In drawing attention to this point, I am mobilising Midgley's own holism to underline the difference between humans and other species.

One of the most striking dimensions of our capacity to transcend the immediate environment is the temporal depth and temporal complexity of day-to-day existence. We are tensed beings. Our present behaviour is directed by an explicitly recalled past—*qua* past—not reducible to effects of past causes. Episodic memory, for example, is memory that is aware of itself not only as being about the past, but as also being about one's own past. While it would, of course, be difficult to assess whether animals do have episodic or even auto-noetic memories (memories about ourselves as individuals, memories in which we are seen as present), the evidence suggests that they have poor episodic recall because they have great difficulty deliberately accessing the contents of their own episodic memories independently of environmental cues (see Donald 2005: 741). Deliberate accessing of episodic memories presupposes a robust sense of an enduring self, of an 'I' that extends over long stretches of time, and there is nothing else in its behaviour that would seem sufficient justification for believing that, say, a chimpanzee has this sense and an associated ability to rack its own brain. Non-human primate life seems to be 'one damn thing after another'.

There have been bold attempts to ascribe a sense of an explicit future to a species as remote from humanity as the Western scrub jays (a member of the crow family) on the basis of its food caching behaviour (e.g., Raby et al. 2007). There is, however, no other evidence of a sense of future tense in these organisms. The caching could be unconsciously programmed. It certainly does not prove that the birds have an intuition of selves continuing into a future. Even less does it indicate that they have an explicit sense of 'the future' analogous to the days in which humans house a shared or communal not-yet. Which is why, as Wittgenstein put it: 'We say a dog is afraid his master will beat him; but not, he is afraid his master will beat him tomorrow' (1963: 166).' There is little evidence of anything comparable in non-human species to a collective past of shared memories, or group histories and myths. These phenomena are manifestations of deeper, more antique differences. They are, what is more, also the necessary conditions of the long chains of the individual and collective 'in orders to' characteristic of our everyday behaviour, marking the increasing distance of our actions from reactions, reflexes, drives, and tropisms. They express an active engagement with the pull of the future—that we ourselves project—rather than a passivity before the push of the past or present. Long chains of 'in order to' distinguish agency from even the most complex, programmed modes of behaviour seen in other species. They not only are shaped by the practical considerations of getting from a present state of affairs to a goal, but also express explicit values, norms, preferences, commitments, for which there is no direct evidence in non-human animals.

There are impressive examples of social behaviour, even among insects. While this often goes far beyond mere dovetailing of pre-programmed modes of working or being together, it is a mistake to think of it as more than superficially analogous to the typical modes of human sociality. Humans are selves with auto-accessible biographies (and even CVs) that are not matched in animals, and the aforementioned temporal depth is but one dimension of the special kind of internal coherence of humans across their lives. Acknowledging this absolutely basic difference must be a starting point for any discussion of the similarities and differences between human society and the 'social behaviour' seen in animals. It leads naturally to the endlessly discussed question of whether, and to what extent, other species have 'a theory of mind'—that is to say, whether or to what extent they ascribe mentality to their conspecifics. It is better perhaps to think of something richer than a theory of mind; namely, the intuition that the other is a self, other than, but comparable in crucial respects to, one's self. Real (that is to say, human) societies—good and bad—are founded upon this intuition.

As we have seen, the evidence from pointing, or rather the lack of it, in other primates (at least in the wild), suggests that awareness of the different viewpoint of another individual—inseparable from acknowledging their equal and independent inner reality—is poorly developed. Call and Tomasello (2008) have presented what they think to be compelling evidence that chimpanzees may ascribe true beliefs to other chimpanzees; they admit, however, that they do not ascribe false ones. But if you cannot entertain the idea that another may have got something wrong, then you cannot really be said to have ascribed a belief to them: beliefs are propositional attitudes that by definition might be erroneous.

There are many other ways in which human consciousness, selves, and societies are unique. One of the most obvious is that we dwell in a landscape of artefacts, tools, machines, developed through cooperative action based upon know-how and know-that, painstakingly acquired and transmitted and actively extended and modified. Our interactions with the natural world are consequently often mediated through seemingly endless chains of intermediate steps. What is more, there is hardly a biological given that we have not transformed and subordinated to (often symbolic) ends that are not evident in other species.

These, then, are some of the reasons why Midgley's opening sentence in *Beast and Man*—that '[w]e are not just rather like animals; we are animals'—should be seen as a challenge to understanding our distinctive nature, not a statement of what we are. Likewise, her claim that 'the gap between man and other animals comes . . . in a slightly different place from the one where tradition puts it, as well as being rather narrower' (1979: xiii). While this points to some important truths, it may also be misleading. Granted, the gap between the human and the non-human does not correspond to the distance between an ensouled Platonic intelligence transcending humble wants rooted in biology (us humans), and fleshly machines activated by beastly drives from which we have long since ascended (them beasts). Even so, differences between ourselves and our nearest primate kin are profound, reaching to the heart of human being. This is evident not only in high-end activities—writing symphonies, falling romantically in love, fretting over transfinite numbers—but in every moment of everyday life—in eating, learning, getting around from A to B, mating, child-rearing, and in acquiring the wherewithal to continue living.

CONCLUSIONS

Beast and Man and Midgley's subsequent works have made a decisive contribution to the humanist project of trying to see ourselves in a non-distorting mirror. She has, however, perhaps conceded a little too much of our humanity to biology, notwithstanding that her philosophy of biology is entirely different from the reductive, gene-eyed views of writers such as Wilson and

Dawkins. For this reason, her much-needed corrective may itself require some correction.

That said, Midgley's writings are a signal contribution to post-religious philosophical anthropology. Her contribution has been important as much for her style of writing as for her clarity of thought and the ease with which she brings extensive knowledge of biology to bear on philosophical questions.

Anyone who toils in this area will make more progress for standing on her shoulders.

NOTES

1. See Midgley 2010 and Brown's chapter in this volume.
2. Alongside books already mentioned, these include Tallis 1991, 2003a, 2003b, and 2004.
3. This very important concept was introduced by Yuri Lotman to capture a development that arises when two worlds genuinely come into communication. The semiosphere has, as we shall illustrate presently, the capacity in humans to expand and evolve indefinitely and independently of the biosphere.
4. Povinelli's conclusions have, however, been hotly criticised by some other primatologists.
5. Povinelli's claims are criticised in Cameron (forthcoming).
6. See 'Abstract Digits', in Tallis 2003a.
7. The arguments are summarised in 'Does Rover Believe Anything?' in Tallis 2014. This addresses the standard positions advanced by Norman Malcolm, George Graham, and Donald Davidson. A similar sceptical view of the capacity of animals to have propositional attitudes is developed by Bermúdez 2009.

REFERENCES

Bermúdez, José Luis, 'Mindreading in the Animal Kingdom', in Robert W. Lurz (ed.), *The Philosophy of Animal Minds* (Cambridge: Cambridge University Press, 2009), 145–64.

Buckner, Cameron, 'In search of balance. Essay review of Daniel Povinelli's *World Without Weight*', *Biology and Philosophy*, forthcoming.

Call, J. and M. Tomasello, 'Does the chimpanzee have a theory of mind? 30 Years Later', *Trends in Cognitive Science* 12(5) (2008): 187–192.

Churchland, Patricia, *Touching a Nerve: The Self as Brain* (New York: Norton, 2014).

Crick, Francis, *The Astonishing Hypothesis. Science and the Search from the Soul* (New York: Touchstone, 1994).

Dawkins, Richard, *The Selfish Gene* (London: Granada, 1976).

Donald, Merlin, 'Précis of *The Origin of the Modern Mind: Three Stages in the Evolution of Culture and Cognition*', *Behavioural and Brain Sciences* 16(4) (2005): 737–791.

Donald, Merlin, 'The Definition of Human Nature', in Dai Rees and Steven Rose (eds.), *The New Brain Sciences: Perils and Prospects* (Cambridge: Cambridge University Press, 2004), 34–58.

Goodall, Jane, *In the Shadow of Man* (London: Collins, 1971).

Kohler, Wolfgang, *The Mentality of Apes* (Harmondsworth: Pelican, 1957).

Leavens, David A., William D. Hopkins, Kim A. Bard, 'Understanding the point of chimpanzee pointing: Epigenesis and ecological validity', *Current Directions in Psychological Science* 14(5) (2005): 185–195.

Midgley, Mary, *Are You an Illusion?* (Durham: Acumen, 2014).

Midgley, Mary, *The Solitary Self: Darwin and the Selfish Gene* (Durham: Acumen, 2010).

Midgley, Mary, *Science and Poetry* (London: Routledge, 2001).

Midgley, Mary, *Beast and Man: The Roots of Human Nature* (London: Methuen, 1979)

Povinelli, Daniel, *World Without Weight: Perspectives on an Alien Mind* (Oxford: Oxford University Press, 2011).

Povinelli, Daniel, *Folk Physics for Apes: The Chimpanzee's Theory of How the World Works* (Oxford: Oxford University Press, 2003).

Raby, C.R., D.M. Alexis, A. Dickinson, & N.S. Clayton, 'Planning for the future by Western scrub-jays', *Nature* 445 (2007): 919–921.

Sartre, Jean-Paul, *Existentialism and Humanism*, trans. Philip Mairet (London: Eyre Methuen, 1958).

Shermer, Michael, 'Sacred science: Using faith to explain anomalies in physics', *Scientific American*, 16 June 2008, 38.

Skinner, B.F., *Beyond Freedom and Dignity* (New York: Knopf, 1971).

Tallis, Raymond, *Aping Mankind: Neuromania, Darwinitis and the Misrepresentation of Humanity* (Durham: Acumen, 2011).

Tallis, Raymond, *Michelangelo's Finger: An Inquiry into Everyday Transcendence* (London: Atlantic, 2010).

Tallis, Raymond, *The Kingdom of Infinite Space. A Fantastical Journey Round Your Head* (London: Atlantic, 2009).

Tallis, Raymond, *I Am: A Philosophical Inquiry into First-Person Being* (Edinburgh: Edinburgh University Press, 2004a).

Tallis, Raymond, *Why the Mind Is Not a Computer: A Pocket Lexicon of Neuromythology* (Exeter: Imprint Academic, 2004b).

Tallis, Raymond, *The Hand: A Philosophical Inquiry into Human Being* (Edinburgh: Edinburgh University Press, 2003a).

Tallis, Raymond, *The Knowing Animal: A Philosophical Inquiry into Knowledge and Truth* (Edinburgh: Edinburgh University Press, 2003b).

Tallis, Raymond, *The Explicit Animal: A Defence of Human Consciousness* (Basingstoke: Macmillan, 1991).

Tomasello, M. 'Having Intentions, Understanding Intentions, and Understanding Communicative Intentions', in P. Zelazo, D.R. Olson, and J.W. Astington (eds.) *Developmental Theories of Intention: Social Understanding and Self-Control* (Cambridge: Cambridge University Press, 1999), 63–75.

Wilson, E.O., *Sociobiology: The New Synthesis* (Cambridge, Mass.: Harvard University Press, 1975)

Wittgenstein, Ludwig, *Philosophical Investigations*, trans. G.E.M. Anscombe (Oxford: Blackwell, 1963).

Wolpert, Lewis, 'Causal belief and the origins of technology', *Philosophical Transactions of the Royal Society of London A* 316 (2003): 1709–1719.

Zlatev, Jordan, Elaine Alenkar Madsen, Sara Lenninger, 'Understanding communicative intentions and semiotic vehicles by children and chimpanzees', *Cognitive Development* 28 (2013): 312–329.

6 Is There Such a Thing as Consensus Morality?

Mary Warnock

In her first, and, in my view, most important book, *Beast and Man*, published in 1978, Mary Midgley licensed us to consider the concept of human nature in a way that would have been a delight to David Hume and a source of amazement to other philosophers of the eighteenth century, many of whom set out to explore the concept. I regard this book as her most important because it was groundbreaking. It explored human nature against the background of evolution, without assuming that the nature of man could be wholly described in biological terms. It caused its readers to contemplate the instincts and desires that human beings retain that are observable also in the species of animals from which they have evolved, and the enormous complexity that these instincts and desires exhibit, in an animal that has acquired language.

Midgley invites us to revisit the ways in which the idea of morality is entangled with the idea of a specifically human nature, in a kind of post-Darwinian rewrite of Books II and III of Hume's *Treatise*. To invoke human nature once again is to suggest that human beings have a lot in common; and this in turn raises the question whether they have enough in common to make possible a kind of common morality, a consensus about what it is to be a good person (or the opposite); or at the very least what it is to be a decent person. It is this question that I shall address in what follows.

CONSENSUS MORALITY?

There are those who immediately recoil from the idea of consensus morality, who indeed hold that it is a contradiction in terms. For, in their view, consensus implies compromise: and morality is necessarily a matter of principle, which allows of no compromises. It's not much of a principle, they argue, unless you are prepared to follow it, though the heavens fall, and though you are the only person among your associates who upholds it. Margaret Thatcher notoriously said, 'I hate consensus'. Such people, if philosophically inclined, would concede that Kant had tried to show that the supreme moral principle, the Categorical Imperative, was as necessarily accepted by any human being capable of morality, as were the laws of logic to those capable of reasoning. Indeed the necessity was the same. True morality was therefore, according to his argument, manifestly a matter of agreement, just as is the proposition that 2+2=4. But Kant's notion of morality was extraordinarily narrow. It was limited to cases where the agent is faced with a choice to do this or that: to lie or tell the truth, to break a promise or keep it, or take more than his share in a situation of scarcity or refrain from doing so. Of course such choices exist; and morally good people generally choose in the way that Kant would have them do, or at least if they choose otherwise they feel shame and remorse. But this seems rather to be because they have been well brought up, that is, taught as children that in certain situations they are subject to temptation and can resist it, than because they must follow the strict dictates of reason, as Kant's theory would have it. The Aristotelian idea of virtues and vices of character, as well as the eighteenth-century idea of 'right feelings', were excluded by him from the sphere of morality. And few would accept this; indeed, it is contrary to the idea of morality that we actually find ourselves and other people using. For, whatever theories they may subscribe to, people who have any concept of morality at all do, as a matter of fact, find themselves admiring noble characters or condemning mean sentiments. Kant's efforts to show that morality *must* be consensus morality as a matter of logic, is not generally accepted, influential though it has been. It must, I think, be counted as a heroic failure. It was heroic, in that it was part of his sustained attempt to show that the human will, the ability to decide to do something and do it, was the only thing in the world not subject to physical determinism, the only thing free from the laws of Newtonian physics.

Those who reject the possibility of a consensual morality do not, in any case, generally think of themselves as rejecting Kantian theory. As I have suggested, they reject the idea that morality can be founded on anything except personal adherence to principle or the personal acceptance of some values as of supreme importance, wherever those values come from, or upon whatever they are founded. And they know very well, as we all do, that principles and values can conflict. Moreover many people hold that it is positively wrong to seek consensus in the field of morality, because one of the values they uphold is tolerance of people whose principles and values are different from, even in direct conflict with, their own. I shall return to the question of tolerance in due course.

First, however, I want to make a distinction between two different, though not wholly separate, nor disparate, concepts, that of public and of private morality. The philosopher and critic, Stuart Hampshire, made this distinction a central part of his moral philosophy, and expounded it most fully in his book *Innocence and Experience*, published in 1989. Here and elsewhere in his writings, Hampshire used the example of Machiavelli, who contrasted the ruthlessness, determination, duplicity, and ambition necessary for a successful ruler, who would, with these weapons, enhance not only his own power and place in history, but, just as much, the security, wellbeing, and cohesion of his people, with, on the other hand, the dictates of the Christian ideals of meekness and innocence, the rewards for which were looked for only in the afterlife. Neither Machiavelli nor Hampshire was much concerned with the particular private virtues extolled by the Christianity of Renaissance Florence or their putative rewards. They were concerned rather with the distinction between the morality of the person engaged in politics, who possessed the power to change things in the public arena, and the morality of someone concerned only to do right within the private arena of his own relationships. This distinction, in my view, remains valid and is, as Hampshire held, too little regarded in moral philosophy.

Hampshire frequently illustrated the conflict that this distinction could cause by the story of a situation in which he found himself after the Second World War. Immediately after the war he was acting as an interrogating officer for the British Government, and it fell to him to interrogate a French traitor, arrested by the Free French, those British allies acting largely under cover throughout the war. The prisoner refused to cooperate unless Hampshire could assure him he would be spared execution, the normal penalty for collaboration with the enemy. Hampshire knew both that the information the prisoner could give would be much in the interests of the allies, and that the man had already been condemned to death. His public duty, as a serving officer, was to tell the man that he would be spared, and receive the information he could give. But the whole message of his private conscience told him that he could not lie to the man on the brink of execution and give him false assurance. He tended to conclude that to follow his private scruples, in these circumstances, would be self-indulgent, and that his duty in the public arena of war should prevail. But whichever way he had decided, he would be troubled for the rest of his life by the feeling that he had betrayed either his own deeply felt principles of decent moral behaviour between individuals or the interest of his country.

In less dramatic circumstances, scarcely a day can go by when a politician does not deceive the public as to his motives for introducing a particular measure, or go back on a promise previously made to preserve some cherished institution or source of public funding, or simply conceal what is happening, where people may feel they have a right to know. And quite often this deceptive, manipulative behaviour, which might be intolerable to the individual politician in his private life, could be justified not merely by the desire to stay in power, but by a genuine concern for the public good. (Even the desire to stay in power may not be an immoral motive; the interests of a government may be not only to retain their seats and their salaries, but also to achieve reasonable stability and to gain time to make effective changes for the good of society. But it has to be said that such benign motives are less and less often credited to serving politicians by the public).

In their private capacity, individual human beings differ greatly from one another, in their tastes, ambitions, sympathies, scruples, and concepts of what it is to be a decent person. (And of course there are those who are virtually unmoved by scruples of any kind, but go only for what seems to satisfy their immediate desires and impulses. However, these people, who undoubtedly exist, do not concern us here because they are, temporarily or permanently, outside the realm of morality, consensual or otherwise).

Where these different kinds of moral sensibility come from, and why, even among those who belong to the same cultural environment, there should still be such differences, is a matter of interest which can probably never be entirely explained. Instead, we tend to fall back on vague expressions such as 'personality' to mark the differences without accounting for them. And zoologists or vets who spend their lives observing other species of animal undoubtedly find that among them, too, there are noticeably different character and personality traits, not only among the apes, but among horses and dogs and doubtless other creatures. Stuart Hampshire, as we have seen, found it almost impossible to lie to a fellow human being about his true and dire situation. On a less heroic scale, I personally find it impossible to tease or make fun of a child in a way that might humiliate him, and I hate seeing others do so. This particular moral scruple doubtless arises from the fact that, being the youngest of a large family, and being subject to what was to me inexplicable teasing, I found such humiliation unbearable. Our spontaneous sympathies, from which our moral sensibilities largely arise, are accounted for by our experiences; and experiences differ. Moral progress is made only when people enlarge their sympathies by imagination as well as by further experience. The fact is that private morality is much more than a set of principles or rules that an individual person consciously adopts. It is bound up in that person's idea of himself in relation to other people, other animals, and the world he lives in. It is part of his personal integrity. This is why the word 'integrity' is so often used to designate the chief characteristic of the morally scrupulous. A person would fall apart, come to pieces, if he did not hold on to some sort of standard of decent behaviour (that this is so was part of the horror of the concentration camps).

Such a conception of private morality seems to render a consensual morality impossible. It also seems to open the door to moral relativism, according to which each person has his own standards, and it is a matter of mere chance if they are the same as someone else's. But of course the expression 'private morality' is not entirely felicitous. Though it is true that the moral sentiments, the natural sympathies, loyalties, and antipathies that one experiences seem to be personal, and to form an important part of one's individuality, yet it is also true that they contain an element of implicit universality. If it were not so, they would have nothing to do with morality. Saying 'I could not bring myself to lie to him' is not like saying 'I could not bring myself to eat insects'. The expression of moral repugnance is set against a background not just of a body and culturally determined culinary or other habits and generally shared tastes, but of a specific, doubtless also partly culturally determined, concept of what it is for anyone to be a decent human being. Such words as 'decent', 'admirable', 'courageous', or 'cowardly', used to express moral judgments and moral comparisons, are not, as was thought in the 1950s, mere expressions of individual preferences, but have an accepted and well-understood meaning. However, the term 'private morality' will have to stand, for all that it is in some respects misleading, since it at least points to a contrast with the morality of the legislator or public servant, however closely the two are linked.

There are those, including many who are not especially pious, who define their own moral principles in terms of what their religion teaches. And there are those who argue that if religion were entirely to disappear, there would be no foundation for personal morality left, and no possibility of enduring or agreed principles, only the aftermath of the old culture which was historically Judeo-Christian, or Muslim, or whatever religion was flourishing in the past in any particular place. After all, many people who are not particularly interested in thinking about the nature of religion or morality, or attempting to analyse either, nevertheless automatically link morality with religion, and therefore regard priests or rabbis as moral experts, knowing better than others the difference between right and wrong. Here is not the place to argue in detail the case for, in principle, separating morality from belief in a God who created the world and gave it its moral laws; it is enough to say that, manifestly, morality existed, and its nature was discussed, historically, outside any of the great monotheistic religions which are especially thought of as the source of morality. For example, ancient Greek religion was not much concerned with morality, though its philosophers were; and, secondly, that if religion were really essential to morality, this would be the death-knell for consensus morality. For there are fundamental issues on which the morality taught by different religions cannot be reconciled. The most important of these is the status of the law itself, that is, whether it comes ultimately from the people and their representatives by due process of legislation, or from the priesthood, interpreting the moral commands of God. It may sound good to talk about people of different faiths living amicably side by side, respecting each others' beliefs, observances, and ceremonies, but we cannot all be expected to 'respect' other people's right to carry out female circumcision, or to issue orders to kill those who have offended by blasphemy. These are moral differences that the virtue of toleration cannot be expected to encompass. These deep differences also lead some to doubt the possibility of any consensus morality, based on human nature.

The social historian David Cannadine recently published a book, *The Undivided Past*, in which he blamed historians for emphasising, even sometimes creating, differences by stereotyping conflicts, as if people who go to war with each other, or struggle against one another in other contexts, were completely defined by their nationality, their class, their gender, or their religion. And he is especially critical of those historians who have had greater overarching theories of history, such as Marx, Arnold Toynbee, or Samuel P. Huntington, whose book *The Clash of Civilizations*, published in 1996, seems to Cannadine to be especially damaging in setting human beings apparently ineluctably one against another. In a review of Cannadine's book in the *New Statesman*, a fellow historian, Roger Overy (2013), pours scorn on such ideas. 'It's difficult to see what Cannadine wants his profession to do now. He calls on academic historians to abandon the artificial divisions of "identity" history, and celebrate a "common humanity that still binds us today." This is 1960s-style cant, a Western delusion that bears no resemblance to the realities of either the recent or the more distant past'. And he goes on, 'There is a common humanity only in the most banal sense that we all eat, sleep, have sex, and die, as do rabbits and gorillas'.

But here I think he is wrong, though I agree that there sometimes seems a certain arrogance in assuming that 'Western values', as they are sometimes called, if they prevailed, would automatically set the world to rights. But all animals, even the most lowly, have certain needs that must be satisfied if they are to survive; and human animals, being complex, have needs that are not only for nutrition, hydration, and suitable climactic environment, but for security to enjoy the ownership of possessions, and freedom to exercise imagination in a huge variety of inventive and aspirational ways. Above all, they have the need for civil society and thus for justice. It is on account of its recognition of such specifically human needs as these that the concept of human rights has gained wide acceptance. It is increasingly commonly held, and recognised in systems of legislation, that there are some rights which people hold simply in virtue of their humanity, that is, their common humanity. And it is true that when a regime is described as having an 'appalling human rights record', we know fairly well what is meant: people subject to the regime are liable to be dispossessed of their property, arbitrarily thrown into prison without trial, tortured, and deprived of freedom of expression and of access to reliable sources of information about their own country or the outside world. And so on. In states where such conditions prevail, there is no such thing as the rule of law. We all, being human, know that these things are nasty; and, as Kingsley Amis once said, 'Nice things are nicer than nasty things'. Broadly speaking, we know the difference.

However, the relation between the existence of a right and that of a law is complicated and controversial, even though the language of human rights is now widely used and, as I have suggested, at least partially intelligible. There is a difference between deriving a right from a common good, and deriving it from a specific law which lays down that a person possesses that right and must not be prevented from exercising it. It is the difference between a wider and a narrower concept of justice. The view prevalent in the eighteenth century, expounded by John Austin, and most influentially by Jeremy Bentham, was that of Legal Positivism. According to this jurisprudence, a right must be conferred by a law. To claim a right except by reference to a specific law of your country was nonsensical and confusing. 'Natural' as opposed to legal rights was a meaningless distinction. We may illustrate positivism by example: in the UK before 1972 there were children who were so severely disabled that they were deemed uneducable, and so were not entitled to education. Other children had a right, by law, to be educated from the age of five, and the Local Authority had a corresponding duty to provide them with schooling. But those children deemed, on assessment, to be incapable of benefiting from schooling had no such right, and there was no correlative duty of provision. However there were those with a wider concept of education, and a greater understanding of what it was possible for the most profoundly mentally disabled children to be taught, who regarded the law as, in the wider sense, unjust to these children and who campaigned, on moral grounds, for the law to be changed. When in 1972 all children, whatever their disabilities, were brought under the aegis of the then Department of Education and Science, a duty was thereby imposed on that department to provide education for all children of school age, and all now have the right to education. A Local Authority that fails to provide such education is, in a narrower sense, acting unjustly towards that child.

Again, it is now widely recognised in Europe and the United States that Jewish families whose property was seized between 1933 and 1945 under the Nazi regime, or who during that time were driven to a forced sale at unduly low prices, are, in a broad sense, entitled to compensation or restitution. In the narrow sense, they have no rights, because there is a legal time limit, long expired, beyond which property may not be reclaimed, even if its provenance can be shown to be illicit. But it is now generally held that, even if a gallery or museum acquired an object in good faith, it may be morally obliged to offer compensation or restitution to the family if a claim is made. (Though obviously, as time goes by, it becomes more and more difficult to establish that the claimant is a member of the family who originally owned the objects, or to trace the history of the sales leading to the acquisition by the gallery). Here there is no question whatever of legal, but only of moral, entitlement.

Benthamite positivism, linking positive law, and only that, to the idea of a right which cannot be conferred otherwise than by such a law, is largely frowned upon now. Bentham held that all laws in any country may be judged good or bad according to a supposedly simple criterion of Utilitarianism, the greatest happiness of the greatest number. If you found yourself subject to a bad law, whose consequences were harmful to most people in society, you were strictly obliged to obey, and had no right to disregard it. However, you could and should criticise it, on Utilitarian grounds. 'Obey instantly; criticise ceaselessly', as Bentham put it. Your criticism could take the form of a claim that you had a right, but that you ought, on moral grounds (and this for Bentham meant Utilitarian grounds) to have a right, and the law ought to be so changed that it would confer the right upon you and others in your position. But partly because Bentham's own Utilitarian criterion for judging a law good or bad was so inadequate (apparently allowing individuals and minorities to be sacrificed to a supposed good of society as a whole), partly because positivism in effect gave no authoritative status to any criticism of a bad law (and, for example, Nazi lawyers could justify appalling atrocities, because the law demanded them), it has come to be generally discarded. A legal system cannot be justified, it is now generally argued, unless it is firmly based on an already existing and logically prior concept of human rights, a concept from which not only law, but morality itself, stems. Old laws gave owners legal rights over their slaves. The abolition of slavery brought in new laws which recognised existing rights possessed by slaves on the grounds that slaves too were human; it did not create these rights. And so, in this country, before it is enacted, a law must now be tested against the Human Rights Act 1998; and every Bill presented to Parliament must be prefaced by a signed declaration by a Minister that it is not in breach of this Act (though whether it is or not so in breach may still fall to be settled by the Court of Human Rights in Strasburg).

Now, though it may be true that the idea of certain identifiable and inalienable rights which belong to all human beings, and only to them, suggests that there is such a thing as shared human nature, with which these rights can be associated and from which they can be derived, to assert this is by no means the same as to assert that all human morality can be derived from human rights, nor that the only morality that has authority and certainty is that of rights. I shall argue that both these propositions are false.

Despite the inadequacy of Utilitarian positivism, it remains true that the idea of a right is logically linked to that of a freedom conferred on someone by law; and this act of conferring a right entails placing on some other person, or some body such as the company for which he works, or the state of which he is a citizen, not to deprive him of that freedom or inhibit him in its exercise. A right is in essence and in origin a legal concept; to determine whether or not your right has been infringed, you need to go to court. It is legitimate, of course, to extend the idea of rights beyond the literally legal sphere. For example, in ordinary domestic life, if my husband promises to meet my train, I have a right to expect that he will be there when it arrives, and to want an explanation if he is not. A promise is a diminished, non-legal form of a contract. Again, if someone gives me a present, I have a right to be annoyed if subsequently he takes it away from me. A gift, I supposed, confers ownership. There are performances, such as promising and giving, that have the power to change people's expectations, and thus their sense of entitlement, and of injustice if these expectations are disappointed. If my husband explains that he was so much caught up in the book he is writing, or even the game he was playing, that he simply lost track of time, then if I am a decent person I shall sympathise, even commiserate with him, not insist on condemning him for breach of promise. Injustice is not the only evil, nor justice the only virtue. Judith Jarvis Thomson (1971) tells the following story to illustrate this point. A box of chocolates has been given to the elder of two brothers. He sits, enviously watched by his younger brother, eating his way through the entire box, without offering to share. Most people, she says, would say that the elder brother ought to offer some to his sibling, that it is mean and callous not to do so. But she adds that it does not follow from this that the younger boy has any right to a share in the chocolates. It may show a nasty side of his brother's character, but he is not unjust. If anyone denies this and says that the younger boy is being treated unjustly, then an important distinction is being blurred, namely the distinction between the story as told, and the case where the elder and younger boys have been given the box of chocolates jointly, and the elder nevertheless refuses to share. In this case, she concludes, 'the small brother . . . has what is from any point of view a clear title to half' (p. 13). She is surely right. In this case we do not admire the elder boy for giving half the chocolates to his brother. He is giving him no more than what is owed him. He is not being generous, but merely showing that he understands what joint ownership means. To say, on moral grounds, that someone ought to behave in a certain way, or has shown moral goodness of character in doing so may have nothing to do with the justice of what he has done. To avoid cruelty is not necessarily the same as to avoid injustice. And greed, callousness, lack of human sympathy are all, different, moral vices.

Moreover, not everything desirable can be claimed as a right. Such conventions as the International Charter of the Rights of Children, though ratified by numerous countries, are more a statement of ideals than a binding treaty, let alone a part of international law. It is an ideal to which, in ratifying the charter, we made clear that we thought was worth aspiring, for instance, the ideal that every child in the world should have enough to eat, a secure family life, an education and time to play. But poverty and ignorance and sometimes cultural assumptions (such as that girls should not be educated) often make these ideals sadly hard or impossible to realize. And if such good things were rights in the proper sense, then someone would have a duty to see that they were provided, or not prevented from being provided. But on whom does this duty fall? There are charities such as UNICEF and numerous religious charities that aim to further the ideals incorporated in the Charter, but no child could sue them if they failed, nor even expect, rather than hope, that they will succeed. It seems to me that to speak of the rights of children in this context is to borrow a certainty and authority that belongs to legal rights, and pretend that it applies as well to such aspirational charters.

I believe, then, that it is confusing to assert that those who courageously demand change, who demand, for example, that Muslim girls should receive an education as well as boys, do so because girls already have that right, and are merely claiming what is rightfully theirs. I would prefer to say that the claim is that they ought to have it. The law ought to be changed to entitle them to education, and the belief that they should be so entitled is based on a moral conviction that all human beings, regardless of gender, are damaged and inhibited by ignorance. When women demanded the vote after the First World War they were demanding a right, not claiming that they already had it.

It may be thought that I am making too much of what is no more than a semantic point. What does it matter whether we say that something is, as the law now stands, incompatible with existing human rights, or that the current law should be changed so that the rights come into existence? Why not simply allow, as others do, that there is a difference between legal and moral rights? Why not say that the Muslim girl demanding education is asserting her moral right, though she knows quite well that she has no legal entitlement to go to school? And I have to agree that this is an intelligible way of putting it. Over the last twelve years, even I, arch-sceptic as I was about the possibility of drawing up a definitive list of human rights, or agreeing on what was and what was not an infringement of them, hostile though I was to the rhetorical appeal to human rights to lend fake authority to a particular demand. . . . even I have had to get accustomed to the language of the 1998 Act. And, as l have said, we most of us understand what sort of thing is meant by 'a bad human rights record'. Moreover, as I have also said, the concept of human rights stretching world-wide, encompassing all cultures and existing because of the nature and needs of humanity itself lends colour to the belief, which I share, that human animals have much in common both with other animals and with each other. And this, in turn, suggests that it may not be fanciful to suppose that we can work towards a consensual ethics. Surely this must be so, if what is thought nasty by all human beings is, more or less, the same. We can surely agree that such things should not be suffered by any peoples, and can prevent them happening.

This, of course, is the problem. In the case of real, legal rights, there is someone who can be prosecuted, if he so acts as to prevent someone from enjoying a right, as a landowner may be prosecuted who fails to keep open a right of way. Or if someone who is incurably ill claims that he has the right to receive assistance with death at the time of his choosing, he can be told flatly by the courts that he has no such right, as the law now stands. If the law is to be changed, it must be parliament, not the courts, which changes it. If he wants to claim a right to assisted dying, he will be told, he must either travel to a legislature where it is permitted, or persuade parliament that the law must be changed.

Worse, there is the fact, already referred to, that if A has a right, B must have a correlative duty not to prevent his enjoying it. This is part of the meaning of the word 'right' and must apply equally to moral as to legal rights, though in the case of moral rights, the duty would presumably be a moral, not a legal, duty. But who is to take the responsibility for the duty to bring to an end an alleged abuse of human rights in a different legislation from one's own? Is putting a stop to such abuse simply to be a matter of putting verbal pressure on the abhorrent regime by crying shame? Or is the pressure of economic sanctions permissible, though it may bring more suffering to those people who are already subject to abuse? Or is every case to be a *casus belli*? Surely not.

It is these considerations that make me, still, a reluctant believer in the effectiveness of the idea of human rights. But I willingly accept the new license they give for the reintroduction of the idea of human nature, and would agree to the proposition that, on account of that nature, there are some ways in which no human being should ever be treated by another, some hardships and indignities to which no human being should be deliberately subjected.

To put it in that way, however, strongly suggests that a claim of infringement of human rights is itself a moral claim. It is morally intolerable to make people suffer in the way that they suffered under, let us say, the Stalinist regime. But if the judgement that a human right has been infringed is a moral judgement it follows that human rights cannot he treated as if they existed separately, as a distinct and fundamental category of human attributes, from which the concept of morality can be derived. They are one and the same. It seems to me that those who would distinguish legal from moral rights are saying exactly that: to claim that someone's moral right has been infringed is to claim that morally speaking, or from a moral point of view, his treatment has been wrong.

If that argument is valid, then in the class of human rights, we have a set of agreed moral values, applicable universally. Anyone, anywhere, who does not pursue these values or who neglects to recognise them may be condemned. And to establish such a set of agreed values was indeed the purpose of those who published the United Nations Declaration of Human Rights in 1948. We are told that there was remarkably little difficulty then in reaching an agreed list. At the time, everyone had clearly in mind the moral outrages that had been committed and the suffering that had been endured in the immediately preceding years. Nothing could more manifestly violate human rights than the treatment that human beings were subjected to in concentration camps, or than, come to that, the wholesale bombing of civilians and the destruction of their cities.

The Declaration of Human Rights, then, was a statement of consensus morality. Further, it was a declaration of public morality. Though issued in the name of more than one legislature, it was issued in the name of a quasi-legislative body, seeking the good not of one country, but of the whole inhabited world. The declaration did not constitute a set of laws (as international laws to regulate fishing or to control air traffic do), but constituted a treaty between states that each must ratify.

But of course not all states are members of the United Nations; and so, though as far as it goes, the existence of such conventions are indeed evidence of consensus morality, they could be thought to show that consensus is possible only between already 'like-minded' people; that the values upheld are the values of the Western world, who would like to impose them on, say, North Vietnam, but have neither authority nor power to do so. And thus human nature, from which these values derive, turns out to be Western human nature, not Human Nature as a Whole. And this is exactly the argument brought by the historian Overy against the historian Cannadine, mentioned above. However, Overy's position seems to imply that different nations, or groups of nations, are simply different and there is no more to be said, because human beings who compose these nations have nothing in common but what they share with all animals. And this is what is wrong with his argument. Midgley has suggested, and I agree with her, that human beings have much more in common than this. Aristotle summed it up in designating humans as political animals. That means that humans are animals naturally drawn to live in cities, or civilised communities. Such is the nature of a Polis. Not only do humans, like many other animals, need to organise themselves in groups: for them, and them alone, there is the need for a stable long-term future, which they can envisage by imagination, describe in language, and incorporate in institutions; and this entails that they need the rule of law.

Here, then, we have come upon the essence of common morality. And it is also essentially a public morality, which seeks above all to maintain justice between people and groups of people. When Aristotle, in his *Nicomachaean Ethics*, went through and analysed a list of human virtues, he found difficulty in fitting justice with the rest. And this is because justice is more an attribute of institutions than of human characters. An individual person may be fair-minded, and impartial in his exercise of such power as he has; and this is certainly a virtue. But, as I have said, it is not the only one. Moreover it seems to be a virtue, as it were, borrowed from the courtroom and the law-making institutions of the Polis. When we bring up or seek to educate children, we want them to respect the law and its impartial application to everyone, but we also want them to be brave, loving, loyal, unselfish, and capable of shame when they fall short in respect of these values. We want them, in short, as Aristotle suggested, to pursue these ideals for their own sake, or because they have come to see for themselves that they are good. Indeed, when Aristotle makes this point, he uses the word 'kalon', not the word 'agathon', the usual word that we translate as 'good'. 'Kalon' is usually translated 'beautiful'; so when Aristotle says that young men must learn to practise the virtues because they are 'kalon' he is saying something powerful. The virtues are to be embraced and gloried in. Here it seems to me that we are in the realm of private morality. As children learn to internalize the values they are brought up to admire, those values become part of their character. If they reject some of the values of their parents or mentors, then this rejection too is part of what they are. I designate this aspect of morality 'private', because of the process of internalisation, which happens when a child grows into a person who 'cannot bring himself' to fail to do what he knows is right, or feels ashamed when he has so failed. This private morality is shared, a matter of consensus in two respects. First, it is shared, more or less, by people brought up within a shared tradition. But there will always be different and sometimes conflicting values within that tradition.

Secondly, it is shared in the sense that it arises out of a shared belief that there exist areas of human behaviour that must be considered from a moral or ethical point of view. This is an important point. For there are those who detach themselves altogether from this field of private morality, or who believe that the concept of morality itself is a kind of pretence, perhaps a hangover from the days when people could be driven to accept rules of behaviour by a fear of the consequences of disobedience to the laws of an all-powerful God. The greatest difference between individuals within society is not a difference between the different moral values that they uphold, but the difference between those who are, as it were, committed to morality and those for whom morality is not a concept they understand, between those who, somehow or other, want to be good and those for whom this idea makes no sense.

However, I would argue that such a detachment from morality runs counter to specifically human nature. Human beings need not only the stability and security that arises from the rule of law, but the stability and security which arises from the very concept of the morally good and evil. Human beings have evolved so that they may not only feel sympathy with others, (for other animals can apparently feel this) but also through language express sympathy, and through imagination form resolutions about a non-existent future which they can plan to bring about. They can say to someone who is suffering, 'I will help you'; and they can sometimes say this, and do it, at a cost to themselves.

Consider the Good Samaritan. Here is a moral story that has nothing intrinsically to do with religion, though it lies at the heart of Christian morality. It has nothing to do with human rights. If the man who lay bleeding in the ditch had a right to be rescued and taken to the inn to recover and to be provided with money for his keep, then the moral goodness of the Samaritan would disappear. He would have been doing no more than was required of him. His goodness lies precisely in the fact that he was acting beyond the call of duty, and putting himself out for the sake of a stranger. The Samaritan is a paradigm case of a good human being, exhibiting a compassion that lies within the power of human beings, as individuals. His action is something that human beings can do.

It is my contention that public morality, justice in the sense of good government, could not exist if there were not a large majority of people who hold that private morality is a reality, not a sham. The possibility of adopting a moral standpoint, what David Hume referred to as 'a steady and general point of view', approving and disapproving without reference to our own interests, is not only real for human beings but a necessary aspect of their nature. This is why what we may describe as Machiavelli's problem, which arises when public and private morality conflict, is both painful and necessary. And since most people, whether historians of philosophy or not, agree with Hume that morality is a matter of feeling, of emotional commitment, tempers are likely to rise when legislation offends against commonly held views of what is morally right. Thus, in times of acute financial crisis, when collapse is all around and imminently threatening the country, a freeze in welfare benefits is inevitable for a responsible government. Yet it is passionately opposed by many who hold that care for the poor, the very young and the very old is not only a private ideal, but, as is often said, the mark of a civilised society. When it is proposed by government that legal aid be denied for appeals in welfare cases, and for civil cases in general, opponents claim that the rule of law itself, which on any definition includes equal access to justice for all citizens, is being undermined. Such clashes are inevitable and salutary. Their occurrence signals that dissent is allowed, on moral grounds, and that the aim is to convince by argument. When, in such cases, consensus cannot be achieved, when the vote is won by those in power, despite all protests, then there is general agreement that the constitution, and the rule of law must prevail. The alternative, which is anarchy, is worse. Where in a specific instance, in this case the freezing of welfare benefits, consensus fails, compromise may begin. But sometimes a government may decide that no compromise is possible. In that case, it is upon the consensus public morality, the respect for the rule of law that they will have to rely.

My unexciting conclusion, then, is that consensus morality is indeed possible, but within limits. First, the language of morality, though intended to be understood as having universal application, in practice derives from particular traditions, and only with difficulty overcomes the barriers that such traditions may erect. The concept of human rights seeks to eliminate these cultural barriers and address the needs of Human Nature as a whole. Yet on further examination, this concept seems to be more a moral aspiration than the discovery of an existing state of affairs. Human rights turn out to be rights that ought to be recognised the world over as belonging to all human beings in virtue of their humanity, but which people living under many legislatures do not yet actually possess. At any rate, the struggle to impose respect for human rights signals that those who engage in it believe in a consensus morality, in the name of which they make the claim that human rights are being infringed.

Two things should be added. First, what I have referred to as public morality, the morality of government and law, is necessarily consequentialist. Lawmakers, in any administration, take on new responsibilities, when they become such. Their duty is to anticipate what will be the outcome of the measures they propose in the, relatively, long term. This is not to say that they are confined within the boundaries of strict Benthamite Utilitarianism. They may be more concerned with the economic stability of the country than with individual happiness. Some general idea of well-being, or flourishing, though it may be connected with the idea of happiness, is not identical with it, and may more plausibly be invoked among their legislative aims. Even where laws are enacted to criminalize some widely perceived moral abuse, such as that of phone hacking by the press, the wrong that is being addressed has to be weighed against interference with the freedom to carry out investigative journalism.

It follows from this, secondly, that there is no place in the moral repertoire of legislators for the ideas of altruism, self-sacrifice, or postponing their own interests to that of others. Nor is there a place for the ideal of standing up for a principle, though the heavens fall. These are concepts applicable, and, I would argue, essential to private morality. But I would further argue that unless there are persons in power, charged with the public obligation to maintain justice and stability, who also at least understand the demands of principle, of honour and honesty, of truthfulness and compassion and the pangs of shame when these are disregarded, the consequentialist public morality of political power is unlikely itself to flourish. But there I may be on shakier ground.

REFERENCES

Cannadine, David, *The Undivided Past: History Beyond our Differences* (London: Penguin, 2013).

Hampshire, Stuart, *Innocence and Experience* (London: Allen Lane/Penguin, 1989).

Midgley, Mary, *Beast and Man: The Roots of Human Nature* (London: Methuen, 1978).

Overy, Richard, 'Reviewed: *The Undivided Past* by David Cannadine', *New Statesman*, 8 March 2013, 46–47.

Thomson, Judith Jarvis, 'A Defense of Abortion', *Philosophy and Public Affairs* 1, (Fall 1971). Reprinted in Parent (ed.), *Rights, Restitution and Risk* (Cambridge, Mass.: Harvard University Press, 1986).

Part III
Minds, Human and Animal

7 Extended Minds and the Nature of Seeing

Rupert Sheldrake

Mary Midgley has eloquently shown how materialist assumptions about minds and the self both distort our understanding of own nature and restrict the scope of science (see, e.g., Midgley 2014). In this essay, I argue that the conventional dogma that the mind is located inside the head is testable scientifically, and the evidence suggests that it is wrong. Our minds are far more extensive than our brains. I suggest that they stretch out beyond brains, and that the concept of fields provides the best starting point for thinking about the extension of minds beyond bodies. Since the nineteenth century, the sciences have been enriched by the concept of fields, which are most generally defined as regions of influence. A magnetic field is both within and around a magnet, extending beyond its surface. The Earth's gravitational field is both within and around the earth, extending invisibly far into the sky, and keeping the moon in its orbit. The electromagnetic field of a mobile telephone is both within the phone and stretches out invisibly beyond it. The space around us is full of invisible radio and TV transmissions, which are vibratory activities within the electromagnetic field, extended far beyond the surface of radio and TV transmitters. I suggest that, in a similar way, our minds are not confined to the inside of our heads but stretch out far beyond our bodies in a field-like way, and so do the minds of other animals. Mental or perceptual fields are different in nature from the recognized fields of physics, but they share with them the property of being extended in space and having effects or influences at a distance.

Despite Midgley's vigorous arguments to the contrary, many leading scientists still regard conscious experience as nothing but the subjective experience of brain activity, or an epiphenomenon of it. Many still believe in what Francis Crick called the 'Astonishing Hypothesis': ' "You," your joys and your sorrows, your memories and your ambitions, your sense of personal identity and free will, are in fact no more than the behaviour of a vast assembly of nerve cells and their associated molecules. . . . This hypothesis is so alien to the ideas of most people alive today that it can truly be called astonishing' (Crick 1994: 3).

This is indeed an astonishing claim. But within institutional science it is commonplace. Crick was no revolutionary: he spoke for the mainstream.

Susan Greenfield, an influential neuroscientist, as she looked at an exposed brain in an operating theatre, reflected, 'This was all there was to Sarah, or indeed to any of us. . . . We are but sludgy brains, and . . . somehow a character and a mind are generated in this soupy mess' (Greenfield 2000: 12–15).

If we follow Crick and treat materialism as a hypothesis, rather than a philosophical dogma, then it should be testable. As sceptics like to say, 'Extraordinary claims demand extraordinary evidence.' Where is the extraordinary evidence for the extraordinary claim that the mind is nothing but the activity of the brain?

There is very little. No one has ever seen a thought or image inside someone else's brain, or inside his or her own. When we look around us, the images of the things we see are outside us, not in our heads. Our experiences of our bodies are in our bodies. The feelings in my fingers are in my fingers, not in my head. Direct experience offers no support for the extraordinary claim that all experiences are inside brains. Direct experience is not irrelevant to the nature of consciousness; it *is* consciousness.

Surprisingly, our direct experience of seeing things provides one of the strongest challenges to the 'Astonishing Hypothesis'.

HOW DOES VISION WORK?

A debate about the nature of vision was going on in ancient Greece 2,500 years ago. It was taken up in the Roman Empire and in the Islamic world, and continued in Europe throughout the Middle Ages and the Renaissance. This debate played an important part in the birth of modern science, and is still alive today.

There were three main theories of how we see. The first was that vision involved an outward projection of invisible rays through the eyes, the 'extramission' theory, which literally means 'sending out.' For example, Empedocles (c. 493–433 B.C.) emphasised this approach. Second was the idea of a 'sending in' of images through light into the eyes, the 'intromission' theory, as supported by atomist philosophers like Democritus (c. 460–c. 470 B.C.). A third group of theories combined an inward movement of light and an outward movement of attention, as in Plato's (c. 424–c.348 BC) theory of vision involving a 'coalescence' of emissions from the eye and from the object of vision (Lindberg 1981: 1–6).

The extramission theory reflects people's experience of vision as an active process. We look *at* things, and can decide where to direct our attention. Around 300 B.C. Euclid, famous for his works on geometry, worked out this idea in mathematical detail. He showed how projection of virtual images from the eye could explain how we see images in mirrors. Unlike light itself, which is reflected by mirrors, visual projections go straight through them. They are not material.

Isaac Newton accepted Euclid's theory, and illustrated it in 1704 in his book *Opticks*. Essentially the same diagram is used in science textbooks today. A typical British physics textbook for secondary schools describes the process as follows: 'Rays from a point on the object are reflected at the mirror and appear to come from a point behind the mirror where the eye imagines the rays intersect when produced backwards' (Duncan and Kennett 2001: 8). There is no discussion of how the eye 'imagines' rays intersecting, or how it 'produces' them backwards. This is essentially Euclid's extramission theory of virtual images, but its implications are left implicit.

Since the early seventeenth century, the intromission theory has been scientifically orthodox, largely thanks to the work of Johannes Kepler (1571–1630), best known for his discoveries in astronomy. Kepler realized that light entering the eye though the pupil was focussed by the lens and produced an inverted image on the retina. He published his theory of the retinal image in 1604. Although this was a major triumph, and a landmark in the development of modern science, it raised questions that Kepler could not answer, and are still unanswered today. The problem was that the images on the retinas of both eyes were inverted and reversed; in other words, they were upside down and the left side was at the right, and vice versa. Yet we do not see two small, inverted, reversed images.

The only way Kepler could deal with this problem was by excluding it from optics. Once the image had been formed on the retina, it was someone else's business to explain how we actually see it (Lindberg 1981: 202). Vision itself was 'mysterious.' Ironically, the triumph of the intromission theory was achieved by leaving the experience of seeing unexplained. This problem has haunted science ever since.

Kepler's contemporary Galileo Galilei (1564–1642) likewise withdrew perceptions from the external world and squeezed them into the brain. He made a distinction between what he called primary and secondary qualities of objects. The primary qualities were those that could be measured and treated mathematically, such as size, weight and shape. These were the concern of objective science. The secondary qualities, such as colour, taste, texture and smell, were not within matter itself. They were subjective rather than objective. Thus our direct experience of the world was split into two separate poles, the objective, out there, and the subjective. This distinction was very influential, and was adopted by many subsequent scientists and philosophers, including John Locke (1632–1704), who wrote in his *Essay Concerning Human Understanding* (Book 2, Chapter 8), 'Such qualities, which in truth are nothing in the objects themselves, but powers to produce various sensations in us by their primary qualities, i.e. by the bulk, figure, texture, and motion of their insensible parts, as colours, sounds, tastes, &c.; these I call secondary qualities.'

After 400 years of mechanistic science, there has been almost no progress in understanding how the brain produces subjective experience, although many details have been discovered about the activities of different regions of the brain. The orthodox assumption is that the brain constructs a picture or model of the world inside itself. This is how an authoritative textbook called *Essentials of Neural Science and Behavior* described the process:

> [T]he brain constructs an internal representation of external physical events after first analyzing them into component parts. In scanning the visual field the brain simultaneously but separately analyzes the form of objects, their movement, and their color, all before putting together an image according to the brain's own rules. (Kandel, Schwartz and Jessell, 1995: 368)

Most contemporary metaphors for the activity of the brain are derived from computers, and 'internal representations' are commonly conceived of as 'virtual reality' displays. As the psychologist Jeffrey Gray put it succinctly, 'The "out there" of conscious experience isn't really out there at all; it's inside the head' (Gray 2004: 10). Our visual perceptions are a 'simulation' of the real world that is 'made by, and exists within, the brain' (Gray 2004: 25).

Although nominally mechanistic, the computer metaphor gives a new lease of life to dualistic thinking, with the 'hardware' of the brain controlled by the 'software' of mental programs. As Midgley pointed out in her *Science and Poetry*, 'Many people find it perfectly natural to say—apparently as a fact and not just as a metaphor—that mind is divided from body exactly as software is divided from hardware. This gives traditional dualism an even stronger grip, which sharply needs our attention' (Midgley 2006: 142).

The idea of visual experiences as simulations inside heads leads to strange consequences, as the philosopher Stephen Lehar (2004) has pointed out. It means that when I look at the sky, the sky I see is inside my head. My skull is beyond the sky! Lehar explains this view as follows:

> I propose that out beyond the farthest things you can perceive in all directions, i.e. above the dome of the sky, and below the solid earth under your feet, or beyond the walls and ceiling of the room you see around you, is located the inner surface of your true physical skull, beyond which is an unimaginably immense external world of which the world you see around you is merely a miniature internal replica. In other words, the head you have come to know as your own is not your true physical head, but only a miniature perceptual copy of your head in a perceptual copy of the world, all of which is contained within your real head. (Lehar 1999: 123)

Despite the theories of academic scientists and philosophers, most people do not accept that all their experiences are located inside their heads. They think they are where they seem to be, outside their heads.

In the 1990s, Gerald Winer and his colleagues in the psychology department at Ohio State University investigated people's beliefs about the nature of vision through a series of questionnaires and tests. They were surprised that extramission beliefs were common among children, and 'shocked' when they discovered that they were also widespread among college students, even among those studying psychology, who had been taught the 'correct' theory of vision (Winer et al. 2002). Among schoolchildren aged 10 to 13, more than 70 per cent believed in a combined intromission-extramission theory, and among college students 59 per cent (Winer et al. 1996). Winer and his colleagues called this a 'striking instance of a scientific misconception,' (Winer et al. 1996a). Education had failed to convert most of the students to the correct belief: 'Given that extramissionists in our studies affirm extramission even though they have been taught about vision, our attention is now directed to understanding whether education can eradicate these odd, but seemingly powerful, intuitions about perception' (ibid.).

Winer and his colleagues seem doomed to failure in their crusade for intellectual cleansing. These 'odd' intuitions about perception persist because they are closer to experience than the official doctrine, which leaves so much unexplained—including consciousness itself.

IMAGES OUTSIDE BODIES

Not all philosophers and psychologists believe the mind-in-the brain theory, and over the years a minority has always recognized that our perceptions may be just where they seem to be, in the external world outside our heads, rather than representations inside our brains (see, for example, Burtt 1932). In 1904, William James wrote as follows:

> [T]he whole philosophy of perception from Democritus' time downwards has been just one long wrangle over the paradox that what is evidently one reality should be in two places at once, both in outer space and in a person's mind. 'Representative' theories of perception avoid the logical paradox, but on the other had they violate the reader's sense of life which knows no intervening mental image but seems to see the room and the book immediately as they physically exist. (quoted in Velmans 2000)

As Alfred North Whitehead expressed it in 1925, 'sensations are projected by the mind so as to clothe appropriate bodies in external nature' (Whitehead 1925: 54).

A recent proponent of the extended mind is the psychologist Max Velmans. In his book *Understanding Consciousness* (2000), he proposed a 'reflexive model' of the mind, which he illustrated by this discussion of a subject (S) looking at a cat:

> According to reductionists there seems to be a phenomenal cat 'in S's mind', but this is really nothing more than a state of her brain. According to the reflexive model, while S is gazing at the cat, her only visual

experience of the cat is the cat she sees out in the world. If she is asked to point to this phenomenal cat (her 'cat experience'), she should point not to her brain but to the cat as perceived, out in space beyond the body surface. (Velmans 2000: 109)

Velmans suggested that this image might be like 'a kind of neural "projection hologram". A projection hologram has the interesting quality that the three-dimensional image it encodes is perceived to be out in space, in *front* of its two-dimensional surface' (Velmans 2000: 113–4). Velmans was ambiguous about the nature of this projection. A hologram is a field phenomenon, a record of the light field produced by the scattering of light rays by an object, from which a three-dimensional image of the original object can be reconstituted by shining light on the hologram. Velmans called this process 'psychological' rather than 'physical' and in the end said he did not know how it happens, but added, 'not fully understanding *how* it happens does not alter the fact *that* it happens.'

My own suggestion is that the outward projection of visual images is both psychological *and* physical. It occurs through perceptual fields. These are psychological in the sense that they underlie our conscious perceptions, and also physical or natural in that they exist outside the brain and have detectable effects. Human perception is not unique in being extended through seeing and hearing. Other animals see things through fields projected beyond the surfaces of their bodies and hear things through projected auditory fields. We are like other animals. (See Ground, this volume). Indeed, as Midgley has pointed out, we are not just like animals, we *are* animals (Midgley 2002).

The senses are not static. The eyes move as we look at things, and our heads and entire bodies move around in our environments. As we move, our perceptual fields change. Perceptual fields are not separate from our bodies, but include them. We can see our own outer surface, our skin, hair and clothing. We are inside our fields of vision and action. Our awareness of three-dimensional space includes our own bodies within it, and our movements and intentions in relation to what is around us. Like other animals, we are not passive perceivers but active behavers, and our perceptions and behaviour are closely linked (see Gibson 1986).

Some neuroscientists and philosophers agree that perceptions depend on the close connection between perception and activity, linking an animal or person to the environment. One school of thought advocates an 'enactive' or 'embodied' or 'sensorimotor' approach. Perceptions are not represented in a world-model inside the head, but are enacted or 'brought forth' as a result of the interaction of the organism and its environment. As Francisco Varela and his colleagues expressed it, 'perception and action have evolved together . . . perception is always *perceptually guided activity*' (Thompson, Palacios and Varela 1992). In the words of the philosopher Alva Noë, 'We are out of our heads. We are in the world and of it. We are patterns of active engagement with fluid boundaries and changing components. We are distributed' (Noë 2009: 183). The psychologist Kevin O'Regan, a committed materialist, prefers this approach to the mind-in-the-brain theory precisely because he wants to expel all magic from the brain. He does not accept that seeing is in the brain, because this would 'put you in the terrible situation of having to postulate some magical mechanism that endows the visual cortex with sight, and the auditory cortex with hearing' (in Blackmore 2005: 164).

Henri Bergson anticipated the enactive and sensorimotor approaches more than a century ago. He emphasized that perception is directed towards action. Through perception, 'The objects which surround my body reflect its possible action upon them' (Bergson 1911: 7). The images are not inside the brain:

> The truth is that the point P, the rays which it emits, the retina and the nervous elements affected, form a single whole; that the luminous point P is a part of this whole; and that it is really in P, and not elsewhere, that the image of P is formed and perceived. (Bergson 1911: 37–8)

My own interpretation is that vision takes place through extended perceptual fields, which are both within the brain and stretch out beyond it. (Sheldrake 2005b) Vision is rooted in the activity of the brain, but is not confined to the inside of the head. Like Velmans, I suggest that the formation of these fields depends on changes in various regions of the brain as vision takes place, influenced by expectations, intentions and memories. When I look at a person or an animal, my perceptual field interacts with the field of the person or animal I am looking at, enabling my gaze to be detected.

Our experience certainly suggests that our minds are extended beyond our brains. We see things and hear things in the space around us. But there is a strong taboo against anything that suggests that seeing and hearing might involve any kind of outward projection. This issue cannot be resolved by theoretical arguments alone, or else there would have been more progress over the last century—or even over the last 2,500 years.

I am convinced that the way forward is to treat fields of the mind as a testable scientific hypothesis rather than a philosophical theory. When I look at something, my perceptual fields 'clothe' what I am looking at. My mind touches what I am seeing. Therefore I might be able to affect another person just by looking. If I look at someone from behind when she cannot hear me or see me and does not know I am there, can she feel my gaze? If people can indeed detect when they are being looked at by someone they cannot see, this would suggest that the minds of the people staring can have effects outside their bodies, at a distance. Such an effect is impossible from a materialist point of view: the mind is confined to the inside of the body, and it cannot have mysterious effects at a distance. The sense of being stared at therefore provides an empirical way of testing the materialist hypothesis that minds are nothing but the activity of brains, confined to the inside of heads. If minds are nothing but the activity of brains then, in the absence of normal sensory clues, people should not be able to detect when they are being stared at.

THE DETECTION OF STARES

In fact, most people have felt someone looking at them from behind, turned around and met the person's eyes. Most people have also experienced the converse: they have made people turn round by staring at them. In extensive surveys in Europe and North America, between 70 and 97 per cent of adults and children reported experiences of these kinds (see Sheldrake 2003).

In surveys I conducted in Britain, Sweden and the United States, these experiences seemed to be most common when people were being stared at by strangers in public places, such as streets and bars. These experiences happened more when people felt vulnerable than when they felt secure.

When people made others turn around by staring at then, both men and women said that curiosity was their most frequent reason for staring, followed by a desire to attract the other person's attention. Other motives included sexual attraction, anger and affection (Sheldrake 2003). In short, the ability to detect someone's attention was associated with a range of motives and emotions.

In some East Asian martial arts, students are trained to increase their sensitivity to being looked at from behind (Sheldrake 2003), and some people observe others for a living. The sense of being stared at is well known to many police officers, surveillance personnel and soldiers, as I found through a series of interviews with professionals. Most were convinced that some people they were watching seemed to know they were being watched, even when the watchers were well hidden. When detectives are trained to follow people, they are told not to stare at their backs any more than necessary, because otherwise the person might turn around, catch their eye and blow their cover (Sheldrake 2003).

Many species of non-human animals also seem able to detect looks. Some pet owners claim that they can wake their sleeping dogs or cats by staring at them. Others have found it works the other way round and that their animals can wake them by staring. Some hunters and wildlife photographers are convinced that animals can detect their gaze even when they are hidden and looking at animals through telescopic lenses or sights. One British deer hunter found that the animals seemed to detect his intention, especially if he delayed shooting when he had them in his rifle sights: 'If you just wait a fraction too long, it will just take off. It'll sense you.'

In their surveys in Ohio, Winer and his colleagues found that more than a third of their respondents said that they had felt when animals were looking at them. About half believed that animals could feel their looks, even when the animals could not see their eyes. (Cottrell, Winer and Smith 1996)

If the sense of being stared at is real, then it must have been subject to evolution by natural selection. How might it have evolved? The most obvious possibility is in the context of predator-prey relations. Prey animals that detected when predators were looking at them would stand a better chance of surviving than those that did not (Sheldrake 1999).

EXPERIMENTAL RESEARCH ON THE SENSE OF BEING STARED AT

Since the 1980s, the sense of being stared at has been investigated experimentally both through direct looking and through closed circuit television (CCTV). In the scientific literature it is variously referred to as 'unseen gaze detection' or 'remote attention' or 'scopaesthesia' (from Greek *skopein* = to view and *aisthetikos* = sensitive).

In direct-looking experiments, people work in pairs, with a subject and a looker. In a randomized series of trials, blindfolded subjects sit with their backs to the lookers, who either stare at the back of their necks, or look away and think of something else. A mechanical signal—a click or a beep—marks the beginning of each trial. Within a few seconds the subjects guess whether they are being looked at or not. Their guesses are either right or wrong, and are recorded immediately. A test usually consists of twenty trials.

These tests are so simple that a child can do them, and thousands of children already have done. In the 1990s, this research was popularized through *New Scientist* magazine, BBC TV and Discovery Channel TV and many tests were conducted in schools and as student projects at universities. All together, tens of thousands of trials were carried out (Sheldrake 2003). The results were remarkably consistent. Typically, about 55 per cent of the guesses were right, as opposed to 50 per cent expected by chance. Although the effect was small, because it was so widely replicated it was highly significant statistically. In more rigorous experiments, subjects and starers were separated by windows or one-way mirrors, eliminating the possibility of subtle cues by sound or even smell. They were still able to tell when they were being watched (Sheldrake 2005a).

The largest experiment on the sense of being stared at began in 1995 at the NEMO Science Centre in Amsterdam. More than 18,000 pairs took part, with positive results that were astronomically significant statistically. The most sensitive subjects were children under the age of nine (Sheldrake 2005a).

Surprisingly, the sense of being stared at works even when people are looked at on screens, rather than directly. CCTV systems are routinely used for surveillance in shopping malls, banks, airports, streets and other public spaces. My assistants and I interviewed surveillance officers and security personnel whose job it was to observe people on screens. Most had noticed that some people could feel when they were being watched (Sheldrake

2003). For example, the security manager in a large firm in London had no doubt that some people have a sixth sense. 'They can have their backs to the cameras, or be scanned using hidden devices, yet they still become agitated when the camera is trained on them. Some move on, some look around for the camera.'

In laboratory tests, many people respond physiologically to being watched through CCTV, even though they are unconscious of their response. In these experiments, the researchers put a subject in one room and a looker in another, where the subject could be watched through CCTV. The subjects' galvanic skin response was recorded, as in lie-detector tests, enabling emotional changes to be detected through differences in sweating; wet skin conducts electricity better than dry skin. In a randomized series of trials, the starers either looked at the subject's image on the TV monitor, or looked away and thought of something else. The subjects' skin resistance changed significantly when they were being looked at (Schmidt et al. 2004). The fact that gaze detection works through CCTV shows that people can detect other people's attention even when they are not being watched directly. These effects of attention at a distance point to a wider view of minds—a literally wider view, in which minds stretch out into the world around bodies; not just human bodies, but the bodies of nonhuman animals, too.

In other words, I am suggesting that the fields of our minds reach out into our environment every time we see something, and that these fields are not just metaphors but have detectable effects as revealed by the sense of being stared at. Moreover, just by paying attention to someone's image on a TV screen, our minds can affect that person, showing that the extension of our minds beyond our bodies is not confined to direct vision, but can extend through our attention to images. This raises the further question as to whether our thoughts, emotions, feelings or intentions directed to someone else, even in the absence of their image, might also be able to affect that person at a distance. Such influences might reveal themselves through what is usually called telepathy, which literally means 'distant feeling.'

TELEPATHY

Most scientifically educated people have been brought up to believe that telepathy does not exist. Like other so-called psychic phenomena, it is dismissed as an illusion. Most people who espouse these conventional opinions, which I used to share myself, do not do so on the basis of a close examination of the evidence. They do so because there is a taboo against taking telepathy seriously. This taboo is related to the prevailing materialist paradigm within institutional science. If all mental phenomena are confined to the inside of the head, telepathy and other psychic phenomena, which seem to imply a mysterious kind of action at a distance, cannot possibly exist.

This prejudice dates back at least as far as the Enlightenment in the eighteenth century, and it is actively defended by sceptical organizations that seek to debunk 'claims of the paranormal' and assume that any evidence for psychic phenomena must be flawed or fraudulent. Nevertheless, telepathy has been investigated scientifically for more than 150 years (Sommer 2015), and there is ample evidence from spontaneous cases and from laboratory research that it really happens (e.g., Radin 2004; Sheldrake 2003). In this essay, I summarize some recent experiments that suggest that telepathy not only exists, but that it is a normal part of biological communication, part of our animal, evolutionary nature.

I first became interested in the subject of telepathy when I realised that it might well exist in the animal kingdom, and might be exhibited more by animals than by people. I started looking at evidence for telepathy in the animals we know best, namely pets, and soon came across numerous stories from dog, cat, parrot and other animal owners which suggested that their animals seemed able to read their minds and intentions.

Through public appeals I have built up a large database of such stories, currently containing more than 5,000 case histories. Many of these stories, from all over the world, are very similar. For example, many cat owners say that their animal seem to sense when they are planning to take them to the vet, even before they have taken out the carrying basket or given any apparent clue as to their intention. Some people say their dogs know when they are going to be taken for a walk, even when they are in a different room, out of sight or hearing, and when the person is merely thinking about taking them for a walk. No one finds this behaviour surprising if it happens at a routine time, or if the dogs see the person getting ready to go out, or hear the word 'walk'. They think it is telepathic because it often seems to happen in the absence of such clues. When hundreds of stories describe the same kind of behaviour, anecdotes turn into a kind of natural history. Of course, this is not necessarily a natural history of what pets actually do, but a natural history of what pet-owners *believe* their pets do.

One of the commonest and most testable claims about dogs and cats is that they know when their owners are coming home, in some cases anticipating their arrival by ten minutes or more, even when the people come at non-routine times, and even when they travel in unfamiliar vehicles such as taxis. In random household surveys in Britain and America, my colleagues and I have found that approximately 50 per cent of dog owners and 30 per cent of cat owners believe that their animals can anticipate the arrival of a member of the household (Sheldrake 1999).

The dog I investigated in most detail was a terrier called Jaytee, who belonged to Pam Smart, in Ramsbottom, Greater Manchester. Pam adopted Jaytee from Manchester Dogs' Home in 1989 when he was still a puppy and soon formed a close bond with him. In 1991, when Pam was working as a secretary at a school in Manchester, she left Jaytee with her parents, who noticed that the dog went to the French window almost every weekday at about 4.30 pm, around the time she set off, and waited there until she arrived some 45 minutes later. She worked routine office hours, so the family assumed that Jaytee's behaviour depended on some kind of time sense. Pam was made redundant in 1993 and was subsequently unemployed, no longer tied to any regular pattern of activity. Her parents did not usually know when she would be coming home, but Jaytee still anticipated her return.

In 1994, Pam read an article about my research and volunteered to take part. In more than 100 experiments, we videotaped the area by the window where Jaytee waited during Pam's absences, providing a continuous, time-coded record of his behaviour which was scored 'blind' by a third party who did not know the details of the experiments. To check that Jaytee was not reacting to the sound of Pam's car or other familiar vehicles, we investigated whether he still anticipated her arrival when she travelled by unusual means: by bicycle, by train and by taxi. He did.

We also carried out experiments in which Pam set off at times selected at random after she had left home, communicated to her by means of a telephone pager. In these experiments, Jaytee still started waiting at the window around the time Pam set off, even though no one at home knew when she would be coming. The odds against this being a chance effect were more than 100,000 to one. Jaytee behaved in a very similar way when he was tested repeatedly by sceptics keen to debunk his abilities (Sheldrake and Smart 2000). The evidence indicates that Jaytee was reacting to Pam's intention to come home even when she was many miles away. We have since replicated this work with other dogs. Telepathy seems the only hypothesis that can account for the facts (Sheldrake, 2011).

There is much potential for further research on animal telepathy. And if domestic animals are telepathic with their human owners, then it seems very likely that animals are telepathic with each other, and that this may play an important part in the wild. Some naturalists have already suggested that the coordination of flocks of birds and herds of animals may involve something like telepathy, as may communication between members of a pack of wolves.

In the course of my research on unexplained powers of animals, I heard of dozens of dogs and cats that seemed to anticipate telephone calls from their owners. For example, when the telephone rang in the household of a noted professor at the University of California at Berkeley, his wife knew when her husband was on the other end of the line because Whiskins, their silver tabby cat, rushed to the telephone and pawed at the receiver. 'Many times he succeeds in taking it off the hook and makes appreciative miaws that are clearly audible to my husband at the other end', she said. 'If someone else telephones, Whiskins takes no notice.' The cat responded even when he telephones home from field trips in Africa or South America.

This led me to reflect that I myself had had this kind of experience, in that I had thought of people for no apparent reason who shortly there afterwards called. I asked my family and friends if they had ever had this experience, and I soon found the majority were very familiar with it. Some said they knew when their mother or boyfriend or other significant person was calling because the phone sounded different!

My colleagues and I conducted extensive surveys on apparent telepathy in connection with telephone calls and find that the majority of the population have experienced it. Indeed, it is the commonest kind of apparent telepathy in the modern world. Most people say that it happens with people they know, but not with strangers (Sheldrake 2003).

Two sceptical hypotheses immediately spring to mind. First, could it not be that this kind of apparent telepathy is an illusion produced by a combination of chance coincidence and selective memory? Perhaps people think of others from time to time for no apparent reason. By chance, someone they are thinking of may then ring. People may remember such coincidences, but forget all the times they have thought of someone who did not ring.

Second, when we know other people well, we may have unconscious expectations of when they are likely to ring and hence anticipating their calls may not be a matter of telepathy but some kind of unconscious knowledge.

These are reasonable possibilities, but is there any evidence for them? When I started thinking about these questions I searched the scientific literature, including the literature of parapsychology and psychical research, to see if there were any data on these subjects. I found that there had apparently been no experimental investigations whatsoever. These sceptical hypotheses were completely untested. In fact, the second hypothesis may be untestable. If apparent telephone telepathy is to be explained in terms of unconscious expectations, how could anyone prove the expectations were there in the first place, since they are by definition unconscious? Further, even if these unconscious expectations exist, might they not be a *result* of telepathy rather than an alternative to it?

The only way of resolving these questions was to do experimental tests capable of statistical evaluation. My colleagues and I developed a simple procedure in which participants received a call from one of four different callers at a prearranged time. Participants chose the callers themselves, usually close friends or family members. They knew who the potential callers were, but did not know which one will be calling in any given test, because the caller was picked at random by the experimenter. They had to guess who the caller is before the caller said anything. By chance they would have been right about one time in four, or 25 per cent of the time. In many of these trials, the participants were videotaped continuously to make sure that they did not receive any other telephone calls or emails that could give them clues as to which caller had been selected.

Under videotaped conditions, the average hit rate was 45 per cent, which is extremely significant statistically (Sheldrake and Smart 2003). I also carried out a similar experiment for a British TV show, in which the participants were five sisters, members of the Nolan sisters group, a girl band popular in the 1980s. In this experiment the hit rate was 50 per cent, twice the chance level (Sheldrake, Godwin and Rockell 2004).

My colleague Pam Smart and I carried out a series of trials in which two of the four callers were familiar, and the other two were strangers, whose names the participants knew, but whom they had not met. With familiar callers, the hit rate was more than 50 per cent: highly significant statistically.

With strangers it was near the chance level, in agreement with the observation that telepathy typically takes place between people who share emotional or social bonds (Sheldrake 2003)

Our findings in telephone telepathy tests have been replicated at the universities of Amsterdam, Holland (Lobach and Bierman 2004) and Freiburg, Germany (Schmidt et al. 2009) with statistically significant positive results.

Experiments on telephone telepathy provide a good opportunity to test for the effect, or lack of effect, of distance. In the experiments conducted within Britain, we found no indication that callers who were closer were more effective than those who are far away. But telephones permit experiments to be carried out with callers on the other side of the earth, up to 12,500 miles away. For these experiments we recruited subjects in London who had recently come to England from Australia and New Zealand, on the opposite side of the earth, and also from South Africa and other distant countries. We compared the subjects' success rates with friends and family members overseas with friends in Britain. The hit rate with callers thousands of miles away averaged 61 per cent, compared with 36 per cent with friends in Britain (Sheldrake and Smart 2003). Subjects were actually *more* successful with callers farther away than with those who were much nearer. Why? The most probable explanation is that the majority of the overseas callers were people to whom the subjects were particularly strongly attached, such as mothers and boyfriends, while the callers in Britain were mainly new acquaintances.

Phenomena very similar to telephone telepathy occur in connection with emails and SMS messages, and in a series of experimental tests, my colleagues and I have found very similar positive, statistically significant effects (Sheldrake 2014).

The lack of effect of distance on telephone telepathy is in general agreement with previous research on other kinds of telepathy. Telepathic influences did not seem to fall off with distance in experiments either with people (Braude 1979; Cooper 1982) or with animals such as dogs, cats and parrots (Sheldrake 1999). These influences seemed to depend on emotional closeness, rather than spatial proximity.

Telepathy seems to be widespread in the animal kingdom and is part of our biological nature, though our own telepathic powers are generally poor compared with those of dogs, cats, horses, parrots and other species of mammals and birds. I discuss a large body of evidence for telepathy in non-human species in my book *Dogs That Know When Their Owners Are Coming Home, and Other Unexplained Powers of Animals* (1999, second edition 2011).

MINDS BEYOND BRAINS

Telepathy, like the sense of being stared at, is only paranormal if we define as 'normal' the theory that the mind is confined to the brain. But if our minds reach out beyond our brains, just as they seem to every time we look at something, then the sense of being stared at seems normal. Likewise, if through our feelings and intentions we stretch out to other people or to animals, just as they seem to, then phenomena like telepathy seem natural, not supernatural, normal, not paranormal. They are not spooky and weird, on the margins of abnormal human psychology, but are part of our biological nature. Indeed the idea of the extended mind is implicit in our language. The words *attention* and *intention* come from the Latin root *tendere*, 'to stretch', as in *tense* and *tension*. Attention comes from *ad + tendere*, literally meaning, 'to stretch (the mind) toward.' Intention comes from *in + tendere*, 'to stretch (the mind) into.' And extend, from *ex + tendere*, means 'to stretch out'.

Of course, I am not saying that the brain is irrelevant to our understanding of the mind. It is very relevant, and recent advances in brain research have much to tell us. Our minds are centred in our bodies, and in our brains in particular. However, they are not *confined* to our brains, but extend far beyond them.

REFERENCES

Bergson, H. *Creative Evolution* (London: Macmillan, 1911).

Blackmore, S. *Conversations on Consciousness* (Oxford: Oxford University Press, 2005).

Braude, S. *ESP and Psychokinesis: A Philosophical Examination* (Philadelphia: Temple University Press, 1979).

Burtt, E. A. *The Metaphysical Foundations of Modern Physical Science* (London: Kegan Paul, Trench and Trubner, 1932).

Cooper, J. 1982. *The Mystery of Telepathy* (London: Constable, 1982).

Cottrell, J.E. and Winer, G.A. and Smith, M.C. Beliefs of children and adults about feeling stares of unseen others. *Developmental Psychology* 32, 50–61, 1996.

Crick, F. *The Astonishing Hypothesis: The Scientific Search for the Soul* (London: Simon and Schuster, 1994).

Duncan, T., and Kennett, H. *GCSE Physics* (London: Murray, 2001).

Gibson, J.J. *The Ecological Approach to Visual Perception* (Hillsdale, NJ.: Lawrence Erlbaum Associates, 1986).

Gray, J. *Consciousness: Creeping Up on the Hard Problem* (Oxford: Oxford University Press, 2004).

Greenfield, S. *Brain Story: Unlocking Our Inner World of Emotions, Memories, Ideas and Desires* (London: BBC, 2000).

Kandel, E.R., Schwartz, J.H. and Jessell, T.M. *Essentials of Neuroscience and Behavior* (Norwalk CT: Appleton and Lang, 1995).

Lehar, S. 'Gestalt isomorphism and the quantification of spatial perception.' *Gestalt Theory* 21, 122–138, 1999.

Lehar, S. 'Gestalt isomorphism and the primacy of subjective conscious experience', *Behavioral and Brain Sciences* 26, 375–444, 2004.

Lindberg, D.C. *Theories of Vision from Al Kindi to Kepler* (Chicago: University of Chicago Press, 1981).

Lobach, E. and Bierman, D.J. 'Who's calling at this hour? Local sidereal times and telephone telepathy.' *Proceedings of Parapsychology Association Annual Convention, Vienna, 2004*, 2004.

Midgley, M. *Beast and Man: The Roots of Human Nature* (London: Routledge, 2002).

Midgley, M. *Science and Poetry* (London: Routledge, 2006).

Midgley, M. *Are You an Illusion?* (London: Routledge, 2014).

Noë, A. *Out of Our Heads: Why You Are Not Your Brain, and Other Lessons from the Biology of Consciousness.* New York: Hill and Wang, 2009.

Radin, D. *Entangled Minds: Extrasensory Experiences in a Quantum Reality* (New York: Paraview Pocket Books, 2004).

Schmidt, S., Schneider, R., Utts, J. and Walach, H. 'Distant intentionality and the feeling of being stared at: Two meta-analyses.' *British Journal of Psychology* 95, 235–247, 2004.

Schmidt, S., Erath, D., Ivanova, V. and Walach, H. 'Do you know who is calling? Experiments on anomalous cognition in phone call receivers'. *The Open Psychology Journal* 2, 12–18, 2009.

Sheldrake, R. *Dogs That Know When Their Owners Are Coming Home, And Other Unexplained Powers of Animals* (London: Hutchinson, 1999).

Sheldrake, R. *The Sense of Being Stared At, and Other Aspects of the Extended Mind.* (London: Hutchinson, 2003).

Sheldrake, R., Godwin, H. and Rockell, S. 'A filmed experiment on telephone telepathy with the Nolan sisters.' *Journal of the Society for Psychical Research* 68, 168–172, 2004.

Sheldrake, R. 'The sense of being stared at. Part 1. Is it real or illusory?' *Journal of Consciousness Studies* 12, 10–31, 2005a.

Sheldrake, R. 'The sense of being stared at. Part 2. Its implications for theories of vision.' *Journal of Consciousness Studies* 12, 32–49, 2005b.

Sheldrake, R. *Dogs That Know When Their Owners Are Coming Home, and Other Unexplained Powers of Animals.* 2nd ed. (New York: Random House, 2011).

Sheldrake, R. 'Telepathy in connection with telephone calls, text messages and e-mails' In: *Evidence for Psi*, eds. Broderick, D. and Goertzel, B., (Jefferson NC: McFarland, 2014), 93–101.

Sheldrake, R. and Smart, P. 'A dog that seems to know when his owner is coming home: Videotaped experiments and observations'. *Journal of Scientific Exploration* 14, 233–255, 2000.

Sommer, A. (ed.), *Psychical Research in the History of Science and Medicine*, special section in *Studies in History of Biological and Biomedical Sciences* 48, part A, 38-111, 2014.

Thompson, E., Palacios, A. and Varela, F.J. 'Ways of coloring: Comparative color vision as a case study for cognitive science.' *Behavioral and Brain Sciences* 15, 1–26, 1992.

Velmans, M. *Understanding Consciousness* (London: Routledge, 2000).

Whitehead, A. N. *Science and the Modern World* (New York: Macmillan, 1925).

Winer, G.A. and Cottrell, J.E. 'Does anything leave the eye when we see?' *Current Directions in Psychological Science* 5, 137–142, 1996a.

Winer, G.A., Cottrell, J.E., Karefilaki, K.D. and Gregg, V.A. 'Images, words and questions: Variables that influence beliefs about vision in children and adults'. *Journal of Experimental Child Psychology* 63, 499–525, 1996.

Winer, G.A., Cottrell, J.E., Gregg, V.A., Fournier, J.S., and Bica, L.A. 'Fundamentally misunderstanding visual perception: Adults' beliefs in visual emissions.' *American Psychologist* 57, 417–424, 2002.

8 Naturalism, Science and the Philosophy of Mind

Jane Heal

INTRODUCTION

The paper is in effect a footnote to Mary Midgley's work. It revisits themes which she has stressed and highlights once again the importance, for our self-understanding, of appreciating that we are social animals.[1] In many rich and wide-ranging books and articles she has brought out the insights which science, among other great human achievements, can offer into human life and human nature. But she has stressed also that we are liable to misconceptions about what science tells us and about what respect for science requires of us. In this paper, I shall consider one idea presupposed in some recent philosophy of mind and suggest that it may provide yet another case study which bears out this view. The idea in question is that psychological concepts are 'theoretical' in a particular sense, namely that their central usefulness for us is that they enable us to predict the thoughts and behaviour of others.

What I shall try to do is show that this idea is mistaken. I shall also consider the relation of this idea to 'naturalism', a tricky notion which may be understood in various ways. I shall suggest that a plausible, modest and methodological version of naturalism shows the idea to be false. That falsity, in turn, blocks at least some possible ways of being drawn into startling, grandiose and ontological versions of naturalism—that is, ideas about the very nature of reality.

But before coming to this it may be helpful to comment on some key terms in the discussion, including 'psychological concept', 'naturalism' and 'theory'.

By 'psychological concept', we shall mean concepts such as 'believe' 'desire', 'intend', 'want', 'have a yen for', 'care about', 'see', 'think', 'guess', 'forget', 'deliberate', 'choose' and the like. Our quarry is a better understanding of what these concepts do for us. My target is the view that they are a species of scientific concept. The view may be put this way: as physics investigates the forces which make matter move and as chemistry explores what causes different kinds of matter to combine in various ways, so psychological thinking theorises about the inner items and forces, such as beliefs and desires, which produce the behaviour of human bodies.

Respect for science, acceptance of some broadly naturalistic outlook, may seem to favour this view. One direction this line of thought then leads in is to seeing the mind as the brain and identifying our thoughts with brain events. And such physicalism has the advantage of granting us and our thoughts undoubted reality—as much reality as brains have. But, on the downside, it is difficult to recognise ourselves in what we are now offered. Things we care about, we ourselves, our feelings, our values, our choices, our commitments, although it is asserted that they are somehow there in the brain and its states, seem to have become invisible on this picture. It is not surprising that, faced with these perplexities, some people move to a dualist view, postulating an immaterial substance to be the real person and to be the locus for awareness of value and for choice. And yet that seems not at all an attractive move, if we are committed to naturalism, or at least to respecting the advances of physics and the neurosciences in the nineteenth and twentieth centuries.

But does naturalism favour the initial view of psychological concepts which contributes to getting us into this tangle? A central commitment in all versions of naturalism is respect for scientific theorising and empirical investigation of the world we find ourselves in. Nothing in that world is *a priori* off limits for such investigation, certainly not us and our thinking. But so far this is only a methodological stance, willingness to accept empirical investigation of ourselves. It is true, however, that it brings with it a serious commitment. When such empirical investigation is possible, we must follow wherever it leads, however surprising or unwelcome the conclusions. If those conclusions are in conflict with cherished cultural traditions or congenial self-images, then we must reinterpret those traditions and discard those images. And if empirical enquiry validates some stronger ontological version of naturalism, reductive physicalism about the mind, for example, then we will have to bite on that bullet too, however perplexing the view.

But this is all merely conditional. Where does empirical enquiry into the nature of our thinking actually lead? Does it show that in using psychological concepts we are in effect using some proto-scientific theory of the mind?

In a wide sense, 'theory' means only a systematically organised body of knowledge about some subject matter. Physics and chemistry are one variety of such theory. What these sciences aim for is systematic bodies of knowledge, couched in terms of distinctive concepts, which serve us by giving insight into the structures and forces which underlie behaviour in the objects and stuffs around us. The prime merit of such concepts, and the theories in which they are embedded, is the predictive power they give us. For sure, simplicity, elegance and the like are also virtues of concepts and theories. And there are desirable corollaries of having a powerful predictive theory, one of which is the ability to explain, and another of which is the possibility of control, at least in some circumstances. But accurate predictions, the more detailed and accurate the better, are a necessary condition for any of these other good things to come into consideration.

But such scientific theories, impressive though they are, are only one of the many sorts of thing which can be called 'theory'. There are plenty of systematic bodies of knowledge, invoking sophisticated concepts, which do not serve the purposes of prediction. Consider, for example, legal theory and the concept of a jury. A jury is a body of people whose duty is to give a fair verdict on whether some accused person did the wrong with which he or she is charged. The point of having the concept of a jury, and of setting out principles about juries, is not to predict the behaviour of such bodies of people. The central fact about juries is the duty noted above. The concept is thus one with essential normative components. And the point of having it is practical. It is to be able to focus cognitive resources on thinking about these norms, so as to able to arrange for the norms to be fulfilled, either by unpacking what other norms they bring with them (for example, no fair trial unless the defence is heard) or through discovering what empirical conditions are needed for the norms to be fulfilled (for example, a jury will fail to appreciate evidence properly if the members are hungry).

Now we are in a position to distinguish concepts which are predictive theoretical from those which are practical theoretical. The central merit of the former, for example, concepts of physics and chemistry, is that they enable us to formulate systematic bodies of knowledge which deliver predictions, the more detailed and accurate the better. The central merit of the latter, for example, concepts of legal theory, is that they enable us to think about, and work through the implications of, the norms governing practical projects so as to be able to carry out those projects well.

Let us note here that having a practical theoretical concept will often enable predictions to be made. One reason for this is that practical enterprises are typically achieved by the joint contribution of various elements, occurring in distinctive patterns, sometimes spread over time, which are intrinsic to the normative structure of the enterprise. For example, for a jury to give a verdict, the accusation needs to be made, the evidence and defense heard, the deliberation of the jury completed and the verdict delivered. So anyone who grasps the concept can predict that, when a jury returns from deliberating, it is likely to give a verdict. Another reason (already briefly remarked on) is that having a practical theoretical concept allows for making relevant empirical investigations. For example, there can be research into how long a jury can remain alert, whether there are pressures such as intimidation which make it difficult for jurors to render a fair verdict and the like. The research is empirical because these things are not to be worked out *a priori*, but can be known only by systematic observation. Knowing them is worthwhile because they enable the setting up of conditions which make it more likely that juries will do their job well.

But it is important to see that the existence of these predictive elements in our body of knowledge about juries does not make the concept more like one of natural science, does not make it predictive theoretical. This is because these predictive elements do not show that the merit of the concept is enabling these predictions to be made. More generally, the fact that some concept is a sophisticated one, that having it involves grasp of complex structures and of generalisations, and also the ability to make some predictions, does not show that it is a predictive theoretical concept.

So now I can state my central claim more clearly. It is that psychological concepts are often discussed as if they were predictive theoretical. But they are much better regarded as practical theoretical. (In what follows I shall sometimes abbreviate these phrases just to 'predictive' and 'practical'.)

In this brief and speculative paper, I cannot undertake the kind of survey of the literature needed to back the claim that the idea that psychological concepts are predictive theoretical is often presupposed in philosophy of mind. But even if I am misreading the evidence or my suggestion is exaggerated, still there is interest in pursuing the line of thought in the rest of the paper. At the very least, it is not obviously false that some philosophy of mind assumes that psychological concepts are predictive. And if the argument against the view that they are predictive has force, then we can say this: to the extent that a philosophical view represents psychological concepts as predictive theoretical, it is mistaken.

But although a large-scale survey cannot be given, we shall consider just one example to illustrate the dominance of concern with prediction, Daniel Dennett's much discussed idea of the 'intentional stance'.[2] Dennett starts by sketching various different strategies for predicting the behaviour of an object. He contrasts the physical stance, where we try to predict behaviour by looking at the object's physical components, with the design stance, where we look at what it was set up to do by its designers. And finally he introduces the intentional stance, which is what we adopt, according to him, when we use psychological concepts. And of this third stance he says, 'Here is how it works: First you decide to treat the object whose behavior is to be predicted as a rational agent; then you figure out what beliefs that agent ought to have, given its place in the world and its purpose. Then you figure out what desires it ought to have, on the same considerations. . . . A little practical reasoning from the chosen set of beliefs and desires will in many . . . instances yield a decision about what the agent ought to do; that is what you predict the agent will do.' And he summarises his view this way: 'My thesis will be that . . . belief . . . can be discerned only from the point of view of one who adopts a certain predictive strategy' (1987: 17). So, for Dennett, you need to be interested in prediction of the particular actions people will do in order to have any use for the concept of belief and related psychological concepts.

Dennett's view, and the reaction to it, is particularly interesting in connection with the claims of this paper precisely because of the prominence he gives to the normative aspects of the psychological. In noting that the concept of belief (and also of desire and other psychological states) has normative links, he is not unusual. Many philosophers who take psychological concepts to be predictive theoretical would be happy to agree to this and to acknowledge that they are different in this from the concepts of physics and chemistry. What is notable about Dennett is that he makes such normative ideas the very centrepiece of his account.

And yet that account is still focused wholly on prediction. And another striking fact, even more important in relation to the claim that much philosophy of mind assumes a predictive theoretical view of psychological concepts, is the reaction to his proposal. It provoked great interest and many responses. But very few of them remarked on or questioned this focus on prediction. Rather, the debate centred on the issue of whether Dennett's proposal allows enough reality to thoughts and desires. On the view he sketches, an object can be credited with beliefs if it is predictable by the intentional strategy, whatever the interior physical arrangements which underlie its being so. Opponents argued that, for an object to have beliefs, there need to be events in its brain (transformations of sentence-like patterns in the neurons, for example) which provide some physical realisation of the rational relations invoked by the strategy. But both sides of the debate accepted that explaining how certain predictions are reliably possible was what is needed to throw light on psychological concepts.

But the normative nature of the concepts at least ought to suggest the possibility that it is interest in the norms which underpins uses of the concept, not interest in prediction. Being able to predict in detail what someone, oneself or another, will think or do is, of course, sometimes made possible by psychological knowledge. We need not deny this obvious truth. But is Dennett right that belief 'can be discerned only from the point of view of one who adopts a certain predictive strategy'? Or might it perhaps be that it can only be discerned from the point of view of one who is interested in the norms of thinking and in thinking well?

In considering this, let us set aside for the moment our interactions with other people and how psychological concepts might figure there. Let us start instead by considering the fantasy of a long-lived and highly intelligent but wholly solitary creature. This creature is like us in wanting bodily ease, variety of foods, amusement and such like, and also resembles us in wanting to know more about its environment, both to satisfy curiosity and so that it can manipulate that environment to secure more comforts. Let us imagine the creature becoming more and more intellectually sophisticated, as it lives and reflects over many years and centuries. What kinds of concepts will it develop? What will it come to think about?

One kind of thing which would make this creature's life go better from its own point of view is discovery of more facts about the non-animate environment. That will satisfy curiosity and also provide increasing ability to control that environment. So the creature may well develop predictive theoretical concepts, as it reflects on and experiments with wood, stone and water, learns how to smelt ores, to fire pots and the like.

But another kind of thing which would make its life go better is being able to think better. Perhaps, for example, the creature puts much effort into securing something but is then unexpectedly less than satisfied by having it. Or perhaps something envisaged and worked towards is not secured because a tool fails to behave as anticipated. Better thinking might have helped in both cases, in the first case by leading to choice of a better project and in the second by leading to better beliefs about effective means for carrying out the chosen project.

So it will help the creature not just to set goals and form beliefs, but to become conscious of itself as so doing, and to grasp that it can do these things in ways which help or hinder it in living well by its own lights in the long term. Having succeeded in forming psychological concepts such as desire and belief, the creature is able not only to act in the light of its goals and beliefs but to ask 'What goals do I have? Should I have them? What beliefs do I have? Should I have them?' And so it is able to concentrate cognitive resources on how to improve its desires and beliefs. It can ask itself whether it really understands what it is thinking about, and try to explore areas where it suspects it is muddled. Also it can observe empirically what environmental conditions lead to acquiring good or bad thoughts. Getting tired or drunk is not helpful, sleeping well and being alert are. And as a result of all this, it may come to do its thinking better, be more confident that it is starting its deliberation from the right points, is set up to avoid fallacies and the like.

But would grasp of the concepts of desire and belief, and the kind of further knowledge about desires and beliefs which has just been sketched, enable it to predict its own future thoughts or actions? There are of course extremely general things the creature is aware of about the tendencies of desires and beliefs to lead to action. Desire, having something as an end, is what moves to action. Belief, taking the world to be a certain way, is what leads to choice of this or that means to the end. But grasping this kind of generality does not enable detailed prediction of any particular thought or action. And although knowledge about the conditions under which good or bad desires and beliefs are formed may enable the creature to predict, again in general terms, that it is likely to come by good or bad thoughts in these or those circumstances, that also will not enable it to predict what particular thoughts it will arrive at.

It is not wholly impossible that the creature should come to be able to consider some particular episodes of its future thinking or acting and to predict how they will go. For example, the creature might find itself in a position analogous to that of Ulysses with the Sirens, where it foresees that it will face temptation to some disastrous action which it will not be able to resist. But the idea of extending such predictive capacity to cover all, or even large swathes, of future thought and action runs into extreme obscurity. The idea that the benefit of having reflective awareness of one's own thoughts is that it would enable one to predict what those thoughts will make one do, somehow enabling one to bypass deliberating on the basis of them, does not make sense. And the unimportance of prediction is brought out even more forcefully by the fact that the creature can derive many benefits from having psychological concepts, the ones we noted earlier, even if it never engages in any predictive dealings with its own detailed thoughts.

So Dennett's claim, namely that beliefs can be discerned only from the point of view of one who adopts a certain predictive strategy, is false. We have made sense of our creature having the concept of belief, but without attributing to it any interest in adopting a predictive strategy towards its own future detailed thoughts and actions. As we have sketched it, what gives it a point of view from which to identify its beliefs and desires is its interest in acting well, so that its life goes well. So the creature is interested in good future thoughts and actions, and in doing things (engaging in normative reflection, seeking circumstances in which good thinking is not hindered and the like) which will tend to produce good future thought and action. But it is not focused on knowing now what in detail those future thoughts and actions will be.

The crucial point to take forward from this, and from our earlier discussion of juries, is that reflective distance from a practical project is not the same as turning that practical project into subject matter for 'theory' in the sense of 'theory' given by natural science. As we have noted several times, reflective distance from a practical project may indeed enable understanding of the general structure of the project and how the different strands contribute to the whole. Also it may enable formulation of predictions of general kinds about when the project will go well or ill. Furthermore, on occasion, it may lead to ability to give some detailed predictions about this or that episode. But focusing on these facts and thereby being led to take a practical theoretical concept to be predictive theoretical would be a muddle. The central point of having a practical concept is not to get into the incoherent position of having stepped wholly outside some project, to a standpoint where it presents itself as a mere sequence of happenings into the causal structure of which we would like to have insight, the more complete the better. The point is rather to be able to step back temporarily from some aspects of the project so as to focus cognitive resources on such things as the norms implicit in it, what they demand and how to satisfy them, thereby being enabled to carry out the project better.

Does the situation change when we abandon the fantasy of the solitary creature and consider our use of psychological concepts in application to other people? It does not. What is obvious about human beings without deep enquiry is that we are social co-operative creatures. For a start, our young are helpless. They need to be brought up by adults, acting in co-operation with each other, if they are to have the nourishment, security and training to survive and themselves become effective adults. And beyond that, what the young learn as they grow is not how to go off and live by themselves. Rather they learn language, together with many other skills, which then enable them to take part in the co-operative enterprises of preparing meals, building shelters, making tools, telling stories, working out theories, passing legislation, designing clothes, organising ceremonies and the innumerable other activities which human life consists of.

And there is something further about ourselves which we have understood only recently, as the result of empirical investigation in disciplines such as evolutionary biology, palaeobiology, archaeology and anthropology. What these have given us is the perspective of deep time on our existence and current way of life. What they reveal is that, despite the fact that we are different from other animals in having an elaborate culturally informed life, we are social primates, closely akin to other primates still living. We have been shaped by millions of years of evolution, together with an extremely long cumulative and varied cultural history. Our tools, language, cookery, painting, poetry, religion, agriculture, metal working, literature, institutions of learning, complex forms of government and so on and on have not been revealed to us over some short space of time, but have been built up in a process which has taken many hundreds of thousands of years of shared thinking, the results of which are passed on by each generation to the next.

In summary, life, for us human beings, centrally involves our thinking together about what is the case and what we shall do. So one central human relation I have to you as a thinker is that in which you are the other part of some 'we' who are together reflecting about some question. Here, because we are doing the thinking together, predicting your thoughts and behaviours is not the point of being aware of what you think, anymore than it is when I am thinking by myself. Rather the point of having psychological concepts, of each of us being able to think about what the other thinks, is that we are able to see that it is important whether we understand each other, whether the goals we propose to pursue are really worthwhile and whether the beliefs we each bring to the debate are well grounded. So applied by each of us to the other in this context of shared deliberation and action, psychological concepts are just as practical as they are when I apply them to myself.

The fact that we are separate individuals of course introduces many complications, many possibilities of mutual misunderstanding and of conflict, into the situation and into the kinds of reflection in which we deploy psychological concepts. But none of these complications has the power to make psychological concepts morph from being practical theoretical into being predictive theoretical, However much we misunderstand each other, or squabble, murder and double-cross, that does not change the basic fact that we live our lives by acting and thinking together.

If we accept this conclusion, we face some further large issues, about which I shall make only some brief remarks since dealing with them is well beyond the scope of this chapter.

One is how the predictive theoretical view of the psychological came to be so entrenched. It seems likely that its grip goes back a long way, at least to developments in natural science and politics in the seventeenth and eighteenth centuries. We find there great progress in physics and chemistry, with the emergence of a powerful atomistic theory of matter and its structure. We find also developments in political and moral thought, asserting the rights and responsibilities of the individual as against traditional and hierarchical forms of power and knowledge. How these two streams of thought and imagery mingled, how aspirations to a scientific view of the mind and society emerged, what pictures of human beings were then formed, are part of a complex story, which I have neither the space nor the competence to trace in detail. It is of course a story on which Midgley has thrown much light.[3]

The suggestion I want to take forward from this historical speculation is that a view with a recognisably predictive theoretical flavour was already in place by the seventeenth and eighteenth centuries. The appearance of the view is not the upshot of nineteenth- and twentieth-century advances, such as the discovery of the completeness of physics or evolutionary theory or improved understanding of the workings of the brain. Rather, the view is part of the context of ideas into which these discoveries arrived.

If this is correct, then many of the problems which preoccupy us about the relations of 'mind' and 'brain' may have the particular shape they do in part because the predictive theoretical view of the psychological is assumed. Taking psychological concepts to be predictive assumes them to be in the same line of business as the concepts of such sciences as physics and chemistry. So when physics and brain science advance, questions of how the psychological relates to the physical or the chemical become acute. We find ourselves with all the problems of explaining how the mental can affect the bodily, where to fit consciousness in, whether we should defend a version of dualism or must bite the bullet of some form of physicalism. I do not claim that jettisoning the predictive theoretical view of the psychological provides an obvious and immediate dissolution of all these puzzlements. But jettisoning it might be part of opening up other avenues of thought. They are not avenues on which substance dualism comes back again, since that is as much complicit in the predictive theoretical view as physicalism. Rather, these other avenues are ones on which we see more clearly the different logical shapes of our different concepts and are less tempted to jam them inappropriately together.

What then does a commitment to naturalism require of us? As noted earlier, we start with a methodological commitment to willingness to include ourselves in what it is possible to investigate empirically. We are also, of course, committed to accepting what empirical study shows, even if it is unwelcome. And there have indeed been empirical discoveries unwelcome to some. For a start, there are those arising from achieving the perspective of deep time, bringing with it awareness of the age of our earth, the evolution of life and our kinship to the other animals. And secondly, closer to hand, what is evident from empirical studies in intellectual history and anthropology is the chastening realisation of how confident people often are in endorsing some general metaphysical or religious outlook common in their society, when from the perspective of other cultures and later investigation the supposed truth is highly questionable. A third related discovery, possibly unwelcome to those with a high conception of human rationality, concerns how much we fall short of honouring even those norms of thinking we recognise. We have known for as long as we have been reflective that we jump to conclusions, overgeneralise, are forgetful, fall into muddles, are given to self-exculpating rationalisation and the like. It is disconcerting, however, to learn how difficult it is to avoid these and related faults, even when we are aware of them and trying to steer clear.[4]

So empirical study of ourselves has revealed some truths we must take on board, our evolutionary history, our tendency to simplify and be overconfident, the complexity and fallibility of our minds. But we should be extremely cautious, I suggest, about advancing beyond these claims to more sweeping metaphysical pronouncements about mind, brain and value. The very facts just noted, about our tendency to endorse grand outlooks which are later shown to be questionable and our tendency to overgeneralise, should make us wary of the temptations of these views.

Many of the ideas I am recommending here, ones linking the idea of the psychological to norms, values, mutual interpretation and understanding, are familiar in the context of some forms of philosophy of mind, particularly in the post-Kantian and hermeneutic traditions. These ideas have not been much favoured by philosophers of more 'analytic' sympathies, who have sometimes supposed that their commitment to naturalism and empirical enquiry puts these ideas off limits, as *a prioristic* and unempirical. Such analytic philosophers have often proceeded as if their commitment to naturalism and their respect for science makes some form of physicalism the only intellectually honest option. I have been concerned to argue that, on the contrary, the predictive theoretical view of the psychological, presupposed in this strand of thought in analytic philosophy, is itself empirically untenable. The central fact about us and our thinking is that we are ineliminably in the business of trying to work out what to do together, with all the difficulties, but also all the opportunities, which that implies.

NOTES

1. I have in mind here particularly *Beast and Man, Wickedness, The Ethical Primate* and *The Solitary Self*.
2. The classic paper here is 'True Believers' in Dennett 1987: 13–35.
3. Midgley's account of these developments is discussed in Ian James Kidd's chapter in this volume.
4. An excellent book on these matters is Kahneman 2012.

REFERENCES

Dennett, Daniel, *The Intentional Stance* (Cambridge Mass.: MIT Press, 1987).
Kahneman, Daniel, *Thinking Fast and Slow* (London: Penguin, 2012)

9   Minding Animals

Ian Ground

'What finally (you may ask) does distinguish man from the animals? Nearly everything is wrong with this question.' (Midgley 2002: 203)

The philosophical debate about the minds of non-human animals may be thought akin to a labyrinthine transport hub through which pass a host of both familiar and exotic routes, in modes underground, overground and, occasionally, skyborne, allowing all manner of commuters, tourists and pilgrims means of travel to and from a profusion of destinations, near and far. The constant through traffic makes it difficult to linger there, for to do so one must be proficient in a great many tongues and learn the customs of faraway places.

Thus the philosopher who wants to think about the minds of non-human animals—and the human relation to them—must ideally be conversant in arguments and ideas in the philosophies of mind and language, epistemology, the philosophy of science and the metaphysics of experience. In addition, she needs to be familiar with developments and methodologies in the relevant animal and psychological sciences, from general issues such as evolutionary theory through sub-disciplines such as cognitive ethology to particular experimental cases and field studies. She must be both conceptually adventurous and empirically conservative. It helps a great deal too to be able to situate all this in particular and comparative cultural contexts. And finally, it is desirable too to have thought a great deal about what it is to think philosophically, since no sooner do we begin thinking about minds other than our own than questions about these questions—for instance, about what it is for one kind of mind to think about other such kinds—insinuate their way into our reflections and, if left unmanaged, threaten to colonise them completely.

The most obvious thing to say about such a philosopher, thus qualified to make progress through this labyrinth, is that she does not and, given the increasing specialization of our intellectual culture, now never will exist. Still, one philosopher who, travelling widely and in fine style, with the sharpest of eyes for both dead ends and promising openings, has come closest to that ideal and long proved her value as a guide is Mary Midgley.

Midgley's *Beast and Man* was not directly aimed at advancing the philosophical understanding of other animal minds. Its overt purpose was to reframe our understanding of human nature in two related ways. First through a negative account of how our understanding of ourselves both is distorted by and distorts our accounts of other animals. And, second, via a positive account of how the mode of explanation that ethologists offer of other animals might also be illuminating and productive in our own case. In this positive aim, Midgley shares Wittgenstein's[1] ambition to offer a naturalistic study of humanity: not in the form of a commitment to the omnicompetence of scientific explanation but rather in that of what Dan Hutto (2013) has more recently called 'softly spoken naturalism': one that, in its task of revealing the background against which human life makes sense, is essentially pluralistic, holistic and connective in the resources and modes of explanation it brings to bear.

It might be argued that, in her negative aim too, Midgley was engaged in a quasi-Wittgensteinian task—one of philosophical therapy. *Beast and Man* showed that, at every turn, pictures of what it is to be a 'beast' 'hold us captive' (Wittgenstein 2009, sec.115). Midgley's elegant expositions, illuminating connections between otherwise disparate thinkers, perspectives and disciplines, striking metaphors and bracing judgements—all so characteristic of her work—are aimed at breaking the hold of these pictures. Or, at least, of trying to show us that they are only pictures, created and inherited in particular contexts, now perhaps forgotten, offering only partial perspectives and in need of being redrawn, reframed or newly curated to serve our current needs.

But while an account of philosophical problems concerning animal minds was not her central purpose, Midgley does offer radical and, as we shall see, prescient proposals for these issues. In particular, as part of her overall project, Midgley develops a tightly focussed critique of overly simple differentiations between the human and the non-human. In doing so, she offers a richer positive account and presents the concept of a species structural property. What follows in this discussion attempts to relate *Beast and Man* to some themes in contemporary debates and to confront Midgley's positive account of species structural properties with what appears to be a new orthodoxy about the difference between our species and others.

THE ONLY MINDED SPECIES

Perhaps the most general lesson to be drawn from *Beast and Man* is the realisation that, for the best part of the modern philosophical tradition, the philosophy of mind and, as a consequence, moral philosophy too, has been conducted as if, for all intellectual purposes, human beings were the only minded species on the planet. *Beast and Man* taught us some very particular ways in which our intellectual tradition has been Cartesian not just in its content and presuppositions but also in its methodology. Philosophically, we withdrew, like the persona of the *Meditations*, from the actual world—the world where there are not, actually, only we humans—and, mired in doubt, we struggled to recover a world outside the human hearth. We tried to puzzle out our own case—what it is for us to be minded—and, if at all then only sporadically, wondered what the implications of the accounts of our own minds we have offered and disputed were for creatures different from ourselves. And other creatures, moreover, pretty much conceived as a single homogeneous group, set over against us, as non-linguistic, as non-rational, as non-sapient, as simply 'Other'.

Left as a task to be begun later, if ever, was that of explaining any discrepancies between our accounts of our minds and what we say and do, insofar as we live and work with or for other animals. Typically, the philosophical response to our ordinary practice—say, of treating our dog as wanting to go for a walk or as thinking that the cat is up the tree or the more exotic case of seeing that the lionesses are nervous about catching this buffalo—has lain between scepticism about the propriety of such practices and a shrug of the philosophical shoulders. Does the dog think of the cat as the *same* one it saw yesterday? Is a buffalo, for the lioness, a kind of creature or a kind of food or a *kind* of anything at all?

Donald Davidson's response was representative of the more general position. Having argued for a holistic account such that our beliefs have content only in virtue of their location in a rich, open-ended and densely connected web of other beliefs and speakers, we were left with the dilemma of explaining our ordinary judgement that the dog thinks the cat is up the tree. A dog has no concept and therefore, for Davidson, no beliefs, about, going up the conceptual trail, what kind of tree it is, or, going down, what a branch is or a leaf. And even it did have these more general or more specific concepts, the same considerations would reapply to those beliefs and concepts. So it must lack the concept of a tree. Such holism about mind and meaning, whatever its philosophical merits in the human case, forces us into a position where we must grant to other animals either everything or nothing. At best, we are left with Davidson's judgement that 'We have no real idea of how to settle, or how to make sense, of these questions' (Davidson 2001).

For later philosophers promoting related kinds of holism,[2] such as Wilfred Sellars (Sellars 1997), Richard Rorty (Rorty 1981) and Robert Brandom (Brandom 1998), the conclusion to draw was the outright denial that non-linguistic animals could be minded at all with a correlate dismissal of our ordinary practice as systematically anthropomorphic. Lacking any particular concept because, holistically, lacking all, non-linguistic animals, and indeed pre-linguistic children, must be thought of as merely responding differentially to environmental stimuli as, for example, does a thermostat. Non-linguistic beings, lacking the normative licence, including standards of inference and judgement, cannot be thought to be in possession of concepts. They live in environments but do not, as we able, adult, linguistically competent humans do, inhabit worlds. We shall have more to say about the structure of such holistic accounts later.

A philosophical naïf might be surprised to learn that the denial of the whole of the natural world as minded—other than ourselves, but including our own young—without much reference to (and often in conflict with) empirical evidence, was thought consistent with a confidence that, generally speaking, the analytic tradition was making splendid progress in the philosophy of mind. They might think, for example, that if the argument that concept possession requires a normative licence is indeed compelling, then the philosophical challenge is to show how normativity, at least in some form, might be operative and manifest in non-linguistic life. Such a naïf would surely be further astonished by the thought, current in other movements within the discipline, that enough progress had been made on issues about thought, language and meaning in our own case to venture a theory about the prospect of constructing artificial minds. Thus, for a time, as various schools of thought passed through the labyrinth, it would seem to such a naïf that our intellectual culture regarded it as the height of philosophical sophistication to hold that, while computers might think, dogs don't. A more striking case of being 'held captive by pictures', of the kinds identified by Midgley in *Beast and Man*, and conflicting pictures superimposed on another at that, it would be difficult to find.

The result of the methodological species solipsism endemic in the philosophy of mind has been that our intellectual traditions remain deeply conflicted about the nature, and, still, even the existence, of minds or anything worth calling 'mind', other than the human (if that [Midgley 2014]). And now that empirical scientists, many at least, are far less embarrassed than they once were about investigating other animals as minded, a further consequence is yet another dispiriting intellectual disconnect between philosophical inquiry and empirical science.

In the context of this philosophical tradition, *Beast and Man* was—and indeed remains—a reality check. Midgley made clear that a surely saner path was to have begun with just looking around the world, acknowledging that it positively teems with life and seeing too that we are naturally driven to act, as if many of the living creatures it contains are, in some yet to be clarified sense, minded. We might have begun, that is, with our ordinary practice, noted that it already implicitly involves the acknowledgement of other minded creatures and then proceeded to critical reflection on that practice, noting the similarities and differences, small and large, with our own case. We would have aimed to come into some kind of reflective equilibrium with that practice, adjusting, in equal measure, for anthropomorphic error in one direction and anthropocentric bias in the other. We would have seen that we face problems, and difficult ones, of making sense of how much that mindedness encompasses and how it differs or not from our own and in what sense such differences are commensurable. These would have been difficult and interesting empirical problems, probably requiring conceptual innovation, but they would not have been paralysing philosophical problems.

It is worth contrasting Midgley's approach here with that of some *soi-disant* champions of empirical science. Discussing the difficulties we confront when thinking about the lives and behaviours of other animals, Midgley writes:

> whether, and how far, interspecies communication works for feelings and motives is an empirical question. On the whole it does. . . . Difficult cases crop up in every area of inquiry; they never give ground for general skepticism. Interspecies sympathy certainly encounters some barriers. So does sympathy between human beings. But the difficulties arising here cannot possibly mean that any attempt to reach out beyond the familiar it circle of our own lives is doomed, delusive or sentimental. (Midgley 2002: 350–1)

Whereas a noted professor of animal behaviour can write:

> If scientists, at least, finally cease to make the conscious or unconscious assumption that animals have minds, then the consequences can be expected to go beyond the boundaries of the study of animal behaviour. If the age-old mind-body problem comes to be considered as an exclusively human one, instead of indefinitely extended through the animal kingdom, then that problem too will have been brought nearer a solution. (Kennedy 1992: 168)

It is clear that it is the philosopher here is who is the actual champion of the empirical, whereas it is the empirical scientist who harbours an arguably fantastical ambition for philosophical inquiry.

With a broader base for the philosophy of mind, we might have come to see our own kind of mindedness as distinctive and special and yet too as one kind amongst others. We would have surely acquired a much deeper sense of our enlanguagement as part of what Wittgenstein calls our natural history, like 'walking, eating, drinking, playing,' rather than, as we do still think of it really, as the result of a divine or magical enchantment. All this might have been had the philosophy of mind started with looking outward rather than inward.

The good news is that, in recent years, and they are fairly recent, what Midgley drew our attention to as the scandal of anthropocentrism in the philosophy of mind has begun to wane. There is now, evidently, a genuine interest in the philosophical task of making sense of the idea of minds other than our own. With the continuing progress of so called E-approaches to the psychological sciences—ethological, embodied, embedded, enactive, engaged—over traditional I-approaches—individualist, intellectualist and internalist (Hutto 2008)—debate on topics such as basic minds, non-conceptual psychological content and anti-psychological content accounts, there is clearly movement through the labyrinth. And it is movement in the direction envisaged by *Beast and Man*: toward ethological explanation as a philosophical method, emphasising the complex but whole animal as systematically embedded in its environment.

Still one should be wary. First, our conflicted inheritance still weighs heavy on us with the result that there is many a rearguard action being fought. Witness, for example, the 'militant agnosticism' about animal minds recently recommended by Marion Dawkins (Dawkins 2012), for whom the 'hard problem of consciousness' is so intellectually paralyzing that she thinks it is best to eschew talk about whether and how other animals are minded and to serve their welfare through philosophically uncontroversial physiological measurement. What 'welfare' means in a context in which is has been shorn of a connection with being, in any sense at all, minded, is hard to fathom.

Second, there now seems to be emerging a centre of attraction in the philosophy of mind which threatens to re-establish the kind of single all purpose distinction between human and non-human about which *Beast and Man* seeks to warn: the existence of psychological meta-states—psychological states about other psychological states. To understand this development, and to pose the right kind of question about whether and how it should be pursued, we need to trace at least the outlines of the account of species mind that Midgley offered.

STRUCTURAL PROPERTIES

The central notion in Midgley's positive account of animal minds is that of a 'structural property'. Taking a cue from Konrad Lorenz, Midgley defines a structural property as one which 'affects the whole organisation of the life of the species'. The contrast is with non-structural or local properties which 'affect it much less pervasively' (Midgley 2002: 205). Examples given of the former include the 'engineering capacities' of beavers, which grow from the heritage of rodent behaviour and the acuity of birds of prey, which emerges from the needs of flying creatures. An example of the latter, hairlessness.

Thus, according to Midgley, a structural property:

1. Is pervasive
2. May but need not be unique to a species.
3. Whether or not unique, may or may not be 'excellent', that is distinctive of a species
4. Does not alone define a species
5. May be possessed as a matter of degree rather than all or nothing,
6. Draws on elements in the relevant genus.

The crucial point here is that the notion of a structural property is one which makes sense of the life of a species but does so without committing us to an unnecessary emphasis on an essence which can be 'expressed in a simple definition'. As she writes, with characteristic *brio*, 'we can do justice to the miracle of a trunk without pretending that nobody else has a nose' (Midgley 2002: 206).[3]

Midgley then adds to the notion of a structural property, the thought that it is clusters of such properties, which ought to play the dominant part in our explanation of the behaviour of a species or a species member.

> . . . 'explaining behaviour' must refer to structural principles, therefore to long stretches of it and many partial parallels. It is relating it to a context. (Midgley 2002: 224)

Midgley's move here is, at heart, a Wittgensteinian one:

> Could someone have a feeling of ardent love or hope for the space of one second—no matter what preceded or followed this second?—What is happening now has significance—in these surroundings. The surroundings give it its importance. (Wittgenstein 2009: §.583)
>
> 'Grief' describes a pattern which recurs, with different variations, in the weave of our life. If a man's bodily expression of sorrow and of joy alternated, say with the ticking of a clock, here we should not have the characteristic formation of the pattern of sorrow or of the pattern of joy. (Wittgenstein 2009, i 2)
>
> When would we say of a child, for instance, that it is pretending? What all must it be able to do for us to say that? Only when there is a relatively complicated pattern of life do we speak of pretence. (Wittgenstein 1990: 40)

The general lesson from these remarks is that we should cease to think of what we call psychological states as private mental objects hidden from view and about which we can only fruitlessly speculate.[4] Rather, the concept of a psychological state is that of a whole stretch of the agent's life, involving a slew of capacities and contexts bound together through the shape of a particular kind of life lived in a particular kind of world. There may be and often are distinctive experiences, feelings, sensations and perhaps images bound up with such states too, but these too are part of the overall pattern and not the hidden essence of the phenomenon. This too is a kind of holism of course. But here the conceptual connections between parts and wholes—between, say, being in pain and its characteristic expression—is not a matter of *a priori* necessity but acknowledged as rooted in a species natural history. What is distinctive about the use of this kind of holism in *Beast and Man* is that Midgley is clear throughout, as Wittgenstein and Gilbert Ryle[5] were perhaps only haltingly and more recent philosophical holists hardly at all, is that such a claim *must* extend beyond the human case because it is true of us humans only in virtue of the fact that *we are animals*. That is, Midgley's distinctive philosophical claim is that the logically prior notion is that of a cluster of structural properties belonging to a species, and that it is only in virtue of *that* truth that the sorts of claims that Wittgenstein and, to an extent, Ryle want to make about the nature of mind, and for how our psychological concepts work, are true in our case.

In this Midgley adds weight to the now accepted view that, therapeutic considerations aside, the Wittgensteinian move about mind was not at all a kind of linguistic behaviourism. It was, in fact, a consequence of taking our evolutionary history seriously—of taking our animal nature seriously—that naturally points to a conception of philosophy of mind as an ethological endeavour. And that should press the reset button on wholesale epistemological scepticism about other animals just as it much as it does in the classical problem of other minds.

A first consequence of this kind of ethological holism about mind is what might be called soft incommensurability. We *can* make comparisons between species but only between particular species, not between one and *all the rest*. This is because:

> it is really not possible to find a mark that distinguishes man from 'the animals' without saying which animals. (Midgley 2002: 206)

Even in the case of a particular comparison, we should not expect to find a single difference:

> What is special about each creature is not a single unique quality but a rich and complex arrangement of powers and qualities, some of which it will certainly share with its neighbors. And the more complex the species, the more true this is. To expect a single differentia is absurd. (Midgley 2002: 207)

And finally, whilst doing any comparisons, we should be much more sensitive to the anthropocentric character even of the distinctions we do offer:

> It is also essential to remember how immensely [other species] differ from one another. In certain central respects, all social animals, including us, are far more like one another than any is like a snake or a codfish, or even a bee. (Midgley 2002: 206)

It is true that Midgley does talk in these passages about a species being 'more complex'. But it follows from this soft incommensurability that attempts to rank whole species as less simple to more complex in terms of a single universally applicable measure will not succeed. 'More complex' *can* make sense in terms of a particular capacity of a species —a dog's olfactory system is hugely more complex than ours and moreover is a structuring principle[6] for dogs. It may do so also in terms of some internal feature of the way in which a species' capacities are organised, that is, the way in which the structuring takes place. As we will see, it is something like this second idea that forms the basis of a new orthodoxy about a human/non-human divide.

A second consequence of Midgley's account of species structural properties is that we should not expect that any species capacity will be a single universal tool. Given the cluster account of species structural properties, the reach and integration of any such capacity within that cluster will likely be partial and contingent. In this, Midgley anticipated a thesis in cognitive science broadly known as the domain specifity thesis: that many aspects of cognition are supported by specialized, evolutionarily specified, learning 'devices', specific to particular domains of problem, for example, face recognition, predator warnings, motion detection. The general thought is that cognitively engaged organisms are organised vertically with specific capacities and functions lined up with the relevant domain, rather than horizontally with all-purpose faculties that operate across a wide range of domains. Jerry Fodor's influential 1983 book, *The Modularity of Mind* (Fodor 1983), is regarded as the *locus classicus* of this position but, earlier, in *Beast and Man*, Midgley writes:

> Reason, in the sense of logic, certainly can be called a universal tool. But considered as a faculty—as something we are gifted with—it is not so at all. It is a set of highly varied mental capacities, practical and theoretical, which are separable and unevenly distributed among human beings and shaped in specific ways by their lives. (Midgley 2002: 212)

And,

> 'having reason' or 'being rational' is not a yes or no business like having a hammer. It is much more like having insight or energy or initiative or imagination—things that can be possessed in varying degrees and also in very different forms. (Midgley 2002: 212–3)

The fact of vertical alignment of creature capacities with relevant parts of the world reinforces the soft incommensurability. It means that a properly scientific account of resemblance amongst species minds will be akin to Wittgenstein's notion of family resemblance—'a complicated network of similarities overlapping and criss-crossing: similarities in the large and in the small' (Wittgenstein 2009: §66).

Again it is noteworthy how Midgley's account gives philosophical support to a resolutely empirical approach to understanding other animal minds. When it comes to the limits which our existing concepts place on our understanding, it will be a mistake to think that we can tell in advance what will and won't be problematic. The way in which our own species nature limits our understanding of other species is most unlikely to form a single and uniform barrier, as it were, of equal height in all directions. On the contrary, it is almost bound to be uneven and messy, with both obstructions and openings in unexpected places. There will be similarities born of common descent to aid intelligibility but also profound discontinuities in species in other respects close to us. The branches on Darwin's tree of life may grow from different parts of the trunk and yet converge. And twigs on the same branch may grow far apart. This is the point of Midgley's remark that, when it comes to asking for the difference between human and other animals: 'Nearly everything is wrong with this question' (Midgley 2002: 203).

The question now is: do contemporary accounts of the distinction between the human and the non-human falsify Midgley's soft incommensurability claim about species differentia? Let us briefly survey three recent accounts.

COOPERATION, ERROR AND THEORY OF MIND

The first account is the developmental psychologist Michael Tomasello's (Tomasello 2008) groundbreaking work, too rich to do full justice here, which has transformed our understanding of primate cognition. Tomasello demonstrates, with great empirical rigour, our serious underestimation of chimpanzee capacities, including their grasp of causality, the identity of objects, a sense of the future and of the perspectives of others. Moreover, Tomasello also shows the extent to which we have placed far too much importance on language and the lack thereof as a marker of cognitive complexity, whilst at the same time giving too little emphasis to understanding the origins of language in communicative gesture.

That said, an overall aim of Tomasello's work has been to establish, by contrast with our closer species cousins, *the difference* between our kind of mind and theirs. In this, he claims, human co-operative activity is key. The critical point is not that primates do not cooperate: they do, but this, he argues, is *de facto* coordination. The claim is that, insofar as we have the empirical evidence, only in the human case *is the fact of cooperation mutually manifest* between the interactants such that *this fact itself* becomes the platform for further (recursive) cooperative interactions. It is the recursive complexity folded into the patterns of conspecific interactions that, according to Tomasello, lies at the roots of human language. But in the human case, this complexity is boot-strapped into new orders of interaction, which constitutes a defining difference between the human and the non-human. The point to note for the current purpose is that Tomasello's claim is *not* that it is language which enables such boot-strapping reflexivity. But rather that language is only the *outcome* of that process (even if language then goes on to profoundly reshape the interactions from which it sprang). What drives the boot-strapping process is the, according to Tomsello, uniquely human capacity to consciously hold the already recursive interactions as objects of further possibilities for recursion. In terms of the philosophical tradition, the thesis is an amalgam[7] of a Wittgensteinian emphasis on inter-activity as a source of meaning allied to an avowedly Gricean[8] emphasis on the reflexive shape of those interactions.

The second account is a recent attempt by the philosopher Tim Crane (2013) to centrally distinguish the human from the non-human by placing centre stage the Aristotelian emphasis on the human pursuit of 'intellectual epistemic goals', independently of their practical consequences. His expla-nation of what underlies this difference is as follows:

> The significance of language, on this view of things, is not simply that it allows us to communicate, or even that it allows a more sophisti-cated kind of communication—although both these things are true. The other extra thing that language gives us is that it facilitates and gives us a mechanism to articulate the correctness and incorrectness of the thoughts of others. (Crane 2013: 146)

Here, the capacity for pursuing knowledge for its own sake is taken to be dependent upon having a concept of error. But the possession of such a concept is itself dependent on our capacity, not just to reason and to 'act on reasons', but to represent such reasons, whether ours or those of others, to ourselves as further targets of rational evaluation:

> As Daniel Dennett has put it (1988), we are 'reason-representers': we don't just act on reasons, but we represent reasons to ourselves and to others. In doing so, we can evaluate our and their reasons as good or bad; as accurate or erroneous. Seeing ourselves as in the pursuit of knowledge for its own sake requires having the concept of error. (Crane 2013: 146)

Here, again, the thought that does the heavy lifting is that of a recursive mechanism: states taking states of the same kind as their own content. What Crane's account brings out very clearly is that the kind of philosophical holism we surveyed earlier *is itself* an instance of the emphasis on recursion. I can have a belief insofar as I can possess the concept of belief and can deploy that concept in relation to others who in turn apply that concept to me.

The third and final account is an example of the now ubiquitous attempts in the ethological and cognitive sciences to determine whether a given species or a human child of a given age is capable of cognitive activities, which take as their target, in varying ways, the perspectives of others, usually conspecifics: the question of whether an organism has a 'theory of mind' or is capable (in a metaphor which betrays the sometimes crude Cartesian assumptions[9] of such approaches), of 'mind-reading'. In their famously painstaking study (Cheney and Seyfarth 1992) of vervet monkeys, Cheney and Seyfarth summarise their study of vervet social organisation and warning calls:

> In social behaviour the monkeys seem to begin by observing the social behaviour of others. Then, using this raw material, they recognise relationships, classify relationships into types, and adopt a behavioural strategy based on this classification. Similarly, in their vocal communication, the monkeys seem to begin by distinguishing among different calls. They then learn the meaning of each call and classify and compare vocalisations according to their referents. (Cheney and Seyfarth 1992: 310)

So, here we have purposeful observation, comparison and learning, recognition not just of relationships, but of types[10] of relationships, referent tracking and appropriate and relevant responses as a result. Yet when it comes to summarising the differences between vervets and ourselves, we find:

> In sum, many fundamental differences in social behaviour between human and non-human primates depend on the presence, or lack, of a theory of mind: whether individuals can recognize their own knowledge and attribute mental states to others. Apparently monkeys see the world as composed of things that act, not things that think and feel. Although they are acutely sensitive to other animals' behaviour, they know little about the knowledge or motives that cause animals to do what they do. (Cheney and Seyfarth 1992: 308)

Here, the vervet skill set additionally includes acute sensitivity to what their conspecifics do and how they act. But before drawing the general lesson here, we must get one oddity out of the way. Part of what is going on in this passage, as Midgley would surely point out, is a rather extraordinary commitment to a particular picture of what behaviour is and what it is to know something about the 'knowledge or motives that cause animals to do what they do'. It would indeed be nonsensical to say of another human being that they were acutely sensitive to the behaviour of their family or friends, of how they acted, that they understood their relationships, acted themselves in response and appropriately and yet have no inkling at all that others had thoughts and feelings and saw others as only 'things'. For 'things' as opposed to what? Not 'agents', for that is precisely the concept which is supposedly lacked. What then is it to think of something *as a 'thing'*? In fact, what it is to know that others have thoughts and feelings is, *inter alia*, to be sensitive to what they do and how they act, and to see how those actions are related to the context. And our criterion for that understanding being in place crucially involves the capacity to respond appropriately. There is not another thing, over and above all that, and of a quite different kind, which is 'regarding others as having thoughts and feelings'. What could that be, except telepathy? So what is going on in this passage is not the description of a mind so weirdly different from our own that it has the hybrid metaphysical concept of 'things' that 'act', but rather the mistaken and all too human projection of an essentially Cartesian picture of mind and behaviour into the life of another creature.

The lesson here is that, while we should be as pluralistic as we can be about the kinds of 'structural properties' of species mind that there are, that generosity need not extend to thinking that some kinds of species minds, but not ours, are exactly as seventeenth-century human philosophers conceived ours to be. One crucial lesson of *Beast and Man* is that the Cartesian species is of our own invention.

This peculiarity aside, what these passages from Seyfarth and Cheney make clear is a quite general feature of Theory Theory of Mind approaches. Namely that, once again, the key difference is supposed to be the capacity for recursion. For, what is being claimed is that to be capable of thinking of others as having 'mental states' is to be capable of having oneself such states whose content—what they are about—consists in (a reference) to the mental states of others. Thus for it to be possible for me to deceive you, I must believe that you can acquire beliefs. It is, moreover, to think (though the implication is rarely made absolutely explicit in the Theory Theory of Mind literature) that the mental states of others are instances of the very same kind of states of which oneself is capable. Thus, according to this approach (and *contra* Davidson), an animal may indeed have beliefs without having any belief that others have beliefs. But if it does have beliefs that others have beliefs, then it will also be, at least tacitly, committed to the thought that the other's beliefs are the same kind of state—which is to say, play the same kind of role in the other's life as they do in its own, say, for selecting a behavioural strategy in response to the way the world turns. I can deceive you by manipulating the conditions that cause you to acquire beliefs because I know, in general, about the causal conditions under which I acquire beliefs. And to know that is to have beliefs about my own beliefs. This perhaps makes some sense of the claim, which is otherwise deeply mysterious, that a creature does or doesn't have what is worth calling a 'theory' of mind. For a theory is not a list of instances but, *inter alia*, a quite general description under which particular instances fall. On this view, then, any 'theory' I have of the mental states of others implicitly commits me to a meta view of my own states.

It should be said that, in principle, it might be supposed at least possible to possess a 'theory of mind' in which one is not oneself capable of all of the kinds of states for which, in the case of others, the theory licenses inferences. Trivially, an ethologist might acquire a 'theory of mind' about the echolocation states of bats and be able to generate correct predictions about the bat's behaviour whilst knowing that she does not herself have such states. More interestingly, there is evidence that some species signal in modalities to which they themselves are not sensitive. Thus California ground squirrels (Rundus et al. 2007) which are not themselves sensitive to infrared signals, add an infrared component to their snake-directed tail-flagging signals by heating up their tails when confronting infrared-sensitive rattlesnakes, but tail flag without infrared emission when confronting infrared-insensitive gopher snakes. The explanation offered is that by following up some such infrared signalling with aggressive attacks, the squirrels are eventually able to condition their local rattlesnakes to respond to the signalling alone. In this case, a Theory of Mind Theorist would need to concede that an organism's 'theory' *can* invoke at least some states of which it was not itself capable.

Within the Theory Theory of Mind paradigm, such cases will be regarded as exceptional. It follows that what is at issue when we ask whether non-human animals have such a theory about their con- and non-conspecifics is, to a large degree, whether they are capable of forming states which are either directly or indirectly 'about' the very same kind of states of which they are themselves capable. And the default position is that we humans are abundantly capable of such meta-states and other animals, unless proven otherwise,[11] are not.

THE META MOVE

Having examined three different contemporary accounts of what distinguishes 'beast' and 'man', it should now be clear that these accounts have something important in common. They share an insistence on a capacity for meta-cognition or, more broadly, meta-representation as a differentia between human and non-human.

If we generalise over their differences, the argument is this: we should distinguish first-order psychological states from second-order psychological states. First-order psychological states take (perceived) real bits of the world as their content. They are, objectively, simpler than second order states. For second-order states take first-order psychological states as their content and, for that reason, must be more complex than the first-order states which they target. We can disagree about how to describe those higher-order states or which are the most important—self-consciousness, truth tracking states, normative evaluations of inferential relations between first-order states, states which intrinsically refer to the psychological states of others. But these are really only disagreements in detail. What really matters is whether there exists or does not exist a vehicle which has sufficient complexity to allow the possession of such meta-states.

Why is the possibility of a recursion-enabling structure thought so significant? The thought is that if an organisms can, in virtue of the recursive power of its representational systems, represent to itself its own representations of the world, then it is thus enabled to distinguish between its subjective experience of the world and the objective world of which it is experience. And that it will be contended is the essence of what it to be minded. Representational recursiveness is, on this view, just what it is to be minded.

Seen in this light, the various candidates for differentia—'conceptual thought or reason, language, culture, self-consciousness, tool-using, productivity, laughter, a sense of the future' (Midgley 2002: 206)—to which must be added the neo-Cartesian enthusiasm for Theory of Mind—may all be regarded as simply instances of the general meta-representational capacity which, it is then claimed, is the gift of the human alone. Thus, on this view, even our much vaunted rationality is not a stand-alone faculty but rather requires for its operation that meta-cognitive capacity which is what, really, is doing all the heavy lifting. The thought is that an organism could not be capable of acting for a reason—of bringing its thoughts and behaviour under a regimen of normative considerations of truth, consistency, objectivity and efficacy—unless it were first capable of regarding its thoughts and behaviour—its own and/or those of others, as themselves targets of its own thought and behaviour. And so the capacities for cooperative behaviour, the pursuit of knowledge for its own sake and 'mind-reading', are not in themselves the difference between us and other animals but rather functions of, and—from a empirical point of view—indicators of, the fundamental difference, namely the capacity to form boot-strapping meta-states. Even 'conceptual thought' which, in *Beast and Man*, Midgley follows Lorenz in advancing (Midgley 2002: 205) as a species structuring principle for humans and self-consciousness itself will then seem to be just rather vague and slightly misleading ways of talking about the same capacity.

It should in this context be noted that theorists who take this line need not be committed to the thesis that such meta-representation must involve the possession of language. What they are formally committed to is not the possession of language as a necessary condition of the capacity for meta-cognitive states but the possession of some vehicle with the requisite structural complexity to allow the recursive content, a type of which language is an instance. Crane is explicitly committed to the thought that it must be language, for the reason that he 'cannot clearly see any other way in which it can be done' (Crane 2013). Seyfarth and Cheney would prefer to think in terms of mental representations. Tomasello is actively opposed to invoking language at this fundamental level, since it is the very possibility of linguistic communication he is trying to explain. He prefers, at least in more recent writings, to insist on the intrinsic meaningfulness of social interactions in which the dynamics of the social interaction provide the vehicle with the requisite complexity and 'the 'meaning' comes built in'.[12] In this respect at least, Tomasello seems aligned with the anti-representationalist approach that drives 'enactivist' thinking (Hutto and Myin 2013).

Of course, we may say, if it functions like a language, then it is a language. But then we should not be misled by the lack of overt possession of language to conclude that a creature is not therefore capable of the meta-states. The fact that lions don't talk is not in itself decisive on the matter. For it will be replied, by those keen to talk in terms of mental representations, that in the absence of lionese, mentalese or neuralese will do as well. And by those who, with Wittgenstein and Tomasello, stress the intrinsic significance of social interactions, that we have only just begun to fathom the complexities lying in the dynamic reciprocities of conspecific (let alone non-conspecific) interactions even in cases familiar to us such as the meta-signalling evident in canine playbows (Bekoff 1974). What matters is only that there is some vehicle with sufficient structure to allow the recursive process.

Still, it will be said, perhaps by all sides, that, enlanguaged, human beings have used this capacity to levels unique in the natural world. At its most general, it is this claim that can be said to amount to a new orthodoxy for characterising the differentia between the human and non-human.

How then does this accord with Midgley's negative claim in *Beast and Man* that we should beware attempts to identify a single difference and her positive claims regarding species structural properties? The answer must be mixed.

The positive notion of a dynamic cluster of species properties, some of which are structural, remains helpful. If any kind of story about meta capacities is true, then they form just such a structural principle. The worst that could be protested is that Midgley's notion of a structuring principle is insufficiently sensitive, at a theoretical level, to the internal dynamic of such clusters and that there might may be, as the orthodoxy about meta capacities claims, at least one 'principle'—the capacity to form meta states—which is not just structuring of a cluster but self-transformative for such a cluster and not confined to a single or set of species but spread very widely through animate nature. But even here, Midgley's commitment to waving inherited philosophical presuppositions out of the way to get on with the practical empirical business of ethological discovery is entirely capable of embracing such a possibility.

The negative claim that there is no single difference, in the form of a capacity or faculty or a divine or adventitious gift, also remains in place. As some are coming to see, even 'theory of mind is not best considered a unitary ability that one has either completely or not at all' (Horowitz 2011). There is no Rubicon 'twixt ourselves and the rest of minded nature. It is rather, to use a Midgleyesque metaphor, much more of a boggy marsh divided by rivulets and streams and the occasional flood, in which different kinds of minded species find themselves more or less connected and more or less isolated, shaped to different degrees by processes which are natural to the landscape as a whole.

Still, whilst rightly debunking a range of mythological and metaphysical *sources* of the difference between ourselves and other animals, *Beast and Man* perhaps underestimated the extent to which entirely naturalistic processes produce change which is not just biologically but metaphysically dramatic. For the possibility of meta-capacities allows for the possibility of runaway change and to a degree which counts, if anything does, as metaphysically significant. Just as a sufficiently complex structure allows for recursion, so further rounds of recursion may have the effect of increasing the structural complexity. The analogy, much used in the literature (Clark 2010, sec.3.1), is with scaffolding, where the structure forms the support to enable further extensions to the structure. But if each level also has bolstering effects on the level below, allowing, as it were, each level to carry more load, the result is runaway development in which entirely new kinds of activity are possible. The direction of philosophical travel does not much matter here. Thus a representationalist may contend that neuro-representational structures allow linguistic structures, which, in turn, allow social structures, which, in turn, allow the 'second nature' (McDowell 1996) that we acquire in living in cultural structures with each level increasing the capacity of the one below. If we are philosophically unimpressed with the idea of 'neural representations', we may contend instead that our embodied natures shape the character of our social and cultural interactions and then what it is for us to be embodied is itself shaped by those interactions. But via either route the result is that such boot-strapping processes have produced, in the human case, ontologically novel kinds of things in the world: societies and symphonies, mathematics and Mauritian Creole. And this, if anything is, is the kind of difference in degree which makes for a difference in kind.

Even so, in her attack on the idea of a single metaphysically significant differentia, Midgley was right to point out the essential relevance to the philosophy of mind that we, *as other species*, have an evolutionary history. That we, *as other animals*, grow from young. That, because of those facts, our kind of mindedness is partial, adventitious, particular. But equally, to other kinds of mind, related and connected. Philosophy ignores either set of facts at its peril.

CONCLUSION

This discussion has tried to show that a claim about meta-capacities is at the foundation of current accounts about the nature of the difference between ourselves and other animals: the theme which forms the starting point for *Beast and Man*. It has not tried to address which direction in which to take such an account: to follow traditional accounts of mental representations or, as this author would prefer, to eschew mental representation as the foundation of such boot-strapping processes and strike out in a new direction toward a deeper understanding of the dynamics of social interaction. The ambition here has been only to remind ourselves of some of the paths we have, rightly or wrongly, already chosen and to offer a distant view of those that lie ahead.

The problem of our understanding of the minds of non-human animals has been a labyrinth where, as a culture, we have not 'known our way about' (Wittgenstein 2009: §123). Let us at least celebrate our good fortune in having had Mary Midgley to give us, amongst other essentials we need to pack for the journey ahead, a compass with its direction true.

NOTES

1. 'What we are supplying are really remarks on the natural history of human beings; we are not contributing curiosities however, but observations which no one has doubted, but which have escaped remark only because they are always before our eyes' (Wittgenstein 2009, §415).
2. For an extended discussion of holism and animal minds, see Bavidge & Ground (1998: chap.7) and Finkelstein (2007).

3. The elephant trunk is in fact functionally analogous to the nose, tongue, lips, limb and hand of other species. But that only underlines Midgley's point about the complex overlapping of structural properties.
4. Thus Kennedy insists on a sub-Cartesian claim that to behave purposefully is for a mental image, available only to introspection, to be the 'prime cause' of the behaviour. Since there is no direct evidence (how could there be?) for such imagery, in animals, we cannot say that animals behave purposefully (Kennedy 1992: 10).
5. 'Man need not be degraded to a machine by being denied to be a ghost in a machine. He might, after all, be a sort of animal, namely, a higher mammal. There has yet to be ventured the hazardous leap to the hypothesis that perhaps he is a man' (Ryle 1949: 328).
6. As Horowitz points out, because 'smell tells time', 'a dog's olfactory window of what is 'present' is larger than our visual one, including not just the scene currently happening, but also a snatch of the just happened and the up-ahead. The present has a shadow of the past and a ring of the future in it' (Horowitz, Alexandra, *Inside of a Dog: What Dogs See, Smell, and Know*, Kindle iPad Edition (Scribner 2010) loc. 3315), a conclusion borne out by empirical studies of the order in which a dog will follow scent marks (c.f. Wells, Deborah L., and Peter G. Hepper, 'Directional Tracking in the Domestic Dog, Canis Familiaris', *Applied Animal Behaviour Science*, 84 (2003), 297–305 http://dx.doi.org/10.1016/j.applanim.2003.08.009)
7. For a discussion on which element is really doing the work here see Ground (2013).
8. For a critique of neo-Gricean accounts of human non-human differences see Bar-On (2013).
9. A critique of the assumptions of 'theory theory of mind' is outside the scope of this discussion, but see Leudar and Costall (2009), which includes, of particular relevance here, Bavidge, Michael, and Ian Ground, 'Do Animals Need a Theory of Mind?', pp. 167–88. It will be evident that this author is deeply sceptical about Theory of Mind approaches but in the current discussion such concerns are, largely, put on hold.
10. For a much-noted study of abstract conceptual capacities in a surprising place, see Pepperberg (2009).
11. Positive but disputed claims have been made about chimpanzees (Hare et al. 2001), dolphins (see Tomonaga and Uwano 2010), Jays (Dally et al. 2010) and canids (Horowitz 2011). But as the latter points out, 'a definitive test for theory of mind in non-language-using animals has been elusive, and no animal has been uniformly successful at those that exist.' Some philosophers may suspect that this is not entirely the fault of the animals.
12. '[T]he meaning or communicative significance of intention-movements is inherent in them, in the sense that they are one part of a pre-existent meaningful social interaction . . . individuals do not need to learn . . . to connect the signal with its 'meaning'—the 'meaning' comes built in' (Tomasello 2008: 26).

REFERENCES

Bavidge, M. & Ground, I., 1998. *Can We Understand Animal Minds?*, Bristol: Bristol Classical Press.

Bekoff, M., 1974. Social play and play-soliciting by infant canids. *American Zoologist*, 14(1), pp.323–340.

Bar-On, D., 2013. Origins of meaning: Must we "go Gricean"? *Mind & Language*, 28(3), pp. 342–375.

Brandom, R., 1998. *Making It Explicit: Reasoning, Representing & Discursive Commitment: Reasoning, Representing and Discursive Commitment* new edition, Cambridge, Mass.: Harvard University Press.

Cheney, D.L. & Seyfarth, R.M., 1992. *How Monkeys See the World: Inside the Mind of Another Species* new edition., Chicago: University of Chicago Press.

Clark, A., 2010. *Supersizing the Mind: Embodiment, Action, and Cognitive Extension*, Oxford: Oxford University Press.

Crane, T., 2013. Human Uniqueness and the Pursuit of Knowledge: a Naturalist Approach. In B. Bashour and Hans D. Muller, ed. *Contemporary Philosophical Naturalism and Its Implications*. New York: Routledge, pp. 139–54.

Dally, J.M., Emery, N.J. and Clayton, N.S., 2010. Avian Theory of Mind and counter espionage by food-caching western scrub-jays (Aphelocoma californica). *European Journal of Developmental Psychology*, 7(1), pp.17–37.

Davidson, D., 2001. Thought and Talk. In *Inquiries into Truth and Interpretation*, Oxford: Clarendon, 155–171.

Dawkins, M.S., 2012. *Why Animals Matter: Animal Consciousness, Animal Welfare, and Human Well-being*, Oxford: Oxford University Press.

Finkelstein, D.H., 2007. Holism and Animal Minds. In A. Crary, ed. *Wittgenstein and the Moral Life: Essays in Honor of Cora Diamond*, Cambridge, MA: MIT Press, 251–278.

Fodor, J.A., 1983. *The Modularity of Mind: An Essay on Faculty Psychology*, Cambridge, MA: MIT Press.

Ground, I., 2013. "The Play of Expression": Understanding Ontogenetic Ritualisation. In Mind, Language, and Action: Proceedings of the 36th International Wittgenstein Symposium. Kirchberg Am Wechsel: Publications of the Austrian Ludwig Wittgenstein Society.

Hare, B., Call, J. and Tomasello, M., 2001. Do chimpanzees know what conspecifics know? *Animal Behaviour*, 61(1), pp. 139–151.

Horowitz, A., 2011. Theory of mind in dogs? Examining method and concept. *Learning & Behavior*, 39(4), pp. 314–317.

Hutto, D.D., 2013. Enactivism, from a Wittgensteinian point of view. *American Philosophical Quarterly*, 50, pp. 281–302.

Hutto, D.D., 2008. Limited engagements and narrative extensions. *International Journal of Philosophical Studies*, 16(3), pp. 419–444.

Hutto, D.D. and Myin, E., 2013. *Radicalizing Enactivism: Basic Minds without Content* Kindle iPad version, Cambridge: MIT Press.

Kennedy, J., 1992. *The New Anthropomorphism*, Cambridge: Cambridge University Press.

Leudar, I. & Costall, A., 2009. *Against Theory of Mind*, Basingstoke: Palgrave Macmillan.

McDowell, J., 1996. *Mind and World: With a New Introduction,*. Harvard: Harvard University Press.

Midgley, M., 2014. *Are You an Illusion?* London: Routledge.

Midgley, M., 2002. *Beast and Man: The Roots of Human Nature*, London: Routledge.

Pepperberg, I.M., 2009. *The Alex Studies: Cognitive and Communicative Abilities of Grey Parrots*, Cambridge: Harvard University Press.

Rorty, R., 1981. *Philosophy and the Mirror of Nature*. Oxford: Blackwell.

Rundus, A.S., Owings, D.H., Joshi, S.S., Chinn, E., Giannini, N., 2007. Ground squirrels use an infrared signal to deter rattlesnake predation. *Proceedings of the National Academy of Sciences*, 104(36), pp. 14372–14376.

Ryle, G., 1949. *The Concept of Mind*, London: Hutchinson's University Library.

Sellars, W., 1997. *Empiricism and the Philosophy of Mind*, Cambridge, Mass: Harvard University Press.

Tomasello, M., 2008. *Origins of Human Communication*, Cambridge: The MIT Press.

Tomonaga, M. & Uwano, Y., 2010. Bottlenose Dolphins' (*Tursiops truncatus*) Theory of mind as developed by responses to their trainers' attentional states. *International Journal of Comparative Psychology*, 23(3). Available at: http://escholarship.org/uc/item/2dd258ps [Accessed January 14, 2015].

Wittgenstein, L., 2009. *Philosophical Investigations*, 4th ed. P.M.S. Hacker & J. Schulte, eds., Oxford: Wiley-Blackwell.

Wittgenstein, L., 1990. *Last Writings on the Philosophy of Psychology: Preliminary Studies for Part II of the Philosophical Investigations v. 1* Volume 1. Oxford: Wiley-Blackwell.

Part IV

Science and Evolution

10 Doing Science an Injustice
Midgley on Scientism

Ian James Kidd

INTRODUCTION

Central to the work of Mary Midgley has been an abiding concern with the proper role of the sciences in intellectual and cultural life. This is evident in early works, like *Beast and Man*, and still present, some thirty years later, in such writings as *Evolution as a Religion* and *Science and Poetry*. Unfortunately, this interest has a negative motivation, insofar as Midgley judges that both academic and popular understandings of science and its proper place in our life and thought generally go badly wrong. Science, she lamented in a 2010 *Guardian* article, 'really isn't connected to the rest of life half as straightforwardly as one might wish', a sentiment consistently expressed and explored in her writings.

Accordingly, Midgley's focus has typically been on *scientism*. By that term, I refer to exaggerated or distorted conceptions of the nature, scope, and value of science, a definition broad enough to accommodate familiar Midgleyan themes, such as evolution, myth, philosophy, poetry, and other topics, including many treated in other chapters of this volume. *The Guardian*, in fact, credits her as the 'foremost scourge of "scientific pretension"' writing today, and an ardent foe of the many salesmen of scientism.

Certainly Midgley's various writings—on human nature, mind, culture, and other 'big topics'—are united, in part, by a concern to ensure that the sciences inform, but do not imperialistically dominate, our diverse efforts to make sense of ourselves, our world, and our place within it. It is clear that her motivation is an acute critical perception of the power and persistence of confusions about the scientific enterprise: of the development, powers, and limits of its multiple aspects, and relationships to other areas of our life and thought. Equally clear is her sense of the problems and abuses that are the natural companions of such confusions, and the dangers—practical and intellectual, social and spiritual—that they bring with them. Given the central place of science in the modern world, if we get it wrong, then we are likely to find ourselves in serious trouble, and Midgley's diagnosis is that this is precisely the situation we find ourselves in today.

In this chapter, I offer an account of Midgley's critique of scientism that converges on the claim that, among its many faults, scientism is objectionable because it does science an injustice.

THE URGES OF SCIENTISM

It is useful to start by saying a little more about scientism, which has the unhelpful qualities of being as commonly used as it is badly defined. Certainly there have been relatively few attempts by philosophers to attempt anything like a robust definition of scientism—or, perhaps, of various *scientisms*—even though many share Midgley's concern that poorly informed, badly developed conceptions of science are generating needless problems in various areas of philosophy.[1]

Still, we are not left completely empty-handed. I suggest that we might usefully think about scientism as reflecting a set of *urges* or *impulses*, more akin to compulsions than convictions, that can generate and sustain more explicit scientific attitudes, beliefs, and doctrines. Indeed, if, as I'll argue, scientism typically gets science, history, and much else wrong, then its sources cannot be reasoned deliberation and informed reflection. Instead, there may be some underlying urge, impulse, or compulsion. Midgley, in fact, often characterises scientism in terms of a 'spirit', 'attitude', or 'ideology' of a distinctly dogmatic, even pathological kind (M 22, SP 40).[2] Likewise, Susan Haack thinks we do better to think of scientism in terms of *attitudes* of 'exaggerated . . . deference' to, and 'excessive readiness' to laud, science (2007: 18–19).

We might usefully distinguish three broad impulses that can generate and nourish various familiar types of scientism. The first is an *imperialist urge*—a compulsion to extend the concepts, methods, and practices of scientific enquiry into areas in which their effectiveness is limited at best, nil at worst. A typical form that scientism takes is 'scientific imperialism', defined by the philosopher of science, John Dupré, as 'the tendency to push a good scientific idea far beyond the domain in which it was originally introduced, and often far beyond the domain in which it can provide much illumination' (2001: 74). So, too, for Midgley, scientism combines a 'general veneration for the idea of science' with lack of 'any real understanding of its methods' (ER 31).[3] The second impulse fuelling much scientism is a *salvific urge*—an insistence that science, or what enthusiasts *take* to be science, can satisfy our ethical, spiritual, and even 'existential' sensibilities and needs. This reflects an inflated conception of the role of science that Midgley, in 1994 dubs, 'science as salvation'.

The third and final impulse that fuels many forms of scientism is an *absolutist urge*—the compulsion to assign to science the exclusive task of providing complete, absolute, 'totalising' accounts of life, the universe, and everything—indeed, of mind and morals, history and culture, and anything else (what Mikael Stenmark calls 'total scientism'). Many of Midgley's writings on scientism are, for this reason, framed around 'big issues'. *Science and Poetry*, for instance, traces the ways that scientistic distortions can interfere with our understanding of 'personal identity' and 'the unity of our lives' (SP 1).

These three urges—the *imperialist*, *salvific*, and *absolutist*—are not rigidly demarked from one another, and doubtless can be defined and related in any number of ways. Certainly Midgley explores each of them, tracing their historical emergence, their evolution and mutation, and the specific forms they have taken. By doing so, she also offers a powerful positive corrective vision of what it means to 'see science aright' (to adapt the handy phrase of Ludwig Wittgenstein, another stern critic of scientistic excesses). Like all good critics of scientism, Midgley tries to show how science and philosophy can, and should, cooperate sensibly and fruitfully facilitate the work of the other—for instance, by enriching our empirical understanding, or clearing away conceptual confusions. In his *Essay Concerning Human Understanding*, the great British philosopher John Locke called this 'under-labouring', and considered it a vital and noble service by philosophy on behalf of science and society. Although Midgley did not invent this role, she performs it to an exemplary degree.

MYTHS AND THEIR MERITS

Midgley begins her critique of scientism with the idea of *myth*. This might seem odd, given that myths are often contrasted unfavourably with science, or at least with a scientific attitude. If myth is something you rely on when you lack proper evidence about your origins and place in the world, then it precedes science and so is destined to be replaced by it. Midgley, however, urges us to be wary of the apparently obvious. Ideas in regular circulation did not always earn their place through reasoned thought and critical scrutiny, and this 'received view' of myths is a case in point.

Midgley urges that we adopt a richer view of myth. Far from being opposed or ancillary to science, myths are, in fact, 'a central part of it: the part that decides its significance in our lives' (M 1). More fully, a myth is better understood as an 'imaginative vision'—a broad, schematic view of the world, reflective of our projects and purposes, and which is, by virtue of its organising role, both intellectually and imaginatively essential. A myth offers a reasonably coherent prospective picture of the history and direction of a culture and its various activities and ambitions—a picture that is also a plan, like a blueprint. Since such organising visions are essential to the difficult tasks of organising the vast range of practical, social, and intellectual labours that make up any large-scale enterprise—whether scientific or not—it follows that myths are 'not a distraction from our serious thinking, but a necessary part of it' (M xii).

A myth is not, of course, strictly true. Midgley is clear that a myth is a 'partial truth' insofar as it provides a selective account of history and a prospective view of the future. It is not true that science has been wholly progressive, and of course we cannot guarantee that it will be into the future—but, still, the myth of the progress of science has and continues to serve a useful role in our thinking (think, for instance, of the furore aroused by Thomas Kuhn's challenge to the idea of scientific progress in his classic 1963 book, *The Structure of Scientific Revolutions*). Still, Midgley adds, since any given myth is partial and selective, it can 'mislead us if we trust it on its own' (M xiii). Although we need these large-scale imaginative structures to lend order and coherence to our historically and culturally contingent anxieties and aspirations—hopes and dreams, fears and joys—we equally need to exercise vigilant criticism and practical caution. A myth is not a lie, but it can lead us to tell lies, or to fall for them. Myths, in order to do their work, necessarily provide 'particular ways of interpreting the world' that, constantly and implicitly, '[determine] what we think important [and] select for our attention' (M 1–3). But, still, such selection can be too narrow, too hasty, or too dogmatic, and this can lead us into problems.

It is a good principle in life to always ask who and what is being left out of an idea or proposal: every grand vision has its blind spots, a lesson well-taught by feminist thinkers of the last century. We do not and cannot give equal concern and attention to each and every thing and event in the world, or even in our immediate environment, since both the world, and our potential interest in it, is too great for us to manage. Midgley often emphasises the diversity and *messiness* of our relations with our environment, non-human animals, and human peers, and the social sophistication, emotional complexity, and practical difficulties that therefore attend our life (a point emphasised by many chapters in this volume).

It is difficult to balance richness and economy—to take enough in to see things aright, but not obscure essential features—but, still, this does not mean that the tools we develop, such as our myths, should be used without care and thought. Indeed, Midgley warns that certain myths, like certain tools, can be improper, unfit for our purpose, or obsolete: an entrenched myth might eventually start to obscure important new facts about the world, fail to accommodate emerging values, or begin to cause structural problems for our thought as a whole.

A myth in decline can often be repaired or revitalised, but this requires both that people recognise their poor state and that they can begin the work of examining and restoring them. I think that scientistic myths prevent us from doing this by obscuring the fact of their poverty—for instance, by driving out our awareness that there are, in fact, other ways of thinking about human nature. If we adopt a fixed, dogmatic attitude towards our myths, then we lose this sense that they can be subject to *criticism* and, therefore, to *choice*. As Midgley puts it:

> [I]t really is important that people who use [a myth] should recognise its mythical character—should see that it is just one optional vision among others, a slanted, incomplete picture belonging to a particular epoch, a story which always needs others to correct it, not a final universal truth. (SP 200)

As a general rule, one can take a narrow view, just as long as one realises that it is narrow, retaining that sense of a wider picture lurking just beyond one's gaze.

The general concern about the potential for myths to decay is amplified by the fact that 'the myths we live by'—the title of Midgley's 2004 collection—are not always the results of careful design and deliberation. Our myths are shaped by history as much as reason, being products of contingent histories rather than inevitable processes, and so they could have been different, and can still be changed (an emancipatory insight deeply appreciated by Michel Foucault and reflected in his 'genealogies' of modern medical and psychiatric norms, practices, and institutions). Our myths are not always well fitted to the world, partly because that world (not to mention our knowledge of it) is complex and changing, and partly because our myths are often inherited, finding their origins in a cultural and intellectual climate that no longer exists.

For these reasons, our myths ought to be subject to active scrutiny, and Midgley's motto might then be, like that of all good philosophers, 'Constant vigilance!' A myth, though partial, can get a ball rolling, but we still need to be able to see when it has ceased to do good work, which requires that we keep our eye on it.

An obvious question, at this point, is that of how we sensibly choose between competing myths, and two sets of criteria suggest themselves. The first are broadly *intellectual criteria*: we might ask whether certain myths make claims that square with the deliverances of history, science, and philosophy, an idea discussed more fully later in the chapter. The second are *pragmatic criteria*, including the important question of whether certain myths do, or could, generate or sustain attitudes, convictions, and dogmas that are socially, politically, or environmentally injurious. Midgley, for instance, contrasts the myths of Gaia and the Selfish Gene by pointing out that one emphasises our 'separateness from the world around us', and the other, our 'profound dependence on it', and rhetorically asks which myth seems most likely to help ameliorate our current environmental crisis (SP 16).

The intellectual and pragmatic criteria converge, of course, in the case of certain especially pernicious myths that are, by any standard, both false and deleterious. Midgley offers the example of the sexist myths that remain depressingly prevalent within modern societies, rightly noting that such myths are not only 'troublesome and inconvenient', but, at a deeper ethical and intellectual level, 'monstrous' (M 132). Such myths after all are not only false in their empirical claims—about, say, women's cognitive incapacities relative to men—but also because embracing them narrows our ethical vision: if we think in ways that are 'gender-blind', then our capacity for self-reflexive criticism is impaired, and, if this goes on, we may be compelled, quite against our will, to become 'fatalistic chauvinists'. If we shake off such myths, then we find that we are not, in fact, 'burdened, as we might have been, with . . . moral ideas that would completely paralyse our efforts' at ensuring decent treatment of women (M 14).

Myths emerge, on Midgley's analysis, as essential to our life and thought. Our myths not only shape our ideas about history, nature, and culture, but also structure our ethical and intellectual habits. The myths we live by order our patterns of reflection and rebuke—of study and scorn, curiosity and contempt—but, if left unregulated, can narrow and harden our vision and our imagination. The myths we live by are essential to thought and activity, but partial and contingent, and prone to decay and abuse. It is for these reasons that we have to take care with them.

Let's now develop these claims further by turning to myths about science.

SCIENCE, MYTH, AND HISTORY

Many of the great figures in the history of science have been mythopoeists. During the sixteenth century, Sir Francis Bacon, philosopher and Lord Chancellor, forged the rich mythic view of science as a perpetual source of practical and intellectual goods that still enjoys a central role in modern thinking about the scientific enterprise. Given the fledgling status of 'natural philosophy' at the time, this was a remarkably ambitious vision, but it enjoyed evocative presentation in *New Atlantis*: a technocratic utopia in which science (as we know it) fulfilled the promises Bacon made on its behalf.

Modern-day scientists offer mythic visions of their own, and much of Midgley's work has been devoted to exploring and assessing their claims—for instance, that science will afford a 'Theory of Everything', defeat death, and so on. It may still sound odd to suggest an intimacy of science and myth, but this is, as Midgley often points out, because we often tend to think and work with false images of science—as something either 'myth-busting' or 'myth-free'—or, in fact, both. The Enlightenment, for instance, is often trumpeted as being responsible for 'completely eliminating myths', when, in fact, it simply 'develop[ed] its own set of myths'—the Social Contract, say, or Progress—which did much useful work, but now, some 300 years later, are beginning to show their age (M xiii).

It is worth reiterating why science needs myths. A main reason is that science has to seem interesting, promising, or compelling before people can be persuaded to invest in it their energies, hopes, and expectations—a point that we denizens of late modern scientific cultures are apt to forget. The distinguished historian of science, David Knight, reminds us that it is not, straightaway, 'obvious that anyone should do [science] or take it very seriously' as a 'component of culture', since, for many reflective persons, 'connoisseurship, discrimination and wisdom were more important culturally than scientific knowledge' (2009: 1, 238). Indeed, in the early days, the successes of science were few and far between, and so advocates, such as Bacon, had to proffer myths instead. As Midgley puts it, the 'modern scientific vision' captures our imaginations because of its capacity to 'enlarge our mental horizons, distract us from mean preoccupations, raise our aspirations [and] remind us of wider possibilities' (SP 36).

Certain myths are therefore good myths insofar as they inspire and direct our energies and enthusiasms in profitable directions, aligned with our values and visions of the good. But other myths, of course, are bad myths. I want to suggest, following Midgley, that scientism can take the form of *bad myths* about sciences—ones we ought to reject, for they lead us astray. Such scientistic myths distort our understanding, appreciation, and capacity to direct science—something unacceptable in a society in which science has such power to affect the content and course of our life, society, and world.

A rich example of the power and popularity of false scientistic myths is offered by a recent volume, edited by the historian Ronald Numbers, entitled *Galileo Goes to Jail*. As its subtitle explains, it is a study of 'myths about science and religion', specifically an entrenched cluster of what I called bad myths that make empirically false, intellectually distorting claims about science, religion, and their interrelationship. Such myths encourage confusion, antagonism, and bad thinking—things we can ill afford when the topic is as important as science and religion.

The twenty-five chapters of Numbers's book each explore a single myth, including the myth that the medievals believed that the world was flat (Myth 3), that the Church persecuted Galileo for his scientific beliefs (Myth 8), that Newton's mechanistic cosmology eliminated the need for God (Myth 13), that evolution destroyed Darwin's religious faith (Myth 16), and so on. The authors of these chapters then go on to show how and why the myth is false and, equally of interest, the details of how and why they became so entrenched. The importance of such work is of course that, as Numbers puts it, much of the public's understanding (such as it is) of science and religion is shaped by what they take to be 'historical truths', but that are, in fact, 'hoary myths' that publicly minded historians ought to work to 'dispel' (Numbers 2009: 6).

Such false myths are worrisome not simply because they are false, but because they converge in a broader historical narrative that frames contemporary thinking about science and religion. Understanding can often usefully start by placing certain topics or problems within a historical context, but of course that presupposes that the context being appealed to is accurate, as best as we can tell, and, at least, not blatantly false, distorted, or exaggerative. Unfortunately many of the myths repeated by advocates of scientism are of this latter type, a fact that Midgley is alert to; her book *Evolution as a Religion* is, after all, dedicated 'To the memory of Charles Darwin, who did not say these things'. It is striking, in fact, that six of the twenty-five myths discussed in Numbers's book gather around evolution in general, or Darwin in particular.

Such scientistic myths are objectionable because they are false, distorting, and so obscure the complexity of the historical development of the sciences. It is plain wrong to say that science and religion have always been at war with one another, even if the narrative of scientists heroically struggling against dogmatic authorities under the banner of truth and reason has an obvious romantic, propagandistic charm. Midgley recognizes the charm, but insists upon a truer picture, insisting that science needs good myths that accurately reflect its history, rather than 'distorted exaltations' (SS 37). It is, she argues, 'quite dangerous' for any tradition or discipline to acquire an 'overblown reputation based on hype' for, sooner or later, they will 'pay a heavy price in public disillusion and resentment' (SS 37).

Science is perfectly good and noble when it is busily engaged providing knowledge and practical goods; there is no reason why it should also be lumbered with the further tasks of providing for all other aspects of human life and experience. Midgley rightly complains that those who are guilty of scientism have 'usurped the name of Science and have grotesquely exaggerated its power', which is why foes of scientism, like herself, are, in fact, 'fighting . . . not against science, but against false scientistic prophets' (OM 127, 129). As Galileo reputedly quipped, what one ought to want from physics is insight into how the Heavens go, rather than edifying instruction in how to go to Heaven. Another of Midgley's philosophical mottos might therefore be, 'Everything in its proper place'.

The critique of scientism that Midgley offers is also quite consistent with the sorts of intellectual virtues central to scientific enquiry. A good scientist is marked out by care, thought, discipline, and other admirable qualities, and so it is ironic that scientism is, all too often, an attempt 'to advance the cause of science by methods that disgrace it' (ER 78). The attempt to promote or praise science through careless speculation, thoughtless boasting, and undisciplined polemic and promise-making is directly contrary to the spirit or attitude of science.

I suggest that Midgley's critique of scientism is motivated in part by a love of science or, more generally, of the virtues of good intellectual enquiry. If so, scientism is not just a source of needless trouble, but something fundamentally opposed to the spirit of science—indeed, for Hilary Putnam, a 'danger [for] the life of the spirit in general' (1985: 183). Midgley's critique of scientism is therefore robustly 'pro-science' and engaging in scientistic myth-busting is an act of service to science and society.[4]

There are two general principles underlying this claim. The first is the principle that if we are going wrong, especially in something that matters, then we ought to be set right—and, if we go along with scientistic claims and conceits, then we are going wrong. The second principle is that if the nobility of science lies in the fact of its being part of our search for truth, then we ought also to search for the truth about science—the truth about its history, nature, place in our society, and so on. To seek the truth about science reflects not only a respect for consistency, but also, more deeply, a respect for science, for truth, and for other people. If we respect people, then we do not mislead them, or allow others to mislead them, especially if that would lead them into problems and perils that they could profitably avoid.

If that sounds too high-falutin', then one might consider a more practical worry. Midgley notes that some people today 'plainly do *not* think that science is altogether good' (M 8). These include the many people who are sceptical of or resistant to the authority of science and who work hard to spur others to share their attitudes, with climate change deniers being the obvious example. Such sceptics and critics often abuse false images of science and trade on public lack of understanding of science, and such strategies are as insidious as they are effective.[5] Given that these worries have a literally global character, the peddling of scientistic myths and distortions amplifies the already potent difficulties accompanying efforts to properly steward the natural and social worlds. The fact of our being a scientific culture, whatever that means, includes the further fact that the authoritative status of science can be upset and challenged. Midgley, therefore, urges that, if we care about that status, then we must take action, and 'consider the present condition of science, how best to live with its difficulties and responsibilities, and how to shape its further development so as to avoid these distortions' (M 8).

In the next section, I suggest that this calls for closer alliances between science and other scholarly disciplines, especially her *métier* and mine, philosophy.

SCHOLARS AND SCIENCE

The emerging claim is that myths are essential, but dangerous if left unchecked, and many scientistic myths are, nowadays, indeed running unchecked in ways that are problematic. The question arising is, then, whose job is it to 'check' scientism?

It might seem that the obvious answer is that *scientists* ought to take up that job. Certainly many of the critics of scientism to whom Midgley appeals are scientists, including the mathematician and biologist Brian Goodwin, the biologist Denis Noble—a pioneer of 'systems biology'—and the physicist John Ziman, among others. The thought might be that, given that scientists are the ones whose discipline is being abused by scientism, they are the ones who ought to respond to it. Sensible as that claim might seem, it runs into trouble. For a start, scientistic claims are usually made by scientists *qua* science writer or communicator, rather than *qua* scientist; they are speaking 'off duty', as it were, even if their claims benefit from their authoritative status as scientists. Such people claim false credit, lapsing into what Philip Kitcher calls 'universal punditry', a tendency for 'people who have (rightly) been honored for their scientific work to make pronouncements on issues about which they know very little' (2011: §§ 34 and 36). Moreover, scientists are not generally trained in history, philosophy, or the other disciplines that are necessary to challenging scientism. Of course, scientists can and have criticised scientism on scientific grounds—as the three mentioned earlier did—but, given that modern prophets of scientism play on the field of history and philosophy, one really needs training in those areas in order to challenge them. And finally, there is the fact that scientists really do have better things to do—namely, *science*—which, I imagine, most of them would rather do anyway.

In fact, if, as Midgley argues, scientism is a bad thing in part because it lumbers scientists with tasks and duties that they can rightly do without, and that distract from their main business, then proposing that scientists should take on the job of scientistic myth-busting turns out to be yet another imposition of a job that rightly belongs to someone else. Instead, it is more sensible to suggest that anti-scientism is better assigned to the more obvious constituency of *science studies*. By that term, I refer to historians, philosophers, sociologists of science, and other scholars with interests and expertise relevant to understanding the scientific enterprise. These are scholars with the training, motivation, and, perhaps, the professional obligation to contribute to our understanding of science, including the negative task of identifying and correcting failures of that understanding.

The claim that science studies scholars have a special role to play in combatting scientism is arguably confirmed by the fact that many advocates of scientism typically evince a special hostility towards them. The late American mathematician Norman Levitt, author of *Prometheus Bedevilled*, was a vigorous combatant in the 'Science Wars' of the 1990s and rightly urged caution about the excesses of certain trendy relativistic, constructionist, and 'postmodernist' doctrines. But Levitt errs by lumping all philosophers under the 'postmodernist' banner, and instead goes on to slur 'science studies scholars'—a term invariably placed in scare quotes—for their 'effusions', 'faddishness', and 'ideological obsessions', and reserves a special scorn for feminist philosophers of science (1999: 29, 153, 299). Doubtless some philosophers are effusive and faddish, but to derogate all of them, in a single stroke, is to go too far; indeed, as John Dupré points out, Levitt's triumphalist claims about the need to replace non-scientific beliefs and traditions with science is 'disastrous' precisely because he failed to 'tell us what science is' (2001: 113).

Similarly, Steven Hawking and Leonard Mlodinow claimed a few years ago, in their book *The Grand Design*, that 'philosophy is dead' because it 'has not kept up with modern developments in science' (2010: 13). Such sentiments are echoed by distinguished science communicators, such as Peter Atkins and Neil deGrasse Tyson. This claim is another instance of premature pronunciations of the death of philosophy, a discipline which can claim successive obituaries to its name. It also came as a considerable surprise to those many philosophers who do, in fact, know their science very well: many philosophers of mind are well up-to-date on neuroscience; philosophers of physics know their quantum mechanics—and so on. Hawking and Mlodinow's claim is, simply, false.

Indeed, some philosophers are obvious allies for Hawking and Mlodinow. These include two distinguished philosophers of science, James Ladyman and Don Ross, who, a few years ago, declared their 'frank scientism' and urged that areas of philosophy—such as 'analytic metaphysics'—that strayed too far from the deliverances of science ought to be 'discontinued' (2007: vii, 61). The difference between Hawking and Mlodinow and Ladyman and Ross is, of course, that the latter are both philosophically and scientifically informed, such that their views on the status and relationship of philosophy and science are worth taking seriously.

Presumably scientistic writers recognise that science scholars are well able to expose and critique their claims. Otherwise, the vitriolic rhetoric is difficult to explain. This point is also true, in my view, of the attitudes of the 'new atheists' towards serious scholars of religion.[6]

Science studies scholars can correct our images of the nature of science, including its history, methods, and practices, using the resources of their disciplines. Indeed, much of the work of science studies involves precisely the ongoing study of science and the development of increasingly sophisticated analyses of its various aspects. The sociology of knowledge, 'integrated history and philosophy of science', and the proliferation of philosophies of the special sciences—such as chemistry and climate science—are devoted to just this work, which has, I think, at least two aspects.

The first is a 'corrective' aspect, namely to create and to correct our understanding of science, either in some specific aspects, such as its methodology, or more generally, in the production of what Germans call *Wissenschaftstheorie*—'theories of science'. (The fact that many science studies scholars now shy away from offering large-scale theories of science is, itself, a cautionary lesson for scientistic writers, who, alas, show no such caution). The second aspect is 'celebratory', the pleasant task of increasing our appreciation and admiration for the huge intellectual, practical, and social labours of generations of scientists, technicians, and others—science is, after all, worthy of celebration, which isn't, of course, the same as propagandistic triumphalism.

Let me offer two examples of how science studies scholars exercise their corrective and celebratory functions, each of which contrasts, in my view, with rival scientistic myth-making.

The first is the myth of 'methodological monism', the doctrine that Science, with a capital 'S', is both defined and privileged by virtue of the Scientific Method: a unique, singular, formalised set of methodological rules that are, as the self-confessedly scientistic writer Peter Atkins puts it, capable of illuminating 'every and any concept', in a way that no other practice or mode of enquiry does or could (2011: vii). Unfortunately, scholarly studies of the history and practice of science long ago showed that, in fact, there is no such thing as the Scientific Method, thus conceived. The most dramatic expression of this claim was the provocatively titled 1975 book *Against Method*, by the historically engaged philosopher of science Paul Feyerabend. What Feyerabend was 'against', however, was methodological monism, and what he was 'for' was methodological pluralism: the idea, roughly, that there are many different methodologies at work in science, varying according to the many different investigative aims and objects of enquiry, such that monism is, in practice and in principle, a bad idea.

For Feyerabend and others, this pluralistic account of scientific methodology not only was truer to the historical and practical facts, but also did justice to science—for it showed the creativity, diversity, imagination, and richness of the scientific project, and put the lie to the duller positivist image of scientists as, in Midgley's words, 'operatives in an immense . . . falsification factory', mindlessly working with 'a single, prefabricated 'scientific method'' (ER 4). That image is not only false, it impugns the intellectual vigour and achievement of those scientists, and so does them an injustice.[7]

A second myth is that of 'value-free science'—the idea that science is value-free insofar as it is 'clean' of partisan, 'subjective', or otherwise dodgy ethical, social, and political values, and that its authoritative status is justified, in part, by its being value-free—that is, I think, what Levitt has in mind when complaining about the 'ideological' character of 'science studies', and what critics mean when they complain about feminist philosophers 'contaminating' science. It is true that philosophers of science of the first half of the twentieth century helped to forge this ideal, partly due to sincere conviction, partly due to political pressures upon the discipline of philosophy of science during the ideologically tense cultural and political environment of the Cold War.[8] Science is, of course, a part of our world and cannot escape being shaped and informed by wider political and social developments.

Whatever its origins, contemporary philosophers of science agree that the ideal of value-free science is false: scientific enquiry is inevitably structured by, for instance, ethical constraints on permissible methods of investigation—vivisection is unacceptable, even though it is, in principle, a source of knowledge—and social and political values shape the research agenda, especially in times of 'austerity' when public resources are scarce. If science seems value-free, it is because the values in question are so implicit and taken-for-granted that we fail to see them.[9] There is therefore no need to worry about the bare fact that values play a role in science; indeed, as Midgley notes, science 'only begins to have a value' when it is 'brought into contact with some existing system of aims and purposes' (M 21). If science were value-free then, as one philosopher put it, science would be valueless; so, instead, we need only worry about cases where values are playing an illicit role in science, and that is more likely to happen when people remain oblivious to the necessary role of values. Indeed, this particular myth is especially pernicious these days, since critics of the scientific consensus on climate change often exploit it by criticising perceived efforts to 'politicise' science—a complaint that relies on the false idea that science is empty of political values.

These two myths—that science is methodologically unified and value-free—should be 'busted' because they are false and cause harm. Many philosophers of science are now doing just this, and, in so doing, they are contributing their own efforts to combat scientism.

In the last section of this chapter, I want to end by emphasising the more positive aspect of Midgley's anti-scientism. I call it *doing science justice*.

DOING SCIENCE JUSTICE

Midgley offers an image of science that is strikingly consonant with the 'state-of-the-art' in philosophy of science. I suggest that there are four main aspects to this image which are both true insofar as they are supported by the best results of science studies scholarship, and positive insofar as they can usefully guide our thinking about the nature, scope, and value of science in the modern world.

The first aspect of the image is that there is no one thing called 'science', and attempted appeals to 'science' in the singular are liable to mislead us—for instance, by encouraging critics to set science against philosophy, religion or whatever else arouses their discontent. Science is not, says Midgley, 'a monolithic entity' because the various sciences are theoretically and methodologically diverse, and this is not 'disastrous' (M 32). Given the complexity of the world, and the diversity of our interests, such pluralism is, in fact, precisely what one ought to expect. In fact, we would be wise to remember that terms such as *science, art, morality*, and the like enjoy an 'ambiguity', a profitable richness, which can be 'fruitful', but which, if ignored or underestimated, can become 'dangerous' (ER 34). The ambiguous, pluralistic nature of the scientific enterprise is not to its 'discredit', but is certainly 'a real obstacle to inscribing its name on a banner to fight under' (ER 124)

The second aspect is that scientistic myths can lend to science false prestige and power, but at the cost of exaggeration and distortion. The image of science as a 'solitary intellectual citadel', 'the only scene of rational thought', 'mysteriously set . . . above the rest of life' might be intended to convey its authority and independence, but, in practice, tends to encourage 'alienation and fear' (SP 59). Many scientistic myths introduce 'distorted ideas'—such as simplifications of honorific concepts—which cause practical and intellectual problems for the reason that those concepts 'direct a great deal of life and . . . of research' (M 30). These sorts of scientistic myths lead us to have false ideas about the nature and place of science that interfere with the efforts of scientists, policymakers, and the public to locate science relative to other areas of human experience and activity. Worse still, such abuse of the 'prestige of . . . science' has also seen 'a variety of doctrines' use scientific concepts, language, and metaphors to 'gain the authority which rightly belongs to science' (M xii).

The third aspect is the worry that, if we get science wrong by submitting to scientistic myths, then we will get much else wrong, too, given the central place of science within our culture, thought, and life. Midgley notes that science has 'hugely multiplied' both the 'range of matters that concern us' and 'our ability to affect them' (M 11). Yet our newly expanding range of interests and abilities has uncertain and unstable borders and, all too often, 'science, morals, and politics are . . . combined' and 'confused' by failures to properly chart their relations (SP 199). It is therefore important to engage in boundary-marking and that means, in the first instance, abandoning the idea that 'all serious conceptual thought' is identical with science, which is, in turn, 'a distinct, self-sustaining . . . process', isolated from 'the welter of imaginative and emotional activity which fills most of our lives' (M xii-xiii). The world is complicated, and over history human beings have developed a correspondingly complex array of concepts, methods, disciplines, and traditions for meaningfully making sense of, and acting within, it. We ignore that history, forget that achievement, and lose sight of that complexity if we try to reduce all cognitive activity to 'a single fundamental method' (M 76–77).

The fourth and final aspect of Midgley's image of science, following the third, is that our enquiry into the world ought to be pluralistic. This is 'the recognition that there are many independent forms and sources of knowledge', rather than 'one fundamental form that underlies them all' (M 39). It is true that science is pluralistic, but so, too, are many other areas of human cognitive life—ideas are diverse, methods many, theories abound, and though some are closed down or refuted, many others appear in their place. Not all of them are any good, and not all will remain, but a good pluralist does not insist that we ought to create as much as we can and keep everything—surely the mark of an intellectual hoarder—but, instead, to seek only as much and as many resources as we need in order to make proper sense of the world.

The call for pluralism is echoed by other philosophical critics of scientism. A main reason why Feyerabend argued against methodological monism was that it encouraged a false image of science as unified, thereby encouraging pernicious derogation of 'non-scientific disciplines'. If science is pluralistic, then easy talk of its demarcation from other, non-scientific disciplines becomes very difficult. Similarly, Dupré rejects the idea that science has a special 'essence' that distinguishes it from other modes of enquiry, on the grounds that it sustained prejudices against anything not taken to be 'scientific'. In the case of human nature, his special interest, this scientistic assumption that 'Science' is distinct and privileged militates against pluralism.

As Dupré remarks:

> Indeed, the more diverse and varied the contents of our tool-kit, the better chance we have of coming to grips with the really interesting problems about human behaviour [. . .] The only route to a deeper understanding of ourselves is through radical epistemological pluralism. (2002: S293)

The richness and complexity of the world ought to be reflected in the diversity and sophistication of our intellectual and imaginative endeavours. As Midgley says, our science, art, philosophy, religion, and poetry ought to 'do justice to this complexity' (SP 85).

Science emerges from Midgley's writings as a complex, 'ambiguous' term, encompassing a rich and changing structure of theories, methods, and practices, but also, more deeply, a constellation of hopes, ideals, and ambitions: the myths we live by. It is true that not all of these myths are obvious or explicit, some are conflicting and others cooperating, and all of them are shaped by evolving, and often decaying, background 'imaginative visions'. The pluralistic and dynamic nature of science upsets easy claims made on its behalf, such as its allegedly inevitable conflict with religion or its triumphant displacement of philosophy, and scientism is objectionable partly because it perpetuates and profits from these unclarities, uncertainties, and untruths. This is an irony, given that the pursuit of clarity and certainty are scientific ideals, and that champions of scientism claim to be acting in its defence, when, in fact, they are abusing 'the ideal of science itself' (ER 1).

Granted, science is complex and therefore difficult, and so some degree of uncertainty and error are unavoidable—we do not always have ideal accounts of our ideals, and we will, at times, get science wrong, often for quite forgivable reasons. We have to steer between the broad attitudes to science that Haack calls 'Deferentialism' and 'Cynicism', and this can be hard work. Yet very often we need not go astray if we have good guides—those trained science studies scholars who can inform our thinking—if we would but take seriously their deliverances, not as ironclad statements of final truth, but as the best accounts available to us by enquirers whom we ought recognise, in a spirit of basic collegiality, as fellow travellers in the task of understanding the scientific enterprise.

Scientism, then, does science an injustice. Its accounts of the nature, scope, and value of science are too often false, distorting, and badly informed, and, if we take them seriously, then we are led into confusion, conflict, and error. The myth of methodological monism obscures our understanding of the boundaries of scientific enquiry and impugns the explanatory resources of disciplines pejoratively classified as 'non-scientific', thereby needlessly depriving us of a diversity of resources essential to the job of understanding complex phenomena, such as human nature. The value-free ideal distorts our understanding of the nature of science, the relation between scientific enquiry and social concerns and projects, and generates and exacerbates needless intellectual and political controversies, especially concerning issues of literally global significance, such as anthropogenic climate change.

More generally, scientism does science an injustice by premising its prestige upon false accounts of its methods, distorted versions of its history, and exaggerated accounts of its explanatory powers, and by insisting that its authority and status must be sustained by its taking over the concerns and occupations of the vast range of human endeavour. The imperialist, salvific, and absolutist urges that fuel scientism are pushing the idea that science ought to be, all at once, our morality, politics, and our spirituality, and be these things as well as fulfilling its existing practical and cognitive purposes. Scientists do not need to be our confessors, leaders, and counsellors, not least since our history and society are filled with people whose abilities and aspirations naturally invite those tasks.

Midgley's critique of scientism, at least as I have reconstructed it, is not at all 'anti-science'. Quite the contrary, it is resolutely pro-science, insofar as she aims to do justice to science by exposing false claims, correcting wrongs, and seeking the truth. 'We do not need to esteem science less', she writes, 'What we need is to esteem it in the right way' (SS 37). If science is a search for truth, then we ought also to search for the truth about science, and, for many years now, Midgley has been a wonderful guide in this search, for which we must be grateful.

ACKNOWLEDGEMENTS

I am grateful to Mary for useful correspondence about her ideas and for inspiring this piece and to Heather Jones, Tasia Scrutton, and two referees for comments and encouragement.

NOTES

1. Other notable contemporary philosophical critics of scientism include Dupre (2001), Haack (2003), Sorell (1991), and Stenmark (2001).
2. References to Midgley's writings in the text are to *Evolution as a Religion* (ER), *The Owl of Minerva* (OM), *The Myths We Live By* (M), *Science and Poetry* (SP), and *Science as Salvation* (SS).
3. See, for instance, Clark and Walsh (2009), Dupré (2001), and the papers in the symposium on scientific imperialism in *International Studies in the Philosophy of Science*, vol. 27, no. 3, in 2013.
4. I argue that scientism is intellectually vicious in Kidd (2016).
5. See Oreskes and Conway (2010).
6. I make this claim in Kidd (2015).
7. Some philosophers of science do, in fact, still argue for methodological monism, but they are exceptions for doing so. These days, it seems, pluralism reigns.
8. Two exemplary studies are Douglas (2009) and Reisch (2005).
9. An excellent critique of the value-free ideal, both in general and for specific sciences, is Kincaid, Dupré, and Wylie (2007).

REFERENCES

Works by Midgley

ER   *Evolution as a Religion: Strange Hopes and Stranger Fears* (London: Routledge, 2002).
OM   *The Owl of Minerva: A Memoir* (London: Routledge, 2005).
M   *The Myths We Live By* (London: Routledge, 2011).
SP   *Science and Poetry* (London: Routledge, 2001).
SS   *Science as Salvation: A Modern Myth and its Meaning* (London: Routledge, 1992).

Works by others

Atkins, Peter, *On Being: A Scientist's Exploration of the Great Questions of Existence* (Oxford: Oxford University Press, 2011).

Clarke, Steve and Adrian Walsh, 'Scientific imperialism and the proper relations between the sciences', *International Studies in the Philosophy of Science* 23(2) (2009), 195–207.

Douglas, Heather, *Science, Policy, and the Value-free Ideal* (Pittsburgh: University of Pittsburgh Press, 2009).

Dupré, John, *Human Nature and the Limits of Science* (Oxford: Clarendon Press, 2001).

Dupré, John, 'The lure of the simplistic', *Philosophy of Science, Supplement* 69(3) (2002), S284–S293.

Feyerabend, P., *Against Method: Outline of an Anarchistic Theory of Knowledge* (London: New Left Books, 1975).

Haack, Susan, *Defending Science—Within Reason: Between Scientism and Cynicism* (Amherst: Prometheus, 2003).

Hawking, Stephen and Leonard Mlodinow, *The Grand Design* (London: Transworld Publishers, 2010).

Kidd, Ian James, 'Epistemic Vices in Public Debate: The Case of "New Atheism"', in Christopher Cotter and Philip Quadrio (eds.), *New Atheism: Critical Perspectives and Contemporary Debates* (Dordrecht: Springer, 2015).

Kidd, Ian James, 'Is Scientism Epistemically Vicious?', in Jeroen de Ridder, Rik Peels, and René van Woudenberg (eds.), *Scientism: Problems and Prospects* (Oxford: Oxford University Press, 2016).

Kincaid, Harold, John Dupré, and Alison Wylie (eds.), *Value-free Science? Ideals and Illusions* (Oxford: Oxford University Press, 2007).

Kitcher, Philip, *Science in a Democratic Society* (Amherst: Prometheus, 2011).

Knight, David M., *The Making of Modern Science: Science, Technology, Medicine and Modernity: 1789–1914* (Cambridge: Polity, 2009).

Levitt, Norman, *Prometheus Bedevilled: Science and the Contradictions of Contemporary Culture* (New Brunswick, NJ: Rutgers University Press, 1999).

Numbers, Ronald (ed.), *Galileo Goes to Jail and Other Myths about Science and Religion* (Harvard: Harvard University Press, 2009).

Oreskes, Naomi and Eric M. Conway, *Merchants of Doubt: How a Handful of Scientists Obscured the Truth on Issues from Tobacco Smoke to Global Warming* (London: Bloomsbury, 2010).

Putnam, Hilary, *Realism and Reason: Philosophical Papers: Volume 3* (Cambridge: Cambridge University Press, 1985).

Reisch, George A., *How the Cold War Transformed Philosophy of Science: To the Icy Slopes of Logic* (Cambridge: Cambridge University Press, 2005).

Sorell, Tom, *Scientism: Philosophy and the Infatuation with Science* (London: Routledge, 1991).

Stenmark, Mikael, *Scientism: Science, Ethics, and Religion* (Aldershot: Ashgate, 2001).

11 Genes and Geniality
Dawkins, Midgley, and *The Selfish Gene*

Andrew Brown

INTRODUCTION

This chapter explores the longstanding dispute between Mary Midgley and Richard Dawkins concerning *The Selfish Gene*. My question is whether her original criticisms were fair and important. There's no question that her style did not help. The review was aggressive and bad-tempered. She had thought the book 'bloody awful' when she read it, but what had really shocked her was that it had been used by J. L. Mackie (1978), a philosopher whom she took seriously. She read *The Selfish Gene* as,

> a rotten essay in moral philosophy, propped up with bad scientific examples. Many other readers read something much more like the book Dawkins thought he had written—a work of scientific synthesis and explication. (personal communication)

So the shock of her opening assault was considerable:

> What Mackie welcomes in Dawkins is a new, biological-looking kind of support for philosophic egoism. If this support came from Dawkins's producing important new facts, or good new interpretations of old facts, about animal life, this could be very interesting. Dawkins, however, simply has a weakness for the old game of Brocken-spectre moralizing—the one where the player strikes attitudes on a peak at sunrise, gazes awe-struck at his gigantic shadow on the clouds, and reports his observations as cosmic truths' (1979: 439)

Midgley concluded that Dawkins 'merely feeds the egoist assumption into his *a priori* biological speculations, only rarely glancing at the relevant facts of animal behaviour and genetics' (1979: 439). To the extent that he is writing about genes, that may be true—at least the relationship between Dawkins and empiricism is a complicated one, to be explored later. But *The Selfish Gene* was also for many readers an introduction to all kinds of biology, stuffed full of wonderful empirical nuggets, which is partly why Mackie (1978: 460) says he read it.

Underlying all this was the central powerful idea of 'selfishness' as a kind of clockwork, a mechanism whereby the genes all whirring away in one direction, towards their own survival, meshed with the bodies above them and cause them to move—sometimes at least—in the direction of self-sacrifice. It was as beautiful and intellectually satisfying as Copernican astronomy must first have seen. 'Away with all the epicycles! Here is the perspective from which it all makes sense!'

Its power and attractiveness was certainly overlooked by Midgley. The interesting question that her pieces raise was whether Dawkins himself understood the logic of his own ideas. The root of his defence was that no one could possibly take seriously the idea that genes have emotions, plans, or ideas, so that he was entirely free to write as if they did, in order to illustrate the larger truth that biology develops as if it were driven by the interests of the genes. As Dawkins puts it,

> Now a philosopher could reasonably say: 'I don't like your definition, but given that you adopt it, I can see what you mean when you call a gene selfish'. But no reasonable philosopher would say: 'I don't like your definition, therefore I shall interpret your statement as though you were using my definition of selfishness; by my definition your concept of the selfish gene is nonsense, therefore it is nonsense'. This is, in effect, what Midgley has done' (1981: 557).

On the contrary, he says, he is defining selfishness and altruism as biologists do, without any reference to emotion, consciousness or purpose. They are solely behavioural descriptions, referring to a quantity measurable in principle: the degree to which an organism enhances its own qualities of survival and replication. 'My definition', explained Dawkins, 'is concerned only with whether the effect of an act is to lower or raise the survival prospects of the presumed altruist and the presumed beneficiary' (1981: 557).

There are two problems with this defence. The first is whether he does in fact use the term in this way. Sometimes he does, and sometimes he doesn't. When he writes that people who hope to 'build a society in which individuals co-operate generously and unselfishly towards a common good . . . can expect little help from our biological nature' (1976: 3) he is clearly an entirely different author to the man who explained, earlier in the same book, that biologists' talk about 'selfishness' or 'altruism' is 'emphatically not [talk] about emotional nature, whether of human beings, other animals, or genes' (1981: 557). Dawkins is clearly suggesting that genes are acting against the interests of the body in which they are found—this is the respectable sense of gene selfishness—but also that they are promoting selfish emotions and behaviours *vis-à-vis* other bodies—which is precisely the sense that Midgley, and in some moods Dawkins, finds objectionable.

Dawkins's claim has always been that Midgley misunderstood what he was saying. But the real burden of her attack was that he hadn't understood it either.

SELFISHNESS AND COOPERATION

There is a second, more radical attack on his concept of the selfishness of genes, hinted in a passage of Midgley's, and driven home by the man himself at the book's thirtieth anniversary celebration in the London School of Economics. The Midgley hint comes at the end of 'Gene-juggling', and is thus easily overlooked, when she says:

> Dawkins's crude, cheap, blurred genetics is not just an expository device. It is the kingpin of his crude, cheap, blurred psychology . . . Dawkins is no geneticist and . . . all the genetics which he or anyone knows is solidly opposed to his notion of genes as independent units, only contingently connected, and locked in constant internecine competition, a war of all against all. (In spite of some words in the last quotation, he cannot really mean that it is just war between each gene and its own alleles; this would allow co-operation over the rest of the field and destroy his case entirely.) (1979: 449)

Yet the more closely you examine the meanings of 'selfishness' in genes, the more it becomes apparent that most of it is just persiflage. A lot of the time, he does mean only that genes are 'selfish' in the sense that their alleles 'compete' and vary in frequency over time. This is a definition that is almost entirely tautologous—after all, 'the gene' was invented as a term for the competing units of heredity. But it has the rhetorical advantage that these tautologously selfish genes can perform heroic feats of self-abnegation without becoming in the least bit any less selfish. 'I don't know why people make a fuss about calling it the Selfish Gene', mused Dawkins on stage at the thirtieth anniversary bash for the book, 'It could just as well have been called the co-operative gene'

If he believes that 'selfish' could just as well mean 'co-operative', this would explain why he was so offended that Midgley took 'selfishness' to be the organising principle of his book, of his psychology, and of his view of the universe. And in fact there is a long passage in a later book in which he describes how genes are largely selected for their capacity to 'co-operate' with one another.

This is wrapped in a subtle and interesting discussion of the ways in which genes might be said to form alliances. Essentially, he says, their interests coincide completely only with those of the genes which are copied into new bodies at the same time and in the same way. This line of reasoning is more interesting than perhaps he realises. For one thing, it makes multi-level selection inevitable and natural. Selection comes to operate on clusters of genes, and not on individual ones (whether its operation on a single gene could ever be more than a mathematical abstraction and reordering of reality is another question). These clusters, of course, can be of arbitrary size. Once you have demolished the reality and significance of the organism, as Dawkins did in *The Extended Phenotype*, there's no reason to privilege the organism over the group, or even the species. Maynard Smith and Szathmary's *Major Transitions in Evolution* (1997) becomes then a history of the constructions of hierarchies of groups on which selection can operate.

That's not to say that it does always operate like that. Genes are always being selected in many different contexts, and it can't be worked out from first principles which are going to be the most important factors in determining their fate.

It would be wrong, however, to assume that 'Selfishness', in Dawkins, is never anything more than a tautology or a rhetorical flourish. That was a mistake that Midgley made in her original essay. There was an interesting and powerful sense of 'selfish' which worked through the book and gave rise to a great deal of subsequent thought. This was the use of 'selfish' as meaning 'capable of being selected', or 'taking part as a discrete and measurable entity in a Darwinian process'.[1] Dawkins was not of course the first man to see this, but he gave it a name, and from that name came a research programme.

In that sense, it really is a powerful concept, with a vertiginous effect. 'Selfish DNA', as opposed to 'selfish genes', is a phenomenon which theory predicted before it could be absorbed. It is a problem for Dawkins's rhetoric, though, that sufficient 'selfishness' in this sense also destroys the idea of the gene. He sees this, and skips past it with great elegance, by redefining 'gene' as a 'fuzzy chromosomal unit'. That makes room for all sorts of complications which are found on the actual sequence. It's very noticeable that molecular biologists have decomposed the nice simple idea of a gene into all sorts of complicated and tangled mechanisms.

It was brutal and needlessly unfair to describe the genetics of *The Selfish Gene* as 'crude, cheap and blurred'. But they really aren't refined or precise, and the genes in that book are not among the concepts that even pop scientists use nowadays. Matt Ridley, whom no one could accuse of hostility to Dawkins, has a discussion of seven different meanings of the word 'gene' in his 2004 book *Nature via Nurture*. None of them corresponds to Dawkins' original use of the word.

'TO BREAK A BUTTERFLY UPON A WHEEL'

Perhaps the most shocking aspect of her original essay, to people who had been bowled over by Dawkins's original book, was that it had not seemed to provoke in her any thought or wonder. Bad enough that she found it full of error and confusion: these weren't even interesting errors and confusions. 'Up till now', Midgley wrote, 'I have not attended to Dawkins, thinking it unnecessary to break a butterfly upon a wheel' (1979: 458).

This really wasn't the effect that the book had on most people innocent of biology. Speaking purely for myself, it launched me into years of enquiry into sociobiology and its implications. John Maynard Smith, whose wife disliked the title and was unimpressed by the arguments, none the less said twenty years after publication that he had not had a single student since then who had not been converted to biology as a subject by reading the book in their teens. Attempting to argue with the book provoked David Hull to write *Science as a Process* (1990).

The blurb lifted from a *New York Times* review—'This book makes the reader feel like a genius'—distilled the essence of its power, as well as the sales message. Midgley's strictures on the flawed moral philosophy of the book seemed entirely to miss the point of the wonder it felt and conveyed at the intellectual horizons opening up within biology. The book moved into popular culture like a thunderstorm, full of explosions and bright flashes of illumination. Midgley, almost alone at first, pointed out that there was nothing behind the show but vapour, roiling and obscure.

The idea that genes might usefully be termed selfish was controversial even from the beginning. It certainly wasn't original to Dawkins, though the adjective may well have been. It falls quite naturally out of George C. Williams's[2] rather less catchy definition of the gene as 'That which segregates and recombines with appreciable frequency'.[3] What was original to Dawkins, and overwhelming to his readers, was the idea that it mattered so much. That Darwinism was the solution to almost all philosophical and intellectual problems looked absurd when spelled out, even at the time. But that developments in biology were the single most intellectually exciting thing going on in the Seventies was much more plausible and very probably true.

Two or three things ran together here. The first was Dawkins's doctrine of causation. 'We see the wider world as an arena in which . . . genetic fragments play out their tournaments of manipulative skill. Genes manipulate the world and shape it to assist their replication' (1982: 5). The second was his vision of the world being shaped by information acting on dead matter. This aspect of his rhetoric was toned down in later years. It was affected by his fascination for computers and, in turn, by the admiration he received from many people in the computer industry, to whom the idea that biology could be reduced to an algorithmic dance of inert matter seemed hugely attractive and necessarily true.

The metaphysics of information did not trouble anyone very much. Dawkins founded a school of pop science work which assimilates computers to biology by using 'information' in a special way. As with 'Selfishness' and 'Altruism', this effect is produced by switching at almost undetectable speeds between a technical and quantifiable meaning and the normal everyday one.

This fools us just like a film or video does: by changing rapidly between several distinct and static pictures it produces an illusion of progress and movement.

The third, which seemed the most important to Midgley, was I think quite genuinely the least important to Dawkins. This was the confluence of notions of biological 'selfishness' with economic selfishness and the triumph of the market. This was a development during the Seventies and still more the Eighties to which intellectuals of the Left were keenly sensitive, and intellectuals outside those circles either failed to notice or regarded as common sense, as in 'someone had to sort out the trade unions'.

Two factors need to be distinguished here. The first is the degree to which Selfish Genery appeared to provide an intellectual legitimation of the great retreat from collectivism. There's no doubt that this happened. Even the fantasies of 'memetics' tended in the same direction, as removing an individual's identity as a part of society.

The second is Dawkins's own personal responsibility for this development or even his sympathy for it. There's no reason to suppose that either exists at all. So far as his politics can be distinguished from the anti-clericalism, they are a kind of benevolent elitism. Society should be run according to the wishes of civilised North Oxford. These are taken to be non-political.

Friction and misunderstanding were inevitable then from the moment that Midgley saw the Selfish Gene being used in support of a philosophical attack on the postwar consensus.

Suppose, then, that 'Selfish' is redefined in a politically neutral way, as meaning 'acted upon by natural selection'; and 'Gene' similarly redefined to mean 'a length of DNA which is acted upon as a discrete unit by natural selection'. Is there anything left of the argument of the selfish gene except the definite article?

Midgley suggests, I have come to believe correctly, that even when 'self-ish' and 'gene' are redefined in biological terms, there is still a huge hole in the central argument of Dawkins as a philosopher of biology. What is interesting in this context is that no one put the case against him nearly as forcefully as he sometimes did himself. For instance, on page 5 of *The Extended Phenotype*, he wrote that we 'see the wider world as an arena in which . . . genetic fragments play out their tournaments of manipulative skill. Genes manipulate the world and shape it to assist their replication'. Six pages later, in the same book, Dawkins wrote, 'The belief that genes are somehow super-deterministic, in comparison with environmental causes, is a myth of extraordinary tenacity, and it can give rise to real emotional distress'. Similarly, on page 13 of *The Extended Phenotype*, the million-selling author of *The Selfish Gene* asks, 'What did genes do to deserve their sinister, juggernaut-like reputation . . . Why are genes thought to be so much more fixed and inescapable in their effects than television, nuns, or books?'

Despite this, a couple of years later, he reprints the preface to a new edition of *The Selfish Gene*: 'We are survival machines-robot vehicles blindly programmed to preserve the selfish molecules known as genes. This is a truth which still fills me with astonishment.'

This style of rhetoric is closer to scripture than philosophy, in the sense that it contains proof texts for any position which turns out to be necessary. All can be cited without any of them diminishing the authority of the text for believers. That is in fact how Dawkins has always been read by his followers, and most of the traditional atheist arguments against scripture, contrasted with science, can be made with just as much force against the selfish gene.

DNA 007: WHY GENES AREN'T AGENTS, SECRET OR OTHERWISE

One comes back to the idea of genetic agency. For all its headline protestations, the Extended Phenotype has the makings of a very powerful case against the belief that genes can do or cause anything at all in the world. This is entirely independent of their lack of emotions, desires, aims, and so forth, which in this context can safely be discarded as rhetorical devices. It follows from the process of Darwinian selection.

To see the problem, consider Dawkins's discussion of what it means to say that a gene is 'for' something or some characteristic.

Dawkins has two ideas of causality, one of which is part of his intellectual fortifications, the other part of the imaginative and emotional aspect that drives his work. The intellectually respectable, if unoriginal, claim is that 'a working biologist' establishes causality by demonstrating that some factor makes an outcome statistically more likely and that changing this factor changes the likelihood of the outcome. This entirely elides the distinction between necessary and sufficient causes, but that is essential if you are to take seriously the notion of genes as causes of anything.

The distinction that he does make is between the ways in which genes manufacture copies of themselves and the ways in which they influence phenotypes. Only the first appears to him deterministic:

> The first is inflexible apart from the rare possibility of mutation; the second may be exceedingly flexible. I think a confusion between evolution and development is, then, partly responsible for the myth of genetic determinism. (1982: 14)

But, in fact, as often pointed out by Steven Rose (1997), neither process is determined by genes. On the mechanical or biological level the manufacture of fresh strands of DNA and the manufacture of proteins are both carried out by the surrounding cell. Both depend entirely on factors outside the genome. DNA does not copy itself. DNA is copied, and if you wish to disrupt the process, you disrupt the copying mechanism, not the sequence itself. When it comes to the phenotypic effects, it is the cell, through its splicing and transcription mechanisms, which determines what counts as a gene, and which parts of the sequence will be turned into protein. Causality is distributed throughout the system but, providing that the copying mechanism is undisturbed, you can change the DNA all you want and it will still be copied. Dawkins sees this as evidence of the 'immortality' of DNA, but on his own arguments it's also a demonstration of its irrelevance.

What makes a particular sequence fragment the object of selection is entirely determined by its many environments: the cell within which it is found; the organism of which that cell may be a part; the world outside the organism: all these—and not the DNA itself—determine what will be transcribed and when. And the effects of these transcription products are themselves dependent on the same multiple and overlapping environments.

The protein that any given sequence will code for is fixed once the coding sections have been spliced together. But the same protein can play very different parts in different organisms. It may be found in both a nematode and a chimpanzee, but it will be serving very different functions in each.

The use that a body will make of that protein varies enormously and so does the use that the protein will be to the body, which is the aspect on which natural selection can operate. DNA itself is read like scripture by the cell: the 'words' remain inviolable, while the 'meaning' and the use made of them are almost entirely flexible. The most elegant example of this lies in those viruses whose DNA is arranged in a ring, which is read both forwards and backwards to yield different sets of proteins.

None of these complications are visible in Dawkins's simple model of 'replicators' and 'vehicles'. They were avoided or clarified in David Hull's analysis, which looked at selection as a process: an interplay of roles rather than a play with actors. Looking at process is also the only way to analyse selective systems like RNA world, the hypothesised precursor of DNA world, where the molecules that are copied are also those on which selection acts directly. These are Darwinian, but they are not genetic, because they contain no special class of object whose only function is to transmit hereditary characteristics between generations.

Thinking of Darwinian selection as a process makes it clear that causality is distributed all the way round a long chain of necessary causes, not one of which is or could be sufficient. To be 'selfish' in such a system is to have a self that can be acted on, not to act.

And it is in many ways more natural to look for an efficient cause in the mechanisms of selection, not of replication. What's interesting about natural selection is after all the sculpting, rather than the material sculpted. Aerodynamics has shaped a bird's wing much more clearly and comprehensibly than molecular biology.

Consider the argument from parasites. In Dawkins's view, parasite genes make their way in the world because of their effect on the behaviour of bodies other than those in which they are housed. This isn't dramatically new or unprecedented. A great many genes are selected for their effects on bodies not their own—anything connected with predation, for example. The teeth of the sabre-toothed tiger were selected for their effects on the body of its prey. So are the mouthparts of the mosquito.

But the idea that genes for behaviour might be selected for their effect on the behaviour of other animals—although it is implicit in the application of game theory to biology—had never appeared with such force and clarity before Dawkins. The conception of the arms race which he popularised applied as much to behaviour as to physical characteristics.

The shock and intellectual delight of his stories of parasites manipulating the behaviour of their hosts is still vivid to me after thirty years: the ants which climb to the top of a blade of grass and teeter there until eaten by a sheep which is the next host in their parasite's life cycle; the water-fleas which find themselves impelled by their parasites to the surface where they swim in circles until eaten by a duck where the parasite will breed.

But where is the agency in all this? In the parasite, certainly, but in its genes? Sydney Brenner, reviewing the book for *Nature*, went straight for the jugular:

> Does it help to view genes as active agents, manipulating, reaching, battling? I think it only obscures the essential feature of living organisms which distinguishes them from all other complex natural systems and which gives them the capacity for evolution. It is that they are propagated by passing on not themselves but an internal representation of themselves in their genes. Exactly how this correspondence is implemented is what most biologists study; knowing it must be important if only for understanding what genetic variation can generate. To a molecular biologist, all the stuff around the genes is anything but transparent; it is hard to see the replicators through the fog of complicated machinery, nor do they reach out so easily as Dawkins wants them to. (1982: 507)

Brenner had devoted decades to the project of discovering how behaviour arrives from proteins in the tiny transparent worm *C. elegans*. (He reckoned to have solved the question of how proteins arise from genes by 1963). It turns out to be horrendously complicated even in an animal as simple as a flatworm. Once behaviour gets more complex than a worm, the contribution of any particular protein is, to all intents and purposes, impossible to map. The best we can do is to look at everything that breaks when the protein is absent.

The ghastly systemic effects of some of the diseases caused by recessive mutations in a single gene in human babies make clear just how complex the effects of a single protein can be. There is a group of diseases referred to as Batten's syndrome, all caused by malfunctions in a gene on chromosome 12 called CLN1. Babies thus afflicted grow normally until they are about eight months old. Then they start to regress. They lose the ability to crawl, they lose the most of their ability to eat. Acid reflux strips the enamel from their teeth. They will never talk and if they live to four they'll lose their sight. Nothing, and possibly even less than nothing, is added to our understanding by considering the healthy form of CLN1 as a gene whose strategy is to make bodies able speak, talk, move, and see.

The language of strategy and manipulation may not produce any greater understanding even when we are talking about parasites. Obviously it makes dramatic and emotional sense to consider tobacco plants as parasitic on humans, and to suppose that the genes which produce nicotine have somehow manipulated human beings to plant tobacco all around the world. But as an account of the causality involved, it's absurd. You might as well talk of 'the demon drink'. What makes drink demonic is not spirits (in either sense). It is the ways that we use it, and that parts of our minds and hearts use it to the detriment of other parts.

Incidentally, the example of nicotine genes shows how the same protein can have entirely different effects depending on the environment. Presumably, nicotine and other compounds are first selected for their effects on insect and predatory nervous systems, and these effects are aversive. That the same chemical should be attractive to our species was not predictable by even the most cunning mastermind among selfish genes plotting their way down through generations. To the extent that there was agency involved, it was all outside the tobacco plants and still further removed from their chromosomes.

When human farmers decide to plant tobacco or opium, they are undoubtedly spreading certain alleles at the expense of others. But they are not compelled to do so by the genes involved. As part of his rejection of genetic determinism, Dawkins would deny—quite rightly—that they are compelled by their own genes to do so. But it is still more absurd to follow the logic of the Extended Phenotype to its end and suppose that human farmers are compelled to plant their crops by tobacco genes. What is true is that both humans and plants are part of the same selective loop. You cannot consider the selective pressures on nicotine genes as existing solely within the tobacco plant. But wherever they arise they are pressures or currents within the gene pool: they are not the passive objects of a gene's manipulation.

Nor is the feedback loop of selection by humans the only one in which the plant is involved. There are parasites even of tobacco plants.

In any case, we are entitled to ask why there should be a single locus of causality or a single point of measurement for evolution. This criticism is also present in Midgley's original 'Gene-juggling' argument:

> When the mountains of metaphor are removed, in fact, what we find is not so much a mouse as a mare's nest, namely the project of finding a unit which will serve for every kind of calculation involved in understanding evolution; a 'fundamental unit' at a deep level which will displace, and not just supplement, all serious reference to individuals, groups, kin and species, and which (for some unexplained reason) will also be the unit of selfishness or self-interest. (1979: 451)

As other chapters in this volume attest, Midgley is deeply opposed to such reductionist thinking, in biology, philosophy, or indeed anywhere else. She offers an example:

> To see how vacuous, we might ask the parallel question, 'what is the fundamental unit of economics?' A coin? If so how large and of what country? A single worker? A factory? A complete market exchange? A minimal investor? For various purposes and from different angles, we might need to count any of these things. The decision which to count, and how finely to divide them, would depend entirely on the particular problem which we wanted to solve, and for most purposes we would refer to all of them, and would rightly not expect to have to reduce one to another. (1979: 451)

Dawkins may still feel the cruelties of Midgley's original assault as painfully as a pea beneath the mattress of adulation on which he now reclines, but for the rest of us the arguments are clear and contemporary, while the aggravation has long since been buried by time. And considered without animosity, purely as a criticism of the book, Midgley was right in every respect, except to suppose that Dawkins noticed or cared about the meaning that the world 'selfish' might have to the wider world.

NOTES

1. Dawkins argues this explicitly early on in *The Selfish Gene*: 'The fundamental unit of selection, and therefore of self-interest . . . is the gene, the unit of heredity' (1976: 12).
2. http://bioscience.oxfordjournals.org/content/49/8/656.full
3. http://stearnslab.yale.edu/sites/default/files/55._williams_george.pdf

REFERENCES

Brenner, Sydney, 'Beyond selfish genes', *Nature* 296(5857) (1982): 506–507.
Dawkins, Richard, *The Selfish Gene* (Oxford: Oxford University Press, 1976).
Dawkins, Richard, 'In defence of selfish genes', *Philosophy* 56 (1981): 556–573.
Dawkins, Richard, *The Extended Phenotype: The Gene as the Unit of Selection* (Oxford: Oxford University Press, 1982).
Dawkins, Richard, *The Selfish Gene: 30th Anniversary Edition* (Oxford: Oxford University Press, 2006).
Gleick, James, *The Information: A History, a Theory, a Flood* (London: HarperCollins, 2001).
Hull, D.L., *Science as a Process, An Evolutionary Account of the Social and Conceptual Development of Science* (Chicago: University of Chicago Press, 1990).
Mackie, J.L., 'The law of the jungle: Moral alternatives and principles of evolution', *Philosophy* 53 (1978): 455–464.
Midgley, M., 'Gene-juggling', *Philosophy*, 54 (1979): 439–58.

Ridley, Matt, *Nature via Nurture: Genes, Experience, and What Makes Us Human* (London: HarperPerennial, 2004).

Rose, S.P.R., *Lifelines: Biology, Freedom, Determinism* (London: Allen Lane, 1997).

Smith, J.M. & Szathmary, E., *The Major Transitions in Evolution* (Oxford: Oxford University Press, 1997).

Williams, G.C. & Williams, G.C., 'The question of adaptive sex ratio in outcrossed vertebrates', *Proceedings of the Royal Society of London. Series B. Biological Sciences*, 205 (1979): 567–580.

12 Was Plato a Gorilla? Mary Midgley's Search for a Metaphysics of Evolution

Simon Conway Morris

Reality is always turning out to be a great deal more complex than people expect. (M 27)[1]

For philosophers, concepts such as 'hylomorphism' and 'existential fallacy' are an everyday currency. For evolutionary biologists, terms such as *cleistocarpic, heteropycnosis*, or *dikaryotic* roll off the tongue. Either group looks to a private language that reinforces their largely hermetic existence. Faced with these linguistic smokescreens the public try to follow the latest debates, but as often as not a sense of bafflement and excluded frustration descends. Not only transparency but bridge-building becomes a priority, not least when a cadre of distinguished evolutionary biologists begin to make extravagant metaphysical claims. Moreover, their sweeping assertions are not only imposed across their own discipline, but extended far beyond their legitimate intellectual boundaries to distant realms of which they are amateurs but which are then declared to be of nugatory importance, if not entirely meaningless.

For Mary Midgley, this scientific imperialism won't do at all. Rather, however, than strengthening the hermetic bulwarks, she is willing to take the science very seriously and then listen to the claims made on its behalf. For her, as much as for her opponents, Darwin remains a key figure. His ideas underpin a naturalistic programme that sees how much can be learnt of the human condition from our animal cousins and brothers.[2]

So far, so good, but thereafter some very different readings emerge. This is because some Darwinists take the once revolutionary but now mundane observations made by Darwin into some strange territory, making a series of melodramatic claims and asserting an intellectual suzerainty that uniquely confers an enviable capacity for omnicompetence and omniscience. Here Midgley draws the line, deploying her philosophical forces to test, repel, penetrate, batter and dismay her opponents. It can be a *tour de force*, but is this enough? Certainly her dialogue and strictures have exposed both flaws and absurdities in the metaphysics of her opponents. Nor is this destructive, because she has done much to reaffirm our place in the natural order of the world. But, or so I suggest, this adherence to a naturalistic programme eventually imposes some impossible burdens, not least in the questions of consciousness and radical evil.

These questions are neither avoidable nor, I suggest, are they incidental to the themes explored by Midgley. Any naturalistic scheme looks to a story of continuing emergence, as Darwin himself so triumphantly demonstrated. Much that is useful stems from these insights. It is, however, not the only way to view the world. A radically different perspective, and one that is complementary rather than antagonistic to a story of emergence, is to see the world as being empowered to discover pre-existent realities. From this stance, the mundaneness of evolution is transcended by the more interesting observation that it is by these means that the Universe becomes self-aware. Mind is indeed discovered by evolution, but evolution did not make mind.

THE CARTOGRAPHY OF MIDGLEY

Imagine, for the want of a better metaphor, that the dialogue between the sciences (especially evolutionary biology) and the wider world is seen as inhospitable terrain. Across this landscape, any vehicle of discourse must navigate with a considerable degree of care. Wheels have a tiresome habit of falling off, the driver's decision to use a blindfold on occasion is surely unhelpful, whilst it really would help if the passengers just occasionally stopped their incessant chatter and, on the steeper slopes, actually bothered to get out and *push*. Sometimes there is a nagging feeling that we are going in ever-decreasing circles, and after many fruitless miles we should be more than grateful that Midgley has taken over the reins. It is just as well. Who are these passengers? It is a decidedly mixed crew. There sit the ghosts of such luminaries as Nietzsche and Monod, but cheek-by-jowl are the living. Like Monod, they may be the possessors of undoubted scientific authority, but their strident and uncompromising certainties spill over into areas where their competence might, however gently, be questioned. It is a strange enough crew, uniformly equipped with piercing eyes and a distinct tendency to engage in histrionic gestures. For all their alertness, they remain seemingly oblivious of the devastated landscape across which they travel.

Combining a generosity of spirit with a submerged steeliness, Midgley eschews the siren voices with their luring calls for simple solutions. Rather, she insists not only on the centrality of thought, but the sheer scale of the enterprise that awaits us. Her task has been to engage with science, not with its nuts and bolts—nor electron microscopes and Large Hadron Colliders—but its metaphysical foundations. If carefully excavated, they reveal the outlines of a remarkable human enterprise, delineating a map which promises us some reassurance as to who we are and why our hopes and fears are not always idle fancies, but are legitimate. If, however, the preferred tools of the excavator are blunt jackhammers, backhoes in the hands of the partially sighted and the sappers whose chief task is to ensure tremendous detonations, then the results will be disastrous. In this latter case, the map will now be full of holes, not least in missing most of the key, useless to any traveller with a sense of destination but clutched by the deeply fatalistic who deem the world meaningless, but paradoxically seek ever new utopias.

In this essay, I review some of Midgley's contributions, especially as they pertain to Darwinian evolution and our place as 'just another twig' in the Tree of Life. With Midgley, it is difficult to imagine a more intelligent and sympathetic guide to what is for the most part a battlefield, pock-marked in places by abandoned redoubts, elsewhere forbidden territory strewn with mines, but in places marked by scenes of furious engagement. Is it, in the end, all sound and fury signifying nothing? Midgley would insist not. For her, a devotion to such unfashionable topics as the realities of meaning and evil, a clarion-call against ignorance, and her exasperation at those who engage in melodrama in one way or another together introduce us to a perhaps unexpected philosophical programme.

Nor is it one with which I wish to quarrel, but beyond her stated ground I begin to suspect that, for better or worse, there must be a divergence of positions. This is because, whilst I agree that her agenda not only will heal some unnecessarily inflicted wounds but, in taking us a very long way, will keep us happily employed for decades to come, the maps Midgley has provided may ultimately prove to be at best provisional. Not that, I suppose, Midgley would wish to claim that knowledge of any sort is anything other than sketchy, but I fear she would most definitely balk at my diagnosis. Unrelenting as is my admiration of Midgley, I want to question—and ironically as a scientist—whether any naturalistic programme ultimately is capable of closure. In other words, can we be confident that transcendence is any more than one door in the building known as Philosophy? Aquinas remarked that all that he then knew (and which has continued to fuel philosophy) was 'so much straw'. One final point. By this stage my reader may be feeling a sense of growing outrage. Here is a contributor invited to a *Festschrift* who seems to have forgotten it is not some sort of *Kriegschrift*. I am no philosopher, and I freely admit that all my terms of reference, not least those of naturalism and the transcendent, require a great deal of analysis. All I can say as a scientist is that, as Midgley would firmly agree, scientific knowledge, however construed, cannot possibly encompass the whole of human experience. We may need to look beyond ourselves, and not back to animals, in search of ultimate meanings. As she puts it, we have to choose, given the 'enormous enriching of our capacities that gives rise to free will', there is 'much more on the table than we could possibly eat [and so] we have to choose, in a sense in which other species do not' (BM 317). I sense that splendid as the dinner may be, we are still missing the metaphysical banquet.

In my view, slipping through our fingers are questions such as to the nature of consciousness, the roots of our imaginative vision, and the recurrent demands for the transcendent. It is, in the end, a radically different world-picture, offered not to argue that a given perspective is wrong, but to suggest that it is incomplete. It is a view at odds with any naturalistic scheme because, whilst it agrees that on a first reading the construction of our Universe seems to be simply a continuing story of emergence, ultimately the evidence before us demands a different sort of metaphysics. So yes, it is true that, seen from one perspective, the Universe appears a gripping story of an unfolding, not least as is seen in processes of evolution. But why does all this happen in the way it does? What happens if we turn the tables and see the history of the Universe as one of discovery? Perhaps then we arrive at an arrangement which ultimately makes better sense, in terms of both our curiosity and the way things are so ordered. And of this tale there seems to be no end.

That, however, is to get ahead of ourselves. Let us now set out the ground so far as it pertains directly to the work of Midgley. Thus, to be informed that 'Clear expressions of important mistakes are very useful things' (SP 40) is hardly the way most scientists would choose to address each other. Midgley's seemingly brusque observation, however, is far from being dismissive, but rather it epitomizes the life-philosophical. Not that scientists are uninterested in thinking, at least along some lines. Immerse yourself in her writing, however, and you will find no respite from a constant analysis of positions, to appreciate that however extreme an argument may be, somewhere or other it may reveal an important truth. It is not, however, an enterprise based upon the endless grinding of theoretical mills, but rather it is embedded in the insistence that we are creatures of the world. We belong here, emphatically we are not cosmic nomads, but even so still have to face difficult, possibly horrendous, choices. We are not just animals, but pre-eminently thinking animals. When Midgley encounters a group whose 'faith needs no argument, being simply self-evident', then, as she observes, this is to engage in what is 'merely a dogmatic slumber' (ER 20–21). To anybody who is willing to take the effort to engage, dialogue becomes essential.

Nowhere is this more applicable than in science. It might seem obvious, but she is right to point out that the exercise of science is very far from simply piling up the facts as they arrive on the laboratory bench. Rather, as she says, it is not only a 'system-building tendency, with its aesthetic criteria of elegance and order' (ER 103), but where the reductionist method must be kept on a short and strong leash. On the other hand, left to its own devices, the subject in question may 'often compensate by strange, illicit expansions elsewhere' (ER 82). The siren call of simplicity, as if somehow the facts are capable of speaking for themselves, must be avoided at all costs.

THE LIMITS OF SCIENCE

All too often, however, science wanders into regions where it has no right to be. Here, as so often, Midgley does not mince her words. Michael Ghiselin's warped view of evolution—'Scratch an 'altruist' and watch a 'hypocrite' bleed'[3]—is briskly dismissed as 'essentially pure fantasy' (ER 3). Karl Popper, whose attempts to corral the scientific method make him the darling of so many scientists, is seen by Midgley as taking a 'rather extreme and simple negative version of this view' (ER 17).[4] So too she can only wonder at both Steven Weinberg's 'tone of personal aggrievement and disillusion' (ER 87) and J.D. Bernal's 'extraordinary, paranoid revulsion from the human body' (M 45). Taken out of context, these observations may seem to be regrettably *ad hominem*, but each is simply exasperation at some decidedly unbalanced views. As Midgley patiently observes, 'physical scientists [are] rather unpractised in general thinking' (ER 24).

Inevitably, feathers are ruffled and her opponents' voices tend to become rather shrill, but, so far as Midgley is concerned, this is unimportant. There is not only an immensity of work to be done, but it is going to be hands-on stuff. As Midgley remarks, 'we need to call in a philosophic plumber' (SP 37) or—if you prefer another metaphor of labour—we must engage in 'stupendous spadework' and such work is, alas, 'inescapably vast' (ER 21–22). Even with all this effort, the wider picture may still remain frustratingly elusive. Consider her metaphor of visiting an aquarium and moving from one porthole to another: here an octopus clamped to the inside of the glass, there a scurry of swiftly vanishing fish, and elsewhere a pool of translucent light that illuminates a small patch of reef. Plumbing, spadework, peering into an aquarium: all capture the magnitude of the task.

In many quarters, the task runs into the sand almost as soon as we have begun. In the English radio panel show *I Am Sorry, I Haven't A Clue*, almost as popular as the game *Mornington Crescent* is the contest in which the panellists are asked to carefully articulate a succession of words whose inappropriate juxtaposition provokes applause and laughter: 'sock . . . gnu . . . custard . . .', that sort of thing. So too the association 'scientist . . . metaphysics' might not bring the house down, but would at least induce a titter amongst the more susceptible members of the audience. Not so for Midgley. She is rightly insistent that science must inevitably tangle with metaphysics. For the most part, scientists are deeply puzzled by this stance. Are they not the guardians of facts, dispassionate enquirers, throwing down the gauntlet of experimental replication to naïve and credulous bystanders? Midgley has no doubt as to the extraordinary success of the sciences and how repeatedly they have delivered deep and unexpected insights, sometimes to our discomfort. But too often scientists are reluctant to concede that it is impossible for them (or anybody else) to erect a *cordon sanitaire* around their activities. The tensions arise because, as she points out, science all too often claims to be neutral and value-free, but then by routes known only to intellectual smugglers it is then deemed to be the source of *all* values.

The assumptions by which this is achieved remain largely unexamined, in that aforementioned zone of dogmatic slumber. The emperor may nod, but the imperialistic enterprise soon produces some pretty strange fruits.

As Midgley explains, these divide into three main strands, each a direct offspring of the Enlightenment. First, we see an unwavering belief in progress, not least in the construction of genetically modified humans. Next, there are repeated claims for omnicompetence and omniscience: all will be explained, all will be known and the powers our descendants will possess would seem to us as magic. Finally, there is the subscription to a social contract: all are individuals, atomistic, with sacrosanct rights and complete freedom to accept or reject. Midgley would be the last to argue that good cannot result from this Enlightenment programme. Self-evidently it has, as even a nodding acquaintance with today's tyrannies will confirm. When, however, scientists either begin pincer-movements of intellectual aggrandisement or suggest that entire areas of human discourse are irrelevant and/or imaginary, then we might begin to be alarmed.

DOGMATIC OPTIMISM

Not that some scientists see matters this way. For example, Midgley is struck by E. O. Wilson's statements of dogmatic optimism, not because they have much value, but on account of their melodrama. Such is a recurrent theme amongst such luminaries as Crick, Dawkins, Ghiselin, Monod, Weinberg and, as mentioned, Wilson. But in many cases it is more than just melodramatics, and, however unwittingly, all are subscribing to mythopoeic visions of science. As she writes, 'Uncontrolled indulgence in the drama enslaves one to the myth' (ER 28). Myths are unavoidable, indeed essential. As Midgley and many others have insisted, it is the employment of symbolic power and its imaginative range that brings meaning and order to our lives. Their very power, however, means that they can readily confer an authority that, on closer, examination is unwarranted.

So if science would have us believe that we are unconscious agents of our genes, that memes are relevant to the thoughts of Socrates (or Midgley), or that minds can be downloaded, then the mythopoeic vision will most likely lead in an atomistic and/or fatalist direction. Too often it is forgotten that thinking is never a neutral activity, and simply adopting a given world-picture is no guarantee that the end result will be at all comfortable. Beware especially of those apparently neat encapsulations that are offered by the scientific magi. So Midgley stresses, the world is simply too complicated to take them seriously. As she says, if we are to make any attempt to deal with 'life, time, space, law, energy' (ER 104), then only a metaphysics can serve to bind them and explain why we are of any consequence at all.

Not, as already emphasized, that Midgley is opposed to science. It is striking how often she salutes Darwin. In contrast to the customary genuflection, I suspect that in him she finds a like mind: exploratory, curious, open to surprise and also delight, and reluctant to take the evidence beyond its legitimate point. Central to her thinking is that we are a product of naturalistic processes. The corollary is that if we fail to understand our natural setting then we are likely to end up confused. So too we have real bodies and must live in societies. Living cheek-by-jowl, as often as not with people we do not particularly care for (or as likely loathe), demands codes of behaviour. Our cognitive capacities do not work in a vacuum, but evolved in a world where they would be useful. As Midgley remarks, 'We are not pure minds but dependent animals' (M 161). Stated so boldly, these perspectives are unremarkable, but, as already indicated, Midgley sees that a great deal more is at stake. As she says, there can be no objection to the 'bringing of human affairs into the same perspective as the rest of nature. . . . What worries me is the hasty use of certain patterns that have been found useful in biology to explain human affairs where they have only a somewhat artificial application' (M 87). So in a sense, we have come full circle. Is there anything more to say?

The answer depends on how far we are willing to follow Midgley's credo. On many counts, of course, we make no dispute. Take again evolution. Neither she, nor her opponents, doubt its validity. What matters is when some scientists decide to impose a religious dimension. This is very far from the mundane observation that, traced back in time, humans lose any semblance to an ape or a mammal or ultimately even an animal. To arrive at this conclusion may have required decades of unremitting work, but as a metaphysical statement it is entirely humdrum. When, however, evolution is treated as a religion, we are offered (however unwittingly) a mythopoeic vision. Some such metaphysical reading is always unavoidable, but we are entitled to choose between competing versions. Not that anybody would claim that this process is easy. The warblings of various ultra-Darwinists hardly stand up to scrutiny, but part of our difficulty is that it is far from clear how fully we understand evolution. Of course as a process it happens, but that in itself is not necessarily especially helpful. If evolution is like any other science, then we should not be surprised if we are dealing with unfinished business. Thus, I would agree with Midgley that the importance of self-organization in biology remains understated, yet ever since D'Arcy Thomson's magisterial *On Growth and Form*, this topic has remained on the edges of the debate.[5] The same seems to apply to the phenomenon of evolutionary convergence.[6] Midgley is surely right in saying that evolution does indeed have 'some set of positive tendencies' (SS 7). Far from being an unholy mess, life does seem to be endowed with a sort of creativity. Nothing, of course, to do with Henri Bergson's ruminations, let alone the higher lunacies of so-called 'intelligent design', but as Midgley writes, 'matter itself has quite definite, limited ways of shaping itself' (SS 103). So too, just as science as a whole is a 'huge, ever-changing imaginative structure of ideas' (M 3), so evolutionary biology would be ill-advised to rest on its laurels, however well-earned. Just because evolution happens does not mean that we understand everything about it.

RUNNING INTO THE SANDS?

Science is part of that great human exploration. As Darwin saw all too clearly, what we learn can change the way we see the world forever, even if we cannot foresee how. That is the nub of the problem. Products of evolution we certainly are, but the attempts to stitch evolution into one or other metaphysical shroud, however erroneous or melodramatic, are actually very odd. Why, in fact, are we so irredeemably mythopoeic? Let me suggest, and with great respect, that in this context there is more to be said.

In several areas Midgley's programme (so far as her immense tapestry deserves such a description) may perhaps have run into the sands. In a sense, it depends on how one thinks (so to speak) the Universe is constructed. Obviously we are part of it, and 'quark to hominid' provides an absorbing narrative. On the other hand, we continue to discover extraordinary things about the place we inhabit. Elsewhere I have written that in the final analysis, evolution is of any interest only because it was in this manner that the Universe has become self-aware. Is this not rather odd? Again, one narrative will depict this process as one of emergence. So in this context evolutionary biology is well-equipped to explain the origins of synapses, encephalization, Von Economo neurones, cerebrotypes and all the panoply that are evidently prerequisites for a human-like intelligence. In this context, Midgley's view seems to be firmly naturalistic. So she writes of the 'real world . . . not, then, a strange metaphysical spook . . . It is simply the whole of what is out there' (M 28). Perhaps the word 'whole' begs the question. Of course we need a real world, and here her strictures as to the various fantasies entertained by some scientists have real force, but nevertheless I still find our capacity to understand things as perhaps a trifle unexpected. It is not enough to take it all for granted. Here, perhaps, those 'metaphysical spooks' may be more real than we sometimes care to imagine.

Midgley is enormously impressed by Darwin's insight into what links us to the rest of the animal world (and beyond) and what appears to be an insensible gradation. So when we consider morality (and the nature of evil) or the nature of consciousness, she would urge us to enormous efforts, but the solution itself lies, so to speak, in 'joining the dots'. With respect to morality, as she observes, evolution gives us a world where not all is possible, so that some sort of workable solution must emerge. Accordingly, they must be realistic, and not, as she writes, a 'set of alien rules' (SS 28). Such a transition need not be trivial, and she quotes Nietzsche with approval as to how, in his words, humans can become 'a way, an episode, a bridge, a great promise' (SS 60). So too Midgley is struck by Darwin's rumination of how it might be that those swallows that raise a brood late in the season and perforce abandon them as they flee towards warmer lands might, if they reflected upon it, be stricken with 'an agony' of remorse having left '[their] young ones perishing in the bleak north from cold and hunger'.[7] But is this not putting the cart before the horse? That animals might feel remorse seems possible. But I am far less persuaded that there would be any circumstances whereby an ethical swallow would abruptly head back north to seek out its starving brood. If it did, then it would no longer be a swallow.

THE PROBLEM OF EVIL

The point is that, whilst the evolutionary roots of humans are plain to see and much that we take for granted is nascent in one way or another in different groups of animals (apes, crows, dolphins, parrots, etc.), humans are now completely different. Remorse is not only a commonplace and, as one ages, so it tends to become increasingly poignant, if not bitter. Yet heroics, even in old men, are not unknown. But so too is evil, and here I suggest is one fault-line in Midgley's naturalistic programme. To be sure, she gives a spirited defence of evil being at least in part 'a process which makes it inevitable [because] our natural desires must conflict' (W 200). Correspondingly, she suggests, its negativity is not the result of the proximity to some chilling metaphysical abyss but the decidedly more mundane result of increasingly social (and no doubt populous) groups matching their aggression and possessiveness with the demands of territoriality. There must be much truth in this, but I am less convinced that this is the end of the story. Midgley makes much of the odious Adolf Eichmann, who epitomizes the oft-quoted 'banality of evil'.[8] Apparatchik he certainly was, but the Holocaust in which he was a not inconsiderable player is permeated by something that seems to have been much more than the conflict of natural desires. No purpose would be served by either a catalogue of evils or a metric of horrors, but in the case of the Holocaust I find it difficult to avoid the conclusion that something deeper was at work. Not that I wish to claim that other genocides and mass killings deserve second rank in awfulness, nor that the magnitude alone should govern our response. In the trial of Rosemary West (her husband Fred having by then committed suicide) one might say that in the Winchester courtroom the appalling recitals of murders and rapes were in themselves responsible for a palpable sense of evil, but again I am not so sure.[9]

As Midgley often remarks, literature is helpful here. I am much struck, for example, by George Bernanos' grasp of this terrible dimension of human existence. Thus in his *Joy*, and writing of the compelling figure of his heroine Chantal, he observes:

> Like a man who, having fallen asleep at sunrise, wakes in the brutal light of noon with the serenity of dawn still in his eyes, the world, which had been no more than a mysterious word to her [Chantal], was through intuition and the flowering and radiation of pity, now revealed not to her experience, but to her charity. Only the blind

of spirit believe that evil is known to those wretches alone who let themselves, little by little, be devoured by it, who at the end of their mournful labours have only known sin's precarious pleasures, its dull melancholy, its obscure and sterile rumination. Oh vain fall, oh cries never to be heard by the living, cold messengers of the shoreless night. If hell has no answer for the questioning dead, it is not because it refuses to answer (for rigorous, alas, in observance, is the imperishable fire), but it is because hell has nothing to say, will say nothing eternally. Only a certain purity, a certain simplicity, the divine ignorance of saints, catching evil off its guard, can penetrate its thickness, penetrate the thickness of immemorial deceit.[10]

For me, this passage (and indeed somewhat similar ones in the novels of Charles Williams) is deeply unsettling. Bernanos has surely put his finger on something terrible, but known only to humans. I am not for a moment trying to say that animals cannot be mischievous and quite possibly malign. Think, for example, of that episode in Henno Martin's *The Sheltering* Desert.[11] The story concerns two German geologists who flee into the Namibian desert to avoid internment by the allied authorities. It is a moving book, and amongst their trials and tribulations are encounters with baboons who, so far as the escapees could tell, deliberately fouled their water supply. Lists of wrongs, perceived or actual, in either animals or more obviously ourselves may in the end not provide the illumination (if that is quite the word) we seek. One need not doubt that there is a gradation in malice and spite, but to argue that as an end point we find Eichmann, Fred and Rosemary West or any other monster may fail to convince. Once again we are compelled to ask: is evil simply an inevitable evolutionary emergence, given that needs and desires must often be in conflict? Or is it more than that? Malice aforethought, whereas often as not one seems to be engaged in something more like a process of encounter, where initial curiosity can swiftly lead to much darker territory?

THE PROBLEM OF CONSCIOUSNESS

I would not be surprised if Midgley took my ruminations as little more than a regrettable lapse into melodrama. If the idea of some sort of encounter applied only to evil, then I might be reassured. There is, however, an apparently unrelated question that may have relevance not only to this conundrum, but oddly also to that of the question of the nature of consciousness. It revolves the deceptively simple enquiry: can animals think? Given their capacity to make tools, and more generally to memorize, learn, sleep (itself a decidedly non-trivial activity), grieve, and communicate, the answer would seem to be otiose. Things may, however, be a bit more complicated. Drawing on Darwin's insights, especially as set forth in his *The Expression of the*

Emotions in Man and Animals, Midgley notes how it seems as if animals may be possessed by one mood, but, rather than deciding in advance what emotional state be adopted, they seem to have little choice in the matter. That is to say, they live for the moment and have 'a sort of emotional tunnel vision' (W 183). Interestingly, in a discussion of the intelligence of elephants, Benjamin Hart and his co-workers come to a somewhat similar conclusion, in as much whilst these beasts have formidable powers of memory, this does not obviously square with 'conventional tests of cognitive performance . . . [and so] brings to mind studies on the rare Savant Syndrome in humans which is often associated with autism'.[12] I unpack some of the implications of these remarks elsewhere, but the point to ponder is whether in this case (and indeed others) some vital ingredient seems to be lacking.

This might find a resonance with other studies on animal cognition. At this juncture it must, however, be stressed that different camps exist, views can be polarized and definitive results may be elusive. Consider, for example, the cognitive skills exhibited by birds, and more especially various species of corvid (rooks, crows, jays, etc.). Experiments that re-run Aesop's fable of the crow dropping stones into a pitcher to raise the water-level sufficiently to allow drinking (or in the laboratory access to floating worms) at first sight seem strikingly human-like.[13] In their commentary on the study, however, two other experts on bird behaviour, Alex Taylor and Russell Gray, suggest that comparisons to a human cognitive capacity appear to fall short, asking 'what exactly . . . were the rooks thinking when they solved the problem?'[14] Other experiments in which the birds have to use a tool to access another tool that will then give access to the reward may also indicate cognitive limitations. One might protest that these birds never evolved to face such tasks, and much evidence does indeed point to an impressive intelligence. All this is true, but human intelligence has the strange knack of 'lateral thinking', and one can argue that neither the birds nor any other cognitively competent animals actually *understand* what they are doing. In this sense, they are not rational.

A different approach might attempt to ask how deep in the Tree of Life any sort of intelligence can be traced. Certainly the evidence suggests that it long preceded animals.[15] This gives us some confidence that intelligence is not some strange property, but it is of little help when it comes to assessing the precise cognitive capacities of our immediate brothers and cousins, the apes and birds. Of course, however one interprets the evidence, they seem to stand on the very threshold of a fully-fledged mind. But is the difference only one of degree? No doubt if apes and birds were equipped with language, our task would be that much the easier. The fact is, however, that despite the intriguing analogies that exist between birdsong and language, the latter is uniquely human. Is it not actually very odd that this is the case? To many, this must seem that we are doing no more than splitting hairs. Does it really matter? It might, the reason being that it leads to a topic that interests Midgley greatly, that is, *consciousness*.

As we should expect, there is a great deal of—well—common sense in her perspective. A stern critic of Cartesian dualism, she is insistent that reason and feeling work hand-in-hand; a disembodied intelligence is a contradiction in terms. This view, of course, plays no small part as to how she sees science and its attendant myths, not least in its recurrent denials of subjectivity. When, however, we speculate as to how consciousness evolved, we seem to run into difficulties. As Midgley stresses, consciousness is not analogous to digestion: 'Consciousness, then, is not just one more phenomenon. It is the scene of all phenomena, the place where appearances appear' (SP 83). This has more than a whiff of theology, but otherwise unfortunately may not get us very far. For example, consciousness seems difficult to divorce from symbols and metaphor. Whilst it helps to explain how scientists so frequently get in such a muddle as they conjure up inappropriate myths, it hardly explains as a species why we are so irredeemably mythopoeic.

So too it might make us even more suspicious as to what animal consciousness actually involves. Is a naturalistic programme going to work? Am I alone in detecting a somewhat plaintive note when Midgley writes, 'Why is consciousness regarded with suspicion as a sinister extra entity, instead of as the normal function of a developed nervous system?' (M 144). Much might hinge on the word 'developed', but certainly she has no time for consciousness being some sort of epiphenomenon. As she says, this can be regarded only as a 'rather a desperate distortion' (M 39), dismissing Huxley's conceit that consciousness is analogous to the steam whistle of a mighty locomotive. Paul Davies wins a commendation in his attempt to bring physics to bear on the problem, but once again Midgley acknowledges that it cannot of itself be physical. Her remark that 'every movement that Einstein's neurones had made . . . would not have the slightest relevance to understanding his thought' (SS 90) has been widely echoed, but seems to present us with the all-too-familiar impasse that is most familiar from the enigmatic nature of qualia but leads some people to suggest that consciousness may simply be beyond our powers of comprehension. We hear the knock of the philosophical plumber at the door, but hardly know to which part of the house to direct her.

In reviewing this area, we must also acknowledge that much has been published since what is her fullest exposition, that is, the revised edition of *Beast and Man* (1995), but as I read the evidence, the tension between the self-evident continuity between ourselves and animals, as against the obvious differences, is no nearer resolution. Either point of view has legitimacy and an either/or stance will achieve little. Nevertheless, one might suggest that Midgley's understanding, sympathy and perhaps a tinge of envy for our animal cousins, papers over some serious cracks. That they are for all intents and purposes entirely within our power, and we often treat them abominably, is not in dispute. Remarks such as 'My present concern is the strong symbolic barrier that still makes it hard for many people who officially believe in evolution to accept its consequences, to see the kinship between man and other species that becomes so obvious once we start to observe both dispassionately' (BM 189) are echoed and amplified throughout *Beast and Man*. They form an invaluable corrective, but, as she immediately adds, 'Kinship is not identity.'

Rather than trying to force animals back into automata, I wish only to register my caution as to the extrapolation of morals from animal antecedents, that the substrates of mercy, humility, altruism and goodness are so easily grounded. Not that I deny for a moment that the lives of animals are always instructive, and not just to fabulists. Midgley freely acknowledges that there is not one ingredient X, such as you might find in a detergent or toothpaste, that can either define us or allow a clear separation from animals. Such does not exist. Yet when she correctly notes 'Thought is not a luxury from which we must heroically refrain. It is an essential aspect of life' (BM 182), it is not clear to me that this applies to animals. Nor am I sure that rationality is any more 'natural' than mathematics. Thus when she suggests that rationality has 'two distinct elements . . . cleverness and integration' (BM 262), I suspect that it is only half the story. So too to observe that '[a]pes and other creatures can count a little, but they do not much care to do so. They are not going to arrive at the differential calculus' (BM 226) is perhaps to open the question of whether *any* sort of animal numerosity (which we now know to be very widespread) will lead to mathematics of even the simplest kind, let alone calculus. Again, I suggest not. And what applies to rationality and mathematics would, I suggest, find equal force in the case of language. Midgley is, of course, correct to say that it is one part of our 'large and versatile tool kit' (BM 226), but language as an extension from animal gestures and vocalizations may be a far less straightforward notion than it might at first appear to be. She is quite correct to point out that words 'describe functions of the whole thinking subject' (BM 172), but as she also insists that ' '[c]ognition' cannot be 'translated into circuitry" (BM 171), surely the central problem remains. Language is our vehicle for thought, but only we possess it. The same applies to all the other ingredient Xs, not least morality and science. Only we, I suggest, actually *know* anything at all, but where this gift comes from remains unacknowledged.

CONCLUSIONS

Midgley offers us a series of maps, and so a path to recovery. They don't always overlap, and others have sections missing. That is to be expected; as she says, reality is irritatingly more complex than we might like. As a cartographer, her generosity is to be welcomed. As she says, 'New ideas are new imaginative visions' (SP 24), and so help us to arrive at the centrality of human thought. Interestingly, she refers to the famous dream by the chemist August Kekulé that gave him the insight into the cyclical structure of benzene. Elsewhere (e.g., in W 117 and 122) she dwells on the hidden depths of

Robert Louis Stevenson's celebrated tale *The Strange Case of Dr Jekyll and Mr Hyde*. What perhaps is less well-known is that Stevenson's access to this plot was by dreams in successive scenes.[16]

Nor was this an isolated instance. Stevenson recounts that, whilst he was very far from being engaged in some sort of automatic writing, his 'Little People' arrived in his dreams (or even in broad daylight), complete with scenes and people to populate his next story.[17] Many more examples could be given. What, for example, are we to make of the mathematician Ramanujan? Robert Kanigel explores what Ramanujan (and many of his admirers) saw as '*A gift from Heaven* . . . Mystery, magic and dark, hidden workings inaccessible to ordinary thought; it is these that [his] work invariably conjures up, a sense of reason butting hard up against its limits'.[18] In this absorbing discussion, Kanigel also relates that in his dream time Ramanujan saw scrolls held by the god Narasimha. On these, as Kanigel relates, 'the most complicated mathematics used to unfold before his eyes'.[19] In very different ways, writer and mathematician accessed invisible, but totally real, worlds.

This is an essay about Midgley, not dreaming, but my point is that in tacitly dismissing the transcendental realm so, in my opinion, any naturalistic programme must eventually grind to a halt. I cautiously wonder if this might explain Midgley's obvious enthusiasm and fascination with the concept of Gaia as expounded by James Lovelock. Metaphysically, it has obvious attractions. It reconnects us to our world, gives us a sense of proportion, will provide a sense of perspective, if not humility, and is at least open to taking traditional responses to the world around us as valid. I am less sure, however, that by itself this will suffice. Of course, Midgley is correct when she insists that we need to discard the idea that 'all natural things are valueless . . . merely pretty extras' (M 174) and that we need new ways of thinking. But as should be already obvious, can any naturalistic programme, by itself, deliver the goods?

ACKNOWLEDGEMENTS

My thanks to Jane Heal for her useful and constructive comments, Vivien Brown for heroic typing, and the editors for the original invitation.

NOTES

1. I make no claim to have made an exhaustive tour of Midgley's philosophy, and have confined my reading to *Beast and Man: The Roots of Human Nature* (BM), *Evolution as Religion: Stranger Hopes and Stranger Fears* (EaR), *The Myths We Live By* (M), *Science and Poetry* (SP), *The Solitary Self: Darwin and the Selfish Gene* (SS), and *Wickedness: A Philosophical Essay* (W). For those unfamiliar with Midgley's enterprise, in my opinion

there is no better place to start than with *Beast and Man*, not least because of its lightness of touch and gentle irony. Finally, whilst I do not quote it here, the collection of essays brought together in *Heart & Mind: The Varieties of Moral Experience* has a vividness that we can seek only to emulate.

2. See the chapters by Ian Ground and Raymond Tallis, this volume.

3. M.T. Ghiselin, *The Economy of Nature and the Evolution of Sex* (Oakland: University of California Press, 1974), p. 247.

4. A conclusion that would be warmly endorsed by the Australian philosopher David Stove. See Stove's *Popper and After: Four Modern Irrationalists* (Oxford: Pergamon, 1982).

5. D'Arcy Wentworth Thompson, *On Growth and Form* (Cambridge: Cambridge University Press, 1917).

6. This is the observation that very similar structures evolve independently. The camera-eye of humans and octopus is a well-known example. Many more instances can be found on our website Map of Life (www.mapoflife. com), and some of the implications are discussed in my *Life's Solution: Inevitable Humans in a Lonely Universe* (Cambridge: Cambridge University Press, 2003) and more recently in *The Runes of Evolution: How the Universe became Self-aware* (West Conshohocken: Templeton Foundation Press, 2015).

7. Charles Darwin, *The Descent of Man, and Selection in Relation to Sex*, 2nd ed. (London: John Murray, 1889), p. 113.

8. The term owes to Hannah Arendt, *Eichmann in Jerusalem: A Report on the Banality of Evil* (New York: Viking Press, 1963).

9. 'The case exuded evil like a contagion in the vast oak-panelled courtroom'— a quote from the obituary of the presiding judge, Sir Charles Mantel, published in the *Daily Telegraph* (11 May 2010).

10. Translated by Louise Varese (London: The Catholic Book Club, 1949), p. 42.

11. Johannesburg, (South Africa: A.D. Donker, 1983).

12. Hart, B.L., Hart, L.A. and Pinter-Wollman, N., 'Large brains and cognition: Where do elephants fit in?', *Neuroscience and Behavioral Reviews* 32 (2008): 86–98. Quotation from page 96.

13. Bird, C.D. and N.J. Emery, 'Rooks use stones to raise the water level to reach a floating worm', *Current Biology* 19 (2009): pp. 1410–1414.

14. Taylor, A.H. and Gray, R.D., 'Animal cognition: Aesop's fable flies from fiction to fact', *Current Biology* 19 (2009): R731–R732. Quotation from page R732.

15. Nakagaki, T., 'Smart behaviour of true slime mold in a labyrinth', *Research in Microbiology* 152 (2001): 767–770.

16. See his *Across the Plains, with other Memories and Essays* (London: Chatto & Windus, 1892), chapter 8, 'A Chapter on Dreams'.

17. *Across the Plains*, p. 165. He also referred to them as his 'Brownies'.

18. Robert Kanigel, *The Man Who Knew Infinity: A Life of the Genius Ramanujan* (New York: Scribners, 1991), pp. 280–281, original emphasis.

19. Kanigel, *The Man Who Knew Infinity*, p. 281.

Part V

Women and the World

13 On Being a 'Full-Time Feminist'

Mary Midgley and Feminist Philosophy

Liz McKinnell

Mary Midgley is best known for her work on animals, the environment, ethics and science and is not primarily known as a feminist writer. Yet she has published one book dealing with feminist issues, *Women's Choices*, co-authored with Judith Hughes in 1984, sadly the only one of her books that is out of print.[1] In this work, Hughes and Midgley argue for an approach to gender equality based on cooperation and in some cases, more controversially, on compromise. They reject claims made by some radical feminist thinkers (most notably, Shulasmith Firestone comes in for some flak). Elsewhere, Midgley (1988) argues that we should not be afraid to acknowledge the existence of natural differences between the sexes, and she has been critical of some feminist work following the tradition of Derrida, suggesting that the language is unnecessarily obscure (see Anthony 2014). Remarks of this kind are liable to create discord in an area of study that is often fraught with tension already, but in what follows, I will argue that some central themes of Midgley's thought, both in relation to what she has said about women, and in relation to philosophy more generally, are of great importance to feminist philosophy.

Like many feminist thinkers, Midgley believes that we cannot look at contemporary philosophy as though it has no history, and as though it is not written by human beings who occupy particular roles and places within that history. In response to Ted Honderich's view that philosophy might be better if it were 'like science', which wilfully eschews any historical sensitivity, Midgley maintains that, in order thoroughly to understand the concepts that we are working with, we need to understand the history of how those concepts came about (2005: 68–72). Our ways of thinking did not spring fully-fledged into our minds, but are rather a product of patterns of thought that evolved in, and may still be better suited to, times different from our own. If we ignore that history, we are in danger of inheriting the prejudices of the past and of treating the contingencies of our conceptual schemes as though they were bare ahistorical truths. There is, Midgley maintains, no such thing as a purely 'contemporary' philosophy, and the assumption that we do or should operate with one is liable to lead us astray.

ROUSSEAU AND WOMEN

With this in mind, let us consider Midgley and Hughes's analysis of Rousseau's ideas about the education of women in the *Émile* (WC 41–6). Their question is simple: why would a thinker who is in other respects so radical—calling for a dramatic overhaul of power structures in society, the education of the entire male population, and the importance of challenging arbitrary authority—still maintain that women should be educated for constraint and obedience, in such a way that they will not question what is asked of them? Midgley and Hughes are far from the first people to find this puzzling. Mary Wollstonecraft, for instance, who was otherwise very much impressed by Rousseau's thought on the education of boys, argued that Rousseau's exception for the education of girls was both anomalous and profoundly unjust.

It is Midgley and Hughes's contention that Rousseau's mistake springs from a functionalist account of human nature, derived from his Aristotelian inheritance. Just as Aristotle used the idea of the 'function' of certain groups of people to justify both the constraint of women and the institution of slavery, Rousseau argues that it is women's function that justifies his views on their treatment. Beginning with the idea of the freedom and independence of man, Rousseau then argues that he needs a mate. Woman therefore needs to be educated in the way that will best fit her for this role, learning how to make herself pleasant and helpful to men and how to aid the activities that men engage in outside the home, as well as the necessary skills involved in child-rearing. In Midgley and Hughes's view, this functionalist account will inevitably overlook how people are important in their own right. If we determine someone's good by asking what they are *for*, we will overlook what they need for who they *are*.

INSTRUMENTALISM AND NATURE

It is very much in line with Midgley's broader philosophy to argue that we can say much the same in regard to our treatment of animals and other elements of the natural world. If we begin with an instrumentalist account of their value, we will not properly value them at all. This is more than a mere structural similarity: the tendency to exert dominance over nature and the tendency to oppress women are connected through a historical tendency to associate the feminine with the natural. 'Man' is rational, free and is therefore a creature with moral importance and autonomy, whereas woman and nature serve as resources to be efficiently exploited by those men in the pursuit of their chosen aims and objectives.

Echoing the work of many feminist philosophers of science, Midgley makes these connections explicitly when she talks about the tendency to use the language of sexual conquest as a metaphor for scientific progress and discovery:

> I think you don't . . . need to be a full-time feminist to conclude [that] . . . when a school of thought officially dedicated to clear, literal, unemotive speech, regularly uses a lurid language of sexual pursuit, torture and rape to describe the interaction between scientists and the natural world, trouble is also surfacing about the relations between actual men and women. At such a point, an entry into the index under the heading 'gender insecurity' doesn't seem excessive. (SS 87–88)

It is not unusual to find references to 'peering up nature's skirt'. A famous bronze by the sculptor Louis-Ernest Barrias entitled *La Nature se dévoilant à la Science* ('Nature Unveiling Herself Before Science') depicts a young woman, personifying nature, removing layers of clothing to reveal her naked breasts to the observer in the style of the dance of the seven veils. This is a metaphor for the scientific goal of uncovering truth. To seek to understand nature, according to this way of thinking, is both to control her and to strip her bare for the eyes of discerning scientists. Nature, as feminine, becomes an object in the eyes of an intellectual master. Nature is a resource that is drawn upon for the purposes that another has for her.

Here, as in other places, there is a harmony between Midgley's approach and the views of ecofeminists like Val Plumwood (1993), who explore these historical conceptual associations in an effort to trace the joint roots of the oppression of women and of nature.

WIDENING THE MORAL CIRCLE, BUT WHOSE CIRCLE IS IT?

What is notable about functionalist/instrumentalising accounts, is that they begin their discussion of the function of women (or nature) by looking at what women or nature are to be contrasted with (as we have seen, this is a particular conception of rational man). Here we might start to draw a distinction between the case of women and the case of nature: there are female philosophers, politicians and activists, and women can and do articulate how the world looks from their perspective. Nature, however, remains silent in this respect. To our knowledge, we are the only creatures capable of such discourse.

Is this then a question merely of expanding the old moral circle, such that the concepts that used to be restricted to men can also include women? This would be a typical liberal feminist solution, but I believe this is not sufficient, and that it can be shown that Midgley does not think so either. A central theme of her work is that accounts of the self as an isolated (and in some sense unembodied) agent are inherently flawed. This, again, is something that is often most prominent in her work on environmental ethics:

> The notion of our selves—our minds—as detached observers or colonists, separate from the physical world and therefore from each other, watching and exploiting a lifeless mechanism, has been with us since the dawn of modern science (and of the industrial revolution). Descartes taught us to think of matter essentially as our resource—a jumble of material blindly interacting. Animals and plants were machines and were provided for us to build into more machines. (SP 178)

Midgley's view associates the idea of social isolation with alienation from matter, nature and the body. This account connects to the functionalist account of value, in that human individuality is taken to be the one source of intrinsic value, with everything else being subservient to its aims. Thus, the only beings that enter into moral consideration for their own sakes are those who fit the rather flattering image of the Enlightenment man. It is this image, Midgley contends, that needs to be rethought. A closer look at ourselves will reveal that we do not fit the image very well.

First of all, we are dependent upon one another. We require the labour of others for our health and survival, and the company of others for our well-being. Associating with other people is not a free choice that we can make or reject, contrary to what social contract models sometimes seem to suggest. Furthermore, we are dependent upon other people for new people to come into the world. Secondly, we are not simply dependent upon each other, but on an environment that sustains us.

All of this, of course, is quite compatible with functionalist thinking: we each require certain physical conditions and the labour and company of others, but these are valuable merely to the extent that they serve certain purposes for us. But, importantly for Midgley's thinking, this view unrealistically separates the bodily dependent element of ourselves from the idea of an essentially independent self that is supposed to be what we really *are*. We should, claims Midgley, reject what she refers to as 'Descartes' diamond':

> It is a hard, impenetrable but very precious isolated sentient substance which sits at its console in its windowless tower communicating with other, similarly secluded diamonds by signals run up between towers and relayed to these beings by a perpetual miracle. Real people, by contrast, are embodied beings living in a public world (SP 119)

One might reject this view by adopting a materialist view of the self, according to which we are to be understood as composed of matter, but this, Midgley maintains, is no better—it is simply adopting the other side of the Cartesian distinction:

Materialism and idealism are equally the products of dualism. This is why the unstable notion of the isolated self has not gone away. The ghost still haunts the machine because the machine has not changed thoroughly enough to do without it. (SP 119)

Instead, then, we need to think of ourselves neither as immaterial selves nor as impersonal mechanical matter, but rather as embodied people, who need each other and our world. What are the implications of all of this for the idea of our moral circle and how it relates to women? A simple way of putting this is that the conception of the self on which the old functionalist model is built serves nobody very well, and that inviting women to join it will not fix things. It relies upon a picture of the world in which some beings (subjects, men, or people) count for their own sakes, and others (objects, women, matter, or nature) are valuable insofar as they serve those who matter for their own sakes. The mark of the former group is independent agency, whereas the latter are understood as resources for the use and sustenance of that agency. However, there is a further point to be made here. The reason that the model itself has survived for as long as it has is partly to do with the way that it has excluded women. I will elaborate on this in the next section.

WOMEN AS A THREAT TO THE ISOLATED SELF

Let us return to Rousseau. As we have seen, Hughes and Midgley think that Rousseau excludes women from the kind of education that he finds appropriate for men because their function is seen as being instrumental to the good of men. However, this cannot be our complete answer: why would women in particular face this kind of exclusion? Why would it not be applied, for example, to men from certain social classes? Where Rousseau makes this exclusion for women, he is unusually (for his time) inclusive of other groups that are, typically, marginalised or oppressed.

I believe that we might begin to find an answer to this question by looking at Rousseau's account of the state of nature in his *Discourse on the Origin of Inequality among Men*, written in 1754. We need to move carefully here, since Rousseau's 'natural man' is distinct from his conception of man in civil society. Nonetheless, part of the point of the programme of education outlined in the *Émile* is to develop certain natural traits and capacities of the child that are—according to his account—typically lost during his initiation into civil society.

Rousseau's image of man in the state of nature is familiar: natural man has very few needs and desires beyond what he requires for his survival. He does not seek the company of others, and lives a simple, solitary, and independent life. We might find a number of elements of this account implausible: wouldn't this natural man become lonely? What if he fell ill? Rousseau maintains that the loneliness we tend to experience is a product of our socialisation, and not something that natural man would experience. Similarly, natural man will rarely fall ill: it is the habits that we develop in society that make us ill, such as poor diet, lack of exercise, or over-indulgence in food or drink. Natural man is free from such vices, and is therefore not dependent on the care of others, as we often are.

Rousseau faces a further question: how, in this environment, are we to explain how natural man comes to be born and survive infancy? At this stage, there can be no such thing as a family or a community that can serve this purpose. Here is his response:

> Males and females united fortuitously according to encounters, opportunities and desires, they required no speech to express the things they had to say to each other, and they separated with the same ease. The mother nursed her children at first to satisfy her own needs, then when habit had made them dear to her, she fed them to satisfy their needs; as soon as they had the strength to find their own food, they did not hesitate to leave their mother herself; and as there was virtually no way of finding one another again once they had lost sight of each other, they were soon at the stage of not even recognizing one another. (1984/1755: 92)

Rousseau can (perhaps) maintain that natural man is solitary, but he is unable to say the same thing about natural children and at least some natural women. In order to explain the continued survival of the human race, he needs to posit a sustained relationship between mother and child. There is a great effort to make this relationship as minimal as possible. As soon as the child ceases to depend upon the mother for survival, he wanders into the wilderness on his own, and the parental bond is broken. But even this minimal admission threatens the idea that people in their natural state are solitary and independent. Women who have children will not be solitary for substantial periods of time, and all people will be dependent on a woman at some stage in their lives.

Here, the woman becomes an imperfect idea of the natural man at the heart of Rousseau's theory: she represents dependence, communal living, and weakness, since Rousseau regards dependence as incompatible with strength. As he says in response to Hobbes:

> But two conflicting suppositions are here being made about man in the state of nature: that he is robust and that he is dependent. Man is weak when he is dependent, and is set free before he is robust. (1984/1755: 99)

This understanding of Rousseau's view is supported by the fact that he describes sociability and dependence on others as 'effeminate':

> The horse, the cat, the bull, and even the ass are for the most part larger and all have a more robust constitution, more vigour, more strength

and more spirit in the forest than under our roofs; they lose half those advantages on becoming domesticated, and one might say that all our efforts to care for and feed these animals have only succeeded in making them degenerate. The same is true even of man himself; in becoming sociable and a slave, he grows feeble, timid, servile; and his soft and effeminate way of life completes the enervation both of his strength and his courage. (1984/1755: 86)

It seems plausible to suggest that this account of human nature, according to which our strength and independence is threatened by dependence on women, and according to which women are not fully solitary, is partially responsible for the view that the purpose of women's education should be to make them good helpmates for men, since, firstly, unlike men, they were never fully able to participate in unconstrained solitude, and, secondly, they represented a stage in man's life when he was more dependent than the ideal upon which Rousseau's social and political thought is built.

'THE OTHER', AND WHAT WE WOULD RATHER NOT BE

The aspects of humanity that Rousseau associates with weakness or effeminacy are aspects of all of us, male and female. Perhaps Rousseau concedes this up to a point, since he suggests that all of the innovations and developments that human beings are capable of are the products of communal living. Nonetheless, this way of living is in itself for Rousseau a corrupt state, far removed from the initial state of innocence in which men alone could fully partake. Woman is, as is frequently the case, associated with man's fallen state, and in her essential nature cannot participate in the ideal of humanity.

This seems an unhelpful way to proceed, not just because it denigrates women, but also because it mischaracterises men. If we are mutually dependent and vulnerable, we had better find a way of living with this fact without constructing fantasies of absolute freedom. Such fantasies, though, are bewitching things to maintain, and if they can be clung to by lumping all of the less desirable elements of ourselves onto one portion of the human race, then it might be difficult to persuade the other portion to let go of them. This has proved to be the case with the myth of the solitary self, which has persisted in many areas of philosophy, society and politics, despite the fact that even those who denied the existence of society were unable to deny the family.

In regard to this analysis, several different schools of thought within feminist philosophy have emerged. Shulasmith Firestone, one of the targets of Midgley's most vociferous criticism in *Women's Voices*, identifies the oppression of women as founded in biological differences between women and men (Firestone 1971). For her, overcoming the oppression must involve a harnessing of nature itself, through the use of reproductive technology, in order to render natural difference socially insignificant. The ultimate aim would be a technologized society that allowed individuals to be completely autonomous and independent, without any of the constraints imposed upon them by their sexual bodies, reproduction, or the family. In contrast, many prevailing liberal views regard the oppression of women as founded in mere social convention. Biological and reproductive differences are only significant insofar as social attitudes make them so, and such differences are used as false excuses to exclude women from the realm of the solitary independent self.

For Midgley, as for some ecofeminists, neither side of this argument is in the right, since the concepts that each are working with all operate within the same problematic conceptual structure. This structure regards promotion to the realm of the independent self as the significant move to women's emancipation. On Firestone's view, the opposing realm of nature is an enemy to be overcome, and from the liberal perspective, it is mere irrelevant background, which should have no impact upon our social lives, or is perhaps a construction to be dismissed. In both cases, our material, vulnerable and mutually dependent being, especially as it relates to gender, is something to be rejected.

The motivating force behind this notion is the idea that biology and materiality are opposed to human freedom, as is the notion that we are dependent upon each other and upon a planet that sustains us. In fact, it is this very materiality and mutual dependence that allows us to function as human agents. Our materiality *does* limit the possibilities for action, but at the same time it is the enabling condition for our being able to act at all. One way of putting this is that in our free activity, we are *patients* as much as we are *agents*. As Soran Reader puts it, in a brilliant exploration of this theme, 'an ability to act is also a liability to suffer, so that to be able to lift objects is to be liable to be confined by walls' (2007: 589). Acknowledging our materiality and our dependence is not necessarily a threat to our freedom, but it may end up looking like such a threat if we behave as though there is a simple dichotomy between the independent self and the 'dead matter' that surrounds us, and as though at any time we can be only one or the other.

Thus a satisfactory version of feminism must be attentive not only to what constrains and harms women, but also to the views of the world, and of humanity in general, that structure these constraints and harms. We should not then move too quickly towards assuming that simply overcoming the woman-nature association is the right way forward, since the escape from nature would (as it stands) involve entering a realm in which nature is viewed as either a threat, or as something to be conquered. This, as Midgley has frequently observed, is a picture of humanity that does a grave disservice both to ourselves and to our planet.

MIDGLEY AS A 'FULL-TIME FEMINIST'

Earlier, I noted that Midgley holds that one need not be a 'full-time feminist' to notice that something has gone badly wrong in gender relations if the language of sexual violence and conquest is being employed to describe the relationship between scientists and the natural world. But what is a full-time feminist, in the context of philosophy, and would Midgley qualify?

I would contend that the full-time feminist need not write exclusively about questions of gender, and that this might not even be a central focus of their work. Rather, they need to be dedicated to identifying and nullifying gendered biases in their thought and in the thought of others, and to resist the notion that such concerns are irrelevant from a serious philosophical standpoint. On this count, as we have seen, Midgley undoubtedly qualifies. She demonstrates that even (and perhaps especially) in realms where we find explicit professions of 'neutrality' and 'objectivity', the standpoint being adopted can be implicitly gendered.

This highlights the need for the practitioners of philosophy themselves to speak from—or at the least listen to—a diverse range of perspectives. If all philosophers are men, then an unquestioned set of masculine norms may come to be regarded as timeless eternal truths, even where such norms are a bad reflection even of male experience. Once we turn away from Rousseau's privileging of the solitary, invulnerable, masculine self, this will have very concrete applications both in philosophy and beyond. For example, there is a lot of discussion about how to 'balance' academic work with personal and family life, as though these are two competing commitments: it might be argued that this thought (and the unnecessary reality that it reflects) is in part a product of the notion that we are, at heart, something along the lines of 'Descartes' diamond'. But a thinker is not a being who thinks in isolation: they think as part of a history, a community and (very often) a family. A discipline that took account of these facts would not only produce happier philosophers, but also produce better ones.

NOTE

1. References to Midgley's writings in the text are to *Science and Poetry* (SP), *Science as Salvation* (SS), *The Owl of Minerva* (OM), and, with Judith Hughes, *Women's Choices* (WC).

REFERENCES

Anthony, Andrew, 2014, 'Mary Midgley: A late stand for a philosopher with soul', *The Guardian*, [online] (23 March 2014) Available at: http://www.theguardian.com/books/2014/mar/23/mary-midgley-philosopher-soul-human-consciousness [Accessed 17 December 2014].

Firestone, Shulasmith, *The Dialectic of Sex: The Case for Feminist Revolution* (London: Jonathan Cape, 1971).

Midgley, Mary and Judith Hughes, *Women's Choices: Philosophical Problems Facing Feminism* (London: George Weidenfeld and Nicholson, 1984).

Midgley, Mary, 'On Not being Afraid of Natural Sex Differences', in Morwenna Griffiths and Margaret Whitford (eds.), *Feminist Perspectives in Philosophy* (Bloomington: Indiana University Press, 1988), 29–41.

Midgley, Mary, *Science and Poetry* (London: Routledge, 2001).

Midgley, Mary, *The Owl of Minerva: A Memoir* (London: Routledge, 2005).

Midgley, Mary, *Science as Salvation* (London: Routledge, 2013).

Reader, Soran, 'The other side of agency', *Philosophy* 82 (2007): 579–604.

Plumwood Val, *Feminism and the Mastery of Nature* (London: Routledge, 1993).

Rousseau, Jean Jacques, *Émile* [1762], trans. Barbara Foxley (London: Everyman, 1969).

Rousseau, Jean-Jacques, *A Discourse on Inequality* [1755], trans. Maurice Cranston (London: Penguin, 1984).

14 'Slipping Out Over the Wall'
Midgley, Anscombe, Foot and Murdoch

Benjamin J. B. Lipscomb

I first entered this jungle . . . by slipping out over the wall of the tiny arid garden cultivated at that time under the name of British Moral Philosophy. (Midgley 1979: xxxiv)

A GENERATION AND A SCHOOL

Mary Midgley, Elizabeth Anscombe, Philippa Foot, and Iris Murdoch were arguably the first generation of women to make careers in philosophy—if by a 'generation' we mean, not a smattering of isolated individuals, but an identifiable cohort with commonalities in experience and outlook. More than that: they make a school of sorts. They met as undergraduates at Oxford, where they overlapped significantly (three of them at Somerville College) and thus shared a distinctive experience of Oxford in wartime—an experience Midgley credits with pushing at least some of them into philosophy.[1] They remained in touch, to varying degrees, for the rest of their lives. Moreover, all of them devoted significant attention to moral philosophy, and their work in moral philosophy bears the stamp of their common background and shared conversation. Since Midgley noted these connections in her 2005 memoir, *The Owl of Minerva*, it has become common to mention all or some of these women together when remarking on the life of any of them.[2]

Midgley's work, though, has not had the same impact in professional philosophical circles as that of her university friends—though she is arguably better known *outside* the academy than Anscombe or Foot (who are the best known *within*). And most scholars who work closely on Anscombe, Foot, or Murdoch have paid little attention to Midgley. In Roger Teichmann's book on Anscombe's philosophy, Foot and Murdoch appear in the index, but Midgley does not. Midgley is likewise unmentioned in John Hacker-Wright's recent study of Foot's moral thought.[3]

A number of factors have converged to keep Midgley's work from being discussed alongside that of her friends. There is, first, the unusual shape of her career. Anscombe, Foot, and Murdoch had all taken posts (and all at Oxford) by the end of 1948, while Midgley did not begin lecturing at (less prestigious) Newcastle until the mid-1960s. By that time, Anscombe and Foot were routinely accepting guest appointments at top American departments, and Murdoch had quit Oxford University altogether. Or again, consider their publication histories: by the mid-1960s, Anscombe had brought out most of the work for which she is famous, Foot had established herself as the leading critic of R. M. Hare's then-dominant meta-ethical theory, and Murdoch was turning her attention away from philosophy and more exclusively to fiction; but the first of Midgley's more than a dozen books was still over a decade away. It is easy, then, to overlook the generational tie between Midgley and her friends.

The character of Midgley's work has likewise kept it from being discussed alongside Anscombe's, Foot's, and Murdoch's. As the epigraph to this essay attests, Midgley is a deliberately multidisciplinary thinker. A classicist by training, she began in her thirties to read extensively in the emerging field of ethology, even as she pursued side interests in literary criticism, intellectual history, politics, and more. She became convinced that moral philosophers must *relate* various bodies of knowledge to one another if they are to achieve an adequate understanding of human life, human motivation, and (thereby) human success or failure. There was distinguished precedent for this kind of work—and Midgley knew it. For this is, very roughly, how Aristotle approaches ethics—as a biologist studying an animal of particularly absorbing interest, exploring not only how this animal behaves and why, but also what challenges are set before this animal by its nature. But it had become extremely uncommon by the mid-twentieth century. Relatedly, Midgley has always written for an audience broader than any single disciplinary guild. 'Because so many disciplines border [my] topic,' she writes, 'it must necessarily be discussed in plain language' (1979: xxxv).'

Anscombe, Foot, and Murdoch likewise took combined degrees (classics and philosophy, or philosophy, politics, and economics), and they draw on their multidisciplinary preparation in their work. But Anscombe and Foot wrote chiefly for the guild, in its venues, and more-or-less following its conventions, while Murdoch eventually abandoned the guild with a conflicted sense that her own boundary-crossing work was not 'real philosophy'. For years, professional philosophers mostly seconded Murdoch's self-assessment. They persist in this assessment of Midgley, and thus do not seek to relate her work to that of her friends—when they are even acquainted with it.

The philosophical interest of Midgley's work is more evident, though, when one sets it alongside her friends', because her work carries forward a project implicit in their efforts. Her friends' work was chiefly critical—consider Anscombe's 'Modern Moral Philosophy', Foot's 'Moral Beliefs' and 'Morality as a System of Hypothetical Imperatives', Murdoch's 'The Idea of Perfection' and 'The Sovereignty of Good Over Other Concepts'. These justly celebrated essays are attacks on a regnant way of conceiving moral judgment and the moral life; at most, they gesture toward what might take its place. This is understandable, considering that the views they shared were minority views, ones unlikely to receive a hearing if dominant and opposing views were not first attacked. It was also the predictable result of working within the genre of the professional journal article, which is best suited to targeted attacks or incremental refinements, not the elaboration of large, visionary proposals.

Anscombe, Foot, and Murdoch criticized their male contemporaries for their view about 'facts and values'—for supposing that moral judgment need not be (or could not be) grounded in facts about human nature and human needs. Murdoch (especially) and Anscombe (to a lesser extent) worked to diagnose this view, to trace back its sources and their hold on the collective imagination of their contemporaries. Foot, taking inspiration from Anscombe, highlighted the limitations of the theories of language and judgment in which this view was embedded. All three recommended a retrieval of the ancient tradition of reflection on the virtues: the qualities of character human beings need in order to thrive (or to 'flourish', as Anscombe put it) in community with other human beings, working together at typically human pursuits. But this work was, at most, promissory. As Anscombe wrote in 1958, 'it is not profitable for us at present to do moral philosophy' (1981: 26).

Midgley, then—writing from the margins of the discipline—was the first to present a positive proposal for a naturalistic ethics of the kind recommended but not developed by Anscombe, Foot, and Murdoch.[4] Indeed, she was the only one who could, as she was the only one who knew enough biology (the relevance of which was implied in her friends' promissory statements) and enough moral philosophy to try to relate the two fields. In so doing, she anticipated ideas Foot would come to slowly over the ensuing two decades, but would never develop with the thoroughness that Midgley did.

In this chapter, I do two things: first, trace the development of Midgley's thought from her undiscussed and even unknown popular works of the 1950s through the publication of her first book, *Beast and Man*, in 1978; and second, explore how *Beast and Man* and the writings that led up to it both draw on and press beyond the work of Midgley's friends. In each case, my aim is to help readers to a truer appreciation of the connections between Midgley and her friends—whether by filling in the gap that makes it hard to recognize their careers as intertwined or by helping readers interested in Murdoch or Anscombe or Foot perceive how Midgley's project is related to theirs.

MIDGLEY'S EARLY CAREER

One of the things most frequently remarked about Midgley's career is how late it began: that she raised her three sons before returning to philosophy, and began writing only in her 50s. These are important half-truths.

Mary Scrutton and Geoffrey Midgley were engaged in the summer of 1950, a year into their first university appointments—she at Reading, he at Newcastle.[5] A generation-long expansion in British post-secondary education had begun—there were 'jobs for old rope'[6]—and the chair of philosophy at each university anticipated work for two Midgleys.[7] They decided together on Newcastle, and on her taking a hiatus from teaching; they wanted children and she wanted to be mostly at home while the children were small. But the Newcastle department continued to flourish and expand, and in the 1964–1965 academic year, as her eldest headed off to boarding school, Karl Britton asked Midgley if she would join the staff part-time. She was thus back in a university setting at age forty-five. Not young, but not with her children entirely out of the house.

Meanwhile, she had established herself as a minor public intellectual and was doing a great deal of writing, mostly under her maiden name. She abandoned, early on, a doctoral thesis on Plotinus, and invested herself instead in broadcast talks, book reviews, and commentary. Although it was not published in disciplinary journals, some of this writing was philosophical, and anticipated themes of her mature work. It would have been surprising if Midgley or anyone in her position—married to a lecturer in philosophy, going in to lunch regularly with him and his colleagues, and keeping up with Anscombe, Foot, and (especially) Murdoch—did not continue reflecting on the discipline. But Midgley was also, deliberately or not, beginning to work out an array of ideas that would coalesce in *Beast and Man*.

Midgley wrote mainly for the BBC's highbrow Third Programme and for a pair of widely read periodicals likewise aimed at an educated public: *The Twentieth Century* and *The New Statesman* and *Nation*. The most philosophical of these early writings are concentrated in the early to mid-1950s, in the half-decade (roughly) after she stopped teaching and before she began to engage significantly with studies of animal behavior[8] (They were also written when she had one or at most two children). Two related clusters of themes emerge from them. One is meta-philosophical, concerning the appropriate topics and techniques of philosophical reflection. The other concerns the several-sidedness and diversity of human nature.

Both surface in an early piece on sexual difference. Midgley is the only one of her university friends to publish about sex and gender,[9] though these publications are largely unknown. (Her co-authored 1982 book *Women's Choices* is, she notes, 'the only one of my books that is not in print' (2005: 195)). For the seventy-fifth anniversary issue of *The Twentieth Century*, Midgley was commissioned to review fifteen essays on women's rights that had appeared in the journal (then called *The Nineteenth Century*) between 1877 and 1927. While working on this commission, she also composed a talk for the BBC Home Service as part of a series titled 'A Letter to Posterity'.[10]

In her letter, (addressed disarmingly to 'My dear Posterity . . .'), Midgley suggested that institutional discrimination, of the sort defended and attacked in the old essays on women's rights, was effectively finished. 'I'm not saying that there is no injustice', she wrote. 'But . . . it is not the profound difference in status that feels like a difference in species' (1952: 510). In light of this, Midgley asked, what ought to be expected of women now that they have been 'admitted to a thousand mysteries from classical scholarship to engineering'? For, she wrote, women taken as a group 'still have their own peculiarities. They still defeat Plato and those other feminists who would like to think of them simply as men who have accidentally come out the wrong shape.'[11]

Midgley's answer to her own question would be controversial today, more than it was in 1952. She suggested that women are more typically gifted at integrative thought—at bringing disparate types of consideration together and relating them—than at specialization. 'Women by nature and habit are not specialists,' she wrote. 'They are more conscious of the complexity of their subject and less powerful at abstracting.'[12] She acknowledged a personal, even confessional element, to her sense of these differences, insisting how much she valued 'thorough and methodical scholarship. . . .' But it was not her destiny: 'I treat it with that profound and remorseful veneration that all sinners feel for the virtue after which they perpetually struggle in vain.'

Nevertheless, she contended, scholarliness of this sort was not the only intellectual virtue, or even supreme above others. 'Human thinking', she wrote, 'has two movements. There is the abstracting, critical process, which has always been recognised as thinking: and there is another process of imaginative comprehension, of comparing and balancing. . . .' There was already implicit, here and in other writings from the 1950s, a manifesto for the kind of philosophy she would begin to produce in the 1970s: a philosophy precisely of 'imaginative comprehension', of criticizing too-tidy conceptions of human nature and recommending more complex and capacious ones, drawing on multiple disciplines, 'comparing and balancing'.

Midgley was interested in men and women, and in the several tasks of thought, but she was interested also more generally in the diversity and several-sidedness of human nature, and in framing our thinking in *acknowledgement* of this diversity and several-sidedness. Apart from a few early reviews (of H. J. Paton's *In Defense of Reason*, for instance), everything she wrote in the 1950s about other philosophers was about her philosophical heroes, thinkers of past centuries whose thought was marked by this acknowledgement.[13]

An abortive piece—a rejected broadcast talk from 1954—singles out Aristotle for praise. Midgley sketches in her memoir the story surrounding this script. Her usual producer, Russian expatriate Niouta Kallin, rejected it—perhaps the only script of Midgley's she ever rejected[14]—on the still-more-unusual grounds of rejecting its thesis. The thesis was that not only one's sex but also the shape of one's household—whether one had a spouse and/or children—could and often did have consequences for one's thought. Midgley had been thinking about this since around the time she finished her 'Letter to Posterity'. In a July 1952 letter to Kallin, she writes,

'I have an idea . . . nearly formed; i.e. I keep elaborating it when I do the potatoes . . . It is roughly speaking about the element of projection in personal relations and history; how dons inevitably see their subjects as dons, and how much this matters.'[15]

When the script arrived in 1954, it was more pointed than that. It began, 'Practically all the great European philosophers have been bachelors', and after demonstrating this with two lists of famous ancient and early modern figures ('I do not cram the groaning scale with monks and friars'), went on to speculate on the difference this might have made, attending particularly to the differences between Plato (unmarried) and Aristotle (married).[16] Aristotle, she argued, showed a tendency toward 'married opinions', such as that humans are a species 'that goes in pairs, not only for procreation, but for all the business of life'. Moreover, Aristotle was alert to the many forms that human life and human excellence take: men and women; scholars, politicians, and tradespeople. Yes, he ranks men's pursuits above women's, and scholars' above all others: 'But he has grasped the point that natures can *differ* . . . that there were other lives and other virtues besides those of the scholar; that perhaps it did really take all sorts to make a world.' Plato, by contrast, 'always kept the irritable sensibility of the adolescent in resisting the claims of temperaments alien to his own.' Marriage, she argued—a 'willing acceptance of the genuinely and lastingly strange'—has the potential to shake one out of this, to awaken one to the diversity and several-sidedness of life.

These notes are sounded once more in her most straightforwardly philosophical essay of the 1950s, an essay on a thinker who would figure very prominently in the argument of *Beast and Man*: eighteenth-century Anglican bishop Joseph Butler. Butler's 'reverence', Midgley wrote, 'is not only for God', but also 'for the infinitely rich and complex personality of man, for that wealth of powers and impulses, which admits indeed of harmony and direction, but not of the mutilation prescribed by narrower moral systems, and by those professing Happiness as much as any other.' There is an extra element in these remarks that is worth drawing out, because of its significance in Midgley's mature moral philosophy: that the fundamental tasks of moral inquiry and of the moral life are, in each case, *integrative*. The task of inquiry is to understand our nature in its full complexity, drawing on all necessary resources. It is to survey honestly the several sides of our nature, turning from none of them in disgust, but working out how far they permit 'harmony and direction' (1952: 61). The task of living is to carry out such harmonization.

Midgley was falling farther and farther out of step with the philosophical mainstream of her time and place. The premier philosophical community in England—arguably in the whole world—was at Oxford, where her friends remained.[17] And the dominant voice in Oxford in the mid-1950s belonged to J. L. Austin, White's Professor of Moral Philosophy, whose approach to philosophy was sharply opposed to the one she was developing.

The opposition was not, of course, total. Austin's thought bore resemblances to the thought of the later Wittgenstein, and thus to the thought of Midgley and her friends. Because of Elizabeth Anscombe's close connection with Wittgenstein, Midgley, Foot, and Murdoch all had early access to his manuscripts and, what was better, uncounted opportunities for conversation with Anscombe, who opened up the manuscripts and their meaning to her friends. Wittgenstein's late work showed, as Midgley later put it, 'how our thought about language has to be rooted in the complexities of real life, not imposed on it from outside' (2005: 159). Midgley resonated with this approach as soon as she apprehended it. As I have shown, she insisted from her earliest publications on the importance of acknowledging complexity, of not being *reductive*. It is part of what she took from Anscombe, who rejected all 'handy simplifications'. It is naturally difficult to say whether or to what extent Midgley owed her emerging convictions to Aristotle, to Butler, to Anscombe and the later Wittgenstein, or to any other source.

The later Wittgenstein's interests in the complexities of ordinary language, in breaking down too-tidy systems, and in considering language as *behavior*—Austin shared all of these. Austin's difference lay in his personality, in the atmosphere he cultivated around him, and in his method. Urbane, witty, but also formal and used to deference, Austin was revered by most Oxford philosophers (if they did not, like Anscombe, despise him). Philippa Foot called him 'the cleverest thing on two legs'.[18] They related to him, as Geoffrey Warnock put it, as if they were schoolboys and he was their headmaster. Warnock's is not the only testimony of this kind.

Austin describes his method in his famous article, 'A Plea for Excuses'. It had roots both in the patient textual scholarship he had practiced as an undergraduate and as a young tutor in classics, and in his wartime experiences sifting intelligence. Working collaboratively with his junior colleagues (whom he convened every Saturday morning when the university was in session) he tried to get as clear as possible about the subtle differences among clusters of topically related words—'hounding down the minutiae', as he put it. Austin was determined to make progress in philosophy, and surveying the wreckage of philosophical history—all the grand systems constructed and abandoned—he renounced system-building. Or, at any rate, he determined that the only way to build was extremely slowly, piece by piece, scrutinizing our words and through them our concepts. Under his influence, a whole generation of Oxford philosophers came to share his impatience with generalization and synthesis, his intellectual aesthetic of clarity and cleanliness. 'Words are our tools,' he wrote, 'and . . . we should use clean tools' (1961: 129). This outlook drove Murdoch and Isaiah Berlin, who revered Austin, out of philosophy altogether, sure that their own best work did not count.

Midgley was impressed with Austin, too, but was more like Berlin and Murdoch than like the participants in Austin's 'Kindergarten'. What she aspired and felt herself best equipped to do—'imaginative comprehension', trying to fit together disparate bodies of knowledge, and thereby to understand the complexity of our nature—was not regarded as real philosophy by her contemporaries. Even if she had been keeping up with the journals—and as her second, and then her third son was born, she did so less and less—the kind of work that interested her had little standing among her peers.

Midgley published little between 1957 and 1972. She was fully occupied with her third child, and with her return to the classroom. She was also disillusioned. One of her last significant publications before this quiet period was a reflection on her experiences in Oxford, Reading, and Newcastle. Her topic was large atmospheric differences between Oxford and these two 'Redbrick' universities, but her comments had special application to the state of philosophy in the 1950s. What struck her on moving to Reading, she wrote, 'was that it was possible to talk freely. Dons openly admitted that they were interested in subjects other than their own.' Moreover, '[t]he state of being unable to say or write anything for fear one might get it slightly wrong was not common, and where it existed, it was not held in honour. I cannot express how much I liked this' (1956: 160).

Midgley contrasted this with the Oxford atmosphere, in which each scholar

> forms part of a . . . system of mincing machines through which any new work [is] put . . . [and] as Oxford is so sociable, there is no chance for a prospective author of forgetting for a moment how the mincing machines work. Before he can develop an idea, he has begun to think of answers to the criticisms that will be made of it. He would be a man of iron [who] did not spend more time working out what will tell in argument than deciding what he really thinks. (1956:160–1)

Among the bad effects of this way of carrying on, she wrote, is that it 'narrows the subjects studied in an incredible manner.' Her next remark is perhaps the most telling, in terms of the gap she felt between herself and the guild. 'It is so difficult', she wrote, 'to insist that a thing is interesting when one's colleagues are bored with it; so embarrassing to be caught paying attention to what is supposed to be left for the amateurs.' Allowing herself to speak directly about philosophy for a bit, she noted how her contemporaries tended to neglect or misrepresent Aristotle—in particular, his richly integrated treatment of ethics and biology. Why, 'he might ask them, do they suppose he took the trouble to write about four times as much on other subjects as on what they call philosophy?' It 'makes one scream', she wrote (1956:161–2).

So thoroughly exasperated, and with her third son on the way, Midgley absented herself from the professional conversation and turned to other things. She reviewed children's books, wrote a never-to-be-published work of science fiction, and read and read in the field of animal behavior, avidly comparing the field observations and concepts of Lorenz, Tinbergen, Goodall, and others with the 'animal behaviour going on all around me, upstairs, in the garden and on the hearthrug' (2005: 189). She had no clear sense yet of where any of it might lead.

Midgley did, however, keep appreciatively reading her friends, whose path-breaking articles were just beginning to appear. These articles culminated conversations the four of them had started back in the late 1940s. They attacked the anti-naturalist orthodoxy of the time and thereby both cleared space and suggested a direction for Midgley's later work. The key points, for Midgley's purposes, were these:

1. There is no need to accept an anti-naturalist account of moral language and moral judgment. Indeed, important features of moral thought and discourse are mystified if one does not understand them as bearing an essential, 'internal relation' to human needs. (Foot, 'Moral Beliefs')
2. Aristotle showed us, in outline, how to construe this relation. Our good is bound up with the traits and circumstances creatures like us need in order to flourish in a characteristically human life. (Anscombe, 'Modern Moral Philosophy')
3. These points hold even if we limit our investigation to highly abstract evaluative words/concepts like 'good', but they hold more manifestly if we consider the richer body of words/concepts people use in judgments of character. It is instructive at multiple levels to rehabilitate the Aristotelian tradition of reflection on character. (Anscombe and Foot)
4. There can be in any case no neutral analysis of moral language and moral judgment. In foregrounding one or another set of words/concepts, one is inevitably offering a picture of moral life and the conditions for its success or failure. A crucial task for moral philosophers is to attend sensitively to their own and others' controlling images and metaphors. (Murdoch, 'Metaphysics and Ethics' *et passim*)

A few years after joining the department at Newcastle, Midgley's colleague David Russell urged her to offer a course on animal behavior and ethics through the university's adult-education program. Russell shared Midgley's interest in ethology and her sense that a comparative approach, relating human beings to various other animals, was of tremendous value for understanding human nature.[19]

It was the pivot of her career. In teaching these students, of varying ages and backgrounds, all of who were enrolled simply because they were interested in the topic, Midgley began to work out a framework for talking about human nature and human motivation, the framework she had sought since at least 1951. Writing to Niouta Kallin that fall, one year into her new life in Newcastle and six months pregnant with her first son, she had identified her great theme: 'the many-sidedness of human nature, and the inadequacy of *all* current official ways of regarding it'.[20] Now, in the space of a few years, she brought out her first scholarly articles, culminating in 'The Concept of Beastliness' in 1973). The piece caught the attention of Max Black at Cornell University and led to an invitation, first, to spend some time at Cornell, and then, to expand her reflections on ethology and ethics into a book.[21]

EXCURSUS: FOOT AND THE 'TIGHT CORNER'

Meanwhile, Foot had fallen into difficulties, difficulties we need to understand in order to understand the special interest and timeliness of Midgley's mature work. Foot puzzled, throughout her career, over what to say about the problem she called 'the tight corner'.[22] Here is the form the problem took for her in the 1950s and 1960s. Suppose the argument of 'Moral Beliefs' is correct, and there is an essential, internal (i.e., conceptual) connection between moral thought and discourse, on the one hand, and human benefit and harm, on the other. There is, in other words, no understanding the latter without invoking the former. Nevertheless, it looks as if, on some occasions, the characteristic behaviors of virtuous people work against them, putting them in harm's way. A first responder jumping down beside a train track to rescue a man who has fallen, a prosecutor in a corrupt regime, arraigning a drug lord or a compromised public official: these people risk death, risk leaving their families bereft.

In 'Moral Beliefs', Foot appealed to the *general* tendency of virtues like courage and justice to benefit their possessors, and to the psychological difficulty of being only selectively just or brave:

> It is perfectly true that if a man is just it follows that he will be prepared, in the event of very evil circumstances, even to face death rather than to act unjustly. . . . For him it turns out that his justice brings disaster on him, and yet like anyone else he had good reason to be a just and not an unjust man. (2002: 129)

But Foot became dissatisfied with this response after 1960. Might there not be whole life contexts—like Nazi-occupied Europe, which haunted her thought—in which virtue did not pay, even in general? And while it might be psychologically difficult to be selectively virtuous, would it not be more rational, if one could somehow manage it? Or suppose there was someone who simply was not drawn to the standards of virtue. Could that person really be shown to be making a mistake? In 'Moral Beliefs', Foot had asserted, in continuity with the Aristotelian tradition, that reason commended virtue to everyone. This had seemed to her a bulwark against the anti-naturalism of most of her contemporaries, who denied any necessary connection between moral thought and utterance, on the one hand, and human nature and needs, on the other. As Murdoch especially emphasized, the anti-naturalists who dominated British moral philosophy were similar in substance, if not in style, to Jean-Paul Sartre, who understood moral judgments as purely voluntary acts of self-definition. Foot had been determined to confute this view and defend the traditional alternative: that in practicing virtue, we are obeying reason.

By 1972, though, when she published 'Morality as a System of Hypothetical Imperatives', Foot had concluded that her earlier view was propaganda, and might even provoke cynicism 'It is often felt,' she wrote, 'that there is an element of deception in the official line about morality' (2002: 167). More effective, perhaps—and in any case, more soberly true—to deny that anything external to our own formed temperaments bids us to practice virtue, and to think of ourselves instead like the citizens of besieged Leningrad, who could not know if they would prosper by standing together, but who were determined to stand together anyway.

There was something ironic about this turn in Foot's thought. It was not a total rejection of her earlier work, insofar she stood by her technical criticisms of anti-naturalist theories of moral language. But she seemed to have come around to the very view she (and her friends) had hoped to disprove: that ethical commitments are purely voluntary acts of self-definition. Unhappy with her own conclusion, but seeing no way around it, Foot turned for some years away from more general questions in moral philosophy and toward various applied topics.

Foot's conclusion rests, notice, on an appealing but controversial notion of rationality: that what is rational for a person to do is whatever serves his or her private interests, and even his or her private *conception* of those interests. The characteristically Aristotelian idea of our species-nature and the interests of our kind, highlighted by Anscombe in 'Modern Moral Philosophy' and elsewhere, had dropped away.

THE PROJECT OF BEAST AND MAN

Beast and Man is a large book, and as many-sided as the account of human nature it contains. But this is in part an accident of its publication history.[23] After she had completed a draft, Cornell University Press asked Midgley to address E. O. Wilson's new (and controversial) work, *Sociobiology*. Then it sent the resulting manuscript for comment to experts in each of the several disciplines on which Midgley drew: in philosophy, yes, but also in the natural and social sciences. The book grew and grew, until—like Plato has Socrates say of Glaucus the sea god—it became difficult to discern its original shape. But it is discernible if we look closely and attend to Midgley's own framing remarks.

The book begins with a Murdochian appeal to think more carefully about the likeness and unlikenesses between humans and other animals, and to scrutinize the language in which we express these likenesses and unlikenesses. The Western tradition has often been fearful of or disgusted at our animality. But given that 'We are not just rather like animals; we *are* animals' (1979: xxxiii), this is apt to leave us with a misleading and unhelpful sense of ourselves. To think about our lives is to think about our nature, and this cannot be understood in isolation from biological and anthropological concepts. Taking this much as understood, Midgley turns to introduce some basic ethological concepts, such as the distinction between more or less precisely specified ('closed' or 'open') instincts, copiously illustrating the application of these concepts both to non-human animals and to human beings.

Next, drawing heavily on the work of her friends, she attacks various too-narrow conceptions of human nature and of ethics. As creatures with open (flexible, not fully specified) instincts, we can develop our basic repertoire of motives in various ways. But the repertoire itself is given, and it is what we have to work with and from when we reflect practically on human life. As Foot had argued in 'Moral Beliefs' (and Murdoch too in 'Vision and Choice in Morality'), it is absurd to talk of choosing or inventing values. And Midgley will have none of traditional oppositions between reason and the passions. It is the burden of her book to show how what we conventionally call 'reason' and 'passion' form a system in which they each play a role. The ethological imperative is to think structurally and integratively about the species one is studying, asking how this or that motive fits into the whole picture of that animal's 'form of life'. One needn't idealize these motives. One need only insist that they are *explicable*, and have to be dealt with in some way by the animal under consideration. These observations point toward the heart of Midgley's project.

By Midgley's testimony, and by the evidence of her 1973 *précis*, 'The Concept of Beastliness' (her working title for the book was *Beastliness*), the heart of the book is its fourth part, and more particularly its eleventh chapter. In this chapter, 'On Being Animal as well as Rational', as in the earlier article, Midgley offers an account, inspired by Darwin and the ethologists, but no less by Butler, of the place of reason in human life. The details are absorbingly complex, but the overall point is straightforward and has already come into view. Our evolutionary history has bequeathed to us a generous assortment of motives, some more open-ended, others less. It has, moreover, bequeathed to us conceptual and imaginative capacities that ramify the conflicts that would occur anyway between our several motives. We are distinctive (Midgley's argument does not require her to say 'utterly' distinctive) in our ability to anticipate and fret over our conflicting motives, or even to think or imagine our way into new conflicts.

Any animal with a nature this complex and potentially conflicted requires some means of organizing and directing its behavior—that is, of prioritizing and harmonizing its motives. For many animals, this is achieved by the operation of relatively simple, closed instincts. In her 1984 book, *Wickedness*, Midgley offers the example of geese who hatch one nest of young after another all summer, but fly away, leaving their last brood to perish, when something—the temperature, perhaps, or the angle of the light—triggers their migratory instinct. For humans, though, the same faculty that aggravates internal conflicts by allowing us to anticipate or even generate them also enables us to deal with them—to conceive, try out, and criticize various approaches to living as a whole and integrated human being. There is something right, then, about the Kantian thought that we must govern our motives by critical reflection. Likewise there is something right about the Humean thought that critical reflection is not itself a motive. To adapt a remark of Kant's, critical reflection without motives is empty, motives without critical reflection are blind. Indeed, without some organizing principle, be it critical reflection or a simple, closed instinct, our disparate motives would reduce our lives to chaos. Midgley warns us, though, not to hypostasize 'reason' or 'passion' as Kant and Hume did: "Reason' is not the name of a character in a drama. It is a name for organizing oneself' (1979: 248). Butler, who wrote of 'the whole system . . . of affections, including rationality, which constitute the Heart', emerges as the great figure in early modern moral philosophy (quoted in Midgley 1952: 250). Midgley's ethics is thus an ethics of self-integration.[24]

It is also an ethics that anticipates and addresses the difficulties Foot encountered in mid-career, though Foot did not perceive this. Foot eventually saw her way past the view of practical rationality that entrapped her in the early 1970s: the view that any behavior that serves one's interests, or one's sense of one's interests, is rational. Drawing on later work by Anscombe, and by her sometime UCLA colleague Warren Quinn, Foot asked: what 'would be *so important* about practical rationality if it were rational to seek to fulfill any, even a despicable desire?' (2001: 10).

But Midgley's integrative conception of practical rationality generates this same thought; moreover, it explains the importance of practical rationality, thereby underwriting Foot's conclusion: that the practice of virtue is practically rational. 'What is it,' Midgley writes, 'that we so respect about rationality? What is so good about it? Why, for instance, does Kant sound convincing when he suggests that it is the *only* thing that can command respect? *We would not be likely to take this view of mere cleverness*' (1979: 251, emphases mine). Midgley here deploys something like the distinction she developed in her earliest publications, between the two movements of thought—the *abstractive* and the *comprehending*—only now both are situated as aspects of our rational nature. And the latter is what commands respect, when we encounter it in ourselves or in others: it is a balanced and disciplined approach to our motives that integrates the person and secures him or her against various threats of fragmentation.

Moreover, practical reasoning as Midgley represents it—a necessary response to our welter of available motives—'would be impossible were not some preferences 'more rational than others'.[25] She expressed this more memorably, and in terms that more plainly anticipate Foot's late views, in 'The Concept of Beastliness':

> Rationality . . . is not an easy concept. It is not the same thing as Intelligence, since you could show great intelligence in the pursuit of something quite irrational. 'Rational' includes reference to aims as well as means; it is not far from 'sane.' (1973:113)

There was no need for Foot to wait for Quinn to teach her this. She could have gotten it from her university friend.

Indeed, for one familiar with both works, it is surprising to see how differently they are treated in professional circles. In crucial respects—in its level of detail and consequent applicability, in its accessibility and potential influence, in its engagement with relevant science and empirical adequacy—*Beast and Man* is more powerful than *Natural Goodness*. But the latter has received much more attention from professional philosophers. This provokes the question, 'why?'

OUTSIDE THE WALL

Why didn't Foot perceive what her friend had accomplished? She as much as anyone bought into the conception of philosophy that Midgley rejected and was more impressed by Austin and more like him in approach than any of her friends; she tried at one point to revive his tradition of Saturday morning discussions.[26] And she had more precise ideas about what counted as philosophy and what didn't. Interviewed about Midgley in 2001, she remarked, '[h]er mind doesn't quite work like most straight Oxford analytic philosophers . . . I think she found her forte being witty and sane on television' (Brown 2001). Midgley, for her part, may well have given offense in 1956 when she wrote, 'Oxford philosophers perpetually . . . argue that philosophy which falls outside their own backyard is—not perhaps valueless, but *unprofessional*' (1956: 162).

There was a sad episode, which might lie behind these remarks, in which Midgley tried (unsuccessfully) to interest Foot in Lorenz and Tinbergen. By rights, Foot *ought* to have been interested. The material connected directly with the naturalism Foot found so promising. Foot, never a quick reader, was dreadfully harried all through the 1950s and 60s with tutorial and administrative responsibilities. She may simply have been being self-protective. But the episode made it that much less likely that Foot would look to Midgley's work for instruction. They remained friends, rooming together on a cruise for Somerville alumnae after they had each retired. And Midgley gave *Natural Goodness* a glowing review in *The Times Higher Education Supplement*. But after 1949, they never collaborated as they might have done. Midgley learned from Foot, but not vice versa.

Only Murdoch seems to have delved seriously into the book. The substantial endorsement she wrote for Midgley's publisher shows a clear perception of its character and significance: how Midgley had positioned herself between scientists with unexamined philosophical presuppositions and moral philosophers who simply neglected science, the strategic importance of her plain-spokenness, the potential contribution of the book to ongoing debates in moral philosophy. But Murdoch was, like Midgley, an outsider. Her endorsement was gratifying to Midgley, and helpful to the book, but not likely to lead mainstream philosophers—even Midgley's other university friends—to engage deeply with Midgley's work. Murdoch wrote to Philippa Foot, recommending the book to her, around the same time; we do not have Foot's reply, but the topic does not surface again.[27] Of Midgley's university friends, only Murdoch saw, or half-saw, the significance of what Midgley had achieved: a synthesis of the work they had all been doing since the late 1950s, and a culmination of conversations that started when they were graduate students. Our position is not so different today.

NOTES

1. Anscombe likely would have ended up in philosophy regardless—the Susan Stebbing, Dorothy Emmett, or Martha Kneale of her generation.
2. Mary Warnock, who came to Oxford just after the war, is sometimes mentioned in these contexts, too. Jean Austin is seldom mentioned, though she was in Anscombe's year and taught in Oxford for a long time. She published little, though.
3. Teichmann, Roger, *The Philosophy of Elizabeth* Anscombe (2008); Hacker-Wright, John, *Philippa Foot's Moral Thought* (2013). I could mention also David Edmond's recent popular discussion of the history of 'trolley cases', *Would You Kill the Fat Man?* (2013). In a chapter on 'The Founding Mothers', Edmonds includes Foot, Anscombe, and Murdoch—though Murdoch wrote nothing on the ethics of killing or on Foot's famous thought-experiment. Justin Broackes's edited collection, *Iris Murdoch, Philosopher* (2012) is a modest exception, as both Broackes and one of his contributors—Murdoch's biographer, Peter Conradi—mention Midgley. None of the other eleven contributors do.
4. Readers of Murdoch may be surprised at my labeling her a 'naturalist', given her wistful fascination with the Platonic Idea of Goodness. There are certainly differences between her vision and Anscombe's, Foot's, or Midgley's. Nonetheless, the commonality is there. Consider how she attacks Sartrean existentialism, on the grounds that it does not take seriously enough the givenness and inertia of our nature. What does she recommend instead? A searching inquiry into our nature and its defects, and into the techniques of attention and habituation that might assist us in overcoming our defects. See 'On 'God' and 'Good'', in *The Sovereignty of Good* (1970). Or see 'Metaphysics and Ethics' in *Existentialists and Mystics* (1997)—in which she repeatedly contrasts her own view with what she calls 'anti-naturalism'.
5. Though he is not my subject, Geoffrey Midgley's publications—particularly a pair of papers from the 1950s on the notion of 'constitutive rules'—are likewise of real interest and originality.
6. Jane Heal, conversation with author, 31 July 2012.
7. Biographical details about Midgley are drawn from *The Owl of Minerva* and from direct interviews and correspondence.
8. Although she clearly conveyed to her editors and producers from the first that she was interested in a wider range of topics than one might expect with a young philosopher. Between 1949 and 1950 she reviewed, for the BBC alone, works by Erich Fromm, Arthur Koestler, and Margaret Mead, plus a biography of Florence Nightingale.

9. Foot in particular disliked being grouped among 'women philosophers'. She was certainly a feminist (as were her friends), proud of Somerville's standing among Oxford's colleges, and closely attentive to differences in treatment, including subtle expressions of appropriate respect. Responding to the letter notifying her of her election to the British Academy, she struck through the word 'Sir' and typed in, next to it, 'Madam' (Foot papers, Somerville College). But she did not want her work to be pigeonholed by being grouped and studied as *feminine*. With less to fear from settled and invidious stereotypes, she was more open to thinking of herself and her work as exhibiting a *generational* perspective (Letter from PF to Peter Conradi, from the Iris Murdoch Archives at Kingston University Special Collections KUAS6/3/41/12 dated 14 May 1998). Mary Warnock takes much the same view.

10. It was a formative moment; in the middle of her work on these pieces, she bore her first child. She would make philosophical use of the experiences of childbearing and child-rearing from then on.

11. For further discussion of Midgley's distinctive feminism, see Liz McKinnell's contribution to this volume, "On Being A Full-time Feminist': Midgley and Feminist Philosophy'.

12. Mary Geach recalls her mother Elizabeth Anscombe contrasting herself with Peter Geach in similar terms: 'she said that he had the more powerful intellect, but that she had the greater ability to see about and around a problem.' 'Introduction' in Geach and Gormally, eds., *From Plato to Wittgenstein* (2011), xx.

13. Beginning—eccentrically, some would say—with her unfinished thesis on Plotinus. Recollecting later, Midgley praised him for his attempt 'to find a wider, more inclusive perspective which could bring together' the physical and the spiritual (2005: 157).

14. If Kallin rejected any other script, there is no evidence of this in the BBC archives.

15. BBC Written Archives Centre RCONT1 —Mary Scrutton—Talks File 1–1942–1962 17 July 1952

16. I am grateful to Mary Midgley for lending me this script and for permission to quote it.

17. Mary Warnock's memoir *People and Places* (2000) is instructive on this, as on many other topics in this period.

18. Interview with Jonathan Ree on BBC Radio 3, 19 September 2000. An article could be written on the notion of cleverness as it operated in the thought and professional behavior of mid-century British philosophers. It included analytical acumen, but also quickness on one's feet and ready wit. An alternative way of putting the point I make below: Midgley neither possessed nor aspired to cleverness in this sense, in an environment in which it was regarded as a cardinal intellectual virtue.

19. See the chapters by Ian Ground and Raymond Tallis, this volume.

20. 7/10/51, BBC Written Archives Centre RCONT1 —Mary Scrutton—Talks File 1–1942–1962 7 October 1951

21. Interestingly, Black was also instrumental in securing Elizabeth Anscombe's first professional publication in 1950, a little-studied article on 'the reality of the past' (Black edited the volume, *Philosophical Analysis*, in which it appeared). The article is (by Anscombe's own admission) an awkward imitation of the style of Wittgenstein. She would publish nothing more of her own for several years, as she worked at translating Wittgenstein's *Nachlass*. When she finally returned to publishing, she had (re)discovered her voice and one of her themes: the bankruptcy of modern action theory and ethics.

22. Already since her death, it has become standard to periodize Foot's career with reference to this problem. See Hacker-Wright, *op. cit.*, but also Rosalind Hursthouse's 2012 memorial essay in the *Proceedings of the British Academy*.

23. Detailed by Midgley both in the prefatory material to later editions and in *The Owl of Minerva*.
24. This brings her interestingly close to the work of authors as diverse as Christine Korsgaard and Alasdair MacIntyre, each of whom regards self-integration (whether construed as efficacious agency or as narrative unification) as *a*, or even *the* central task of human life. As with the point I am about to make concerning Foot, Midgley said these things first—but the philosophical community was not paying attention.
25. *Ibid.*, 249.
26. W. David Solomon, conversation with author, 27 May 2014.
27. Iris Murdoch Archives at Kingston University Special Collections KUAS100/3/78 dated 28 Jul 1978.

REFERENCES

Anscombe, G.E.M., 'Modern Moral Philosophy' [1958], in *Ethics, Religion and Politics: The Collected Philosophical Papers of G.E.M. Anscombe*, vol. 3 (Minneapolis: University of Minnesota Press, 1981), 26–42.

Austin, J.L., 'A Plea for Excuses', in J.O. Urmson and G.J. Warnock (eds.), *Philosophical Papers* (Oxford: Oxford University Press, 1961), 123–152.

Broackes, Justin (ed.) *Iris Murdoch, Philosopher* (Oxford: Oxford University Press, 2012).

Brown, Andrew, 'Mary, Mary, quite contrary', *The Guardian*, 13 January 2001.

Edmond, David, *Would You Kill the Fat Man?* (Princeton: Princeton University Press, 2013).

Foot, Philippa, *Natural Goodness* (Oxford: Clarendon, 2001).

Foot, Philippa, *Virtues and Vices* (Oxford: Oxford University Press, 2002).

Geach, Mary and Luke Gormally (eds.), *From Plato to Wittgenstein: Essays by G.E.M. Anscombe* (Exeter: Imprint Academic, 2011).

Hacker-Wright, John, *Philippa Foot's Moral Thought* (London: Bloomsbury, 2013).

Hursthouse, Rosalind, 'Philippa Ruth Foot, 1920–2010', *Biographical Memoirs of Fellows of the British Academy*, XI (2012): 179–196.

Midgley, Mary, 'A letter to posterity', *The Listener*, 27 March (1952a): 510.

Midgley, Mary, 'Bishop Butler: A reply', *The Twentieth Century*, July (1952b): 61

Midgley, Mary, 'Newcastle: Comments on a case history', *The Twentieth Century*, February (1952c): 159.

Midgley, Mary, 'The Concept of Beastliness', *Philosophy* 48 (1973): 111–135.

Midgley, Mary, *Beast and Man: The Roots of Human Nature* (London: Methuen, 1979).

Midgley, Mary, *The Owl of Minerva: A Memoir* (London: Routledge, 2005).

Murdoch, Iris, *The Sovereignty of Good* (London: Routledge, 1970).

Murdoch, Iris, *Existentialists and Mystics* (London: Penguin, 1997).

Teichmann, Roger, *The Philosophy of Elizabeth Anscombe* (Oxford: Oxford University Press, 2008).

Warnock, Mary, *People and Places* (London: Duckworth, 2000).

Afterword
Which Way Next?

Mary Midgley

Books about *The Philosophy of* X have, I think, often consisted largely of protests about how far X has strayed from the accepted doctrine of the day, varied by a few wails saying that he ought to have diverged a lot further. The classic collections of essays about G. E. Moore and Bertrand Russell seemed to get very excited on these two points. No doubt this was because those philosophers were the alpha wolves of their day, so their positions determined what other people would be allowed to believe. I, however, have never been an alpha wolf. So, as I look through this present collection, I am not too surprised to find only one essay (Ray Tallis's), which makes the first complaint, and one—a very interesting one, Simon Conway Morris's—which makes the second.

By contrast, most of the people here seem quite content to notice that I have long been trying to shift aside the various barriers that surrounded the small garden that is allowed to count as Philosophy. After that, most of them simply use the new paths I have been opening to go out and explore the surrounding woodlands. Some of them, of course, such as Rupert Sheldrake, David E. Cooper, Stephen Clark, Andrew Brown, Francoise Wemelsfelder, Jane Goodall and Mary Warnock have long ago established very useful bases out there—bases which need only to be fully connected with each other to make the whole area habitable. And where these people go, others will surely follow.

Shifts like this in the terrain that philosophers occupy are, of course, nothing new. Perhaps most of those we now think of as established philosophers—Plato, Aristotle, Aquinas, Descartes, Kant, Nietzsche, Russell, Wittgenstein and the rest—all started their work as outsiders, using fierce new brooms to sweep away current topics they thought outdated and moving discussion on to what now seemed most urgent and central. Sometimes their new suggestions caught on; sometimes they didn't. But in any case, between these major upsets, the solid, lawyer-like background of the profession always caught up and took over, weaving the new insights into a further orthodoxy, under whose reign the next lot of philosophers will seethe and shout until the next revolution.

That (as Greg McElwain and Benjamin Lipscombe impressively document here) was the way in which my friends and I did indeed seethe and shout for change when we were graduate students at Oxford in the late 1940s. We were well aware that a revolution was needed. I remember coming home in deep depression from a meeting where a disciple of J. L. Austin had been examining what seemed to be the smallest of all possible verbal questions, but had been outclassed by his hearers, who had managed to find even smaller topics round which to centre the ensuing discussion.

Why (thought I) did you people pick on that particular question in the first place? Did it seem to you in some way important—able to influence large issues that surrounded it? Or was it just the convenient next step on an endless mouse-wheel?

It then occurred to me that this situation was much like what I was seeing in a biological context, in discussions of something called 'the scientific method'. People take this 'method' to consist only in carefully verifying your hypotheses—something that, of course, is anyway not peculiar to the physical sciences. They don't ask where those hypotheses came from in the first place, or how you decided which of them to look at. Those large issues seem to be invisible. Do hypotheses just fall randomly from the sky and sort themselves out by natural selection? Is no discussion of wider issues—fresh visions, alternative directions, varying priorities among new suggestions—necessary or possible?

And it then struck me that this is the sinister consequence of something which in itself is admirable: local perfectionism. At Oxford, it flowed from J. L. Austin's all-consuming passion for exact and perfect clarity in argument. People who become obsessed with this one-sided aim can easily blind themselves altogether to other kinds of questions. They then see any excursion into surrounding possibilities, not just as mildly self-indulgent but as morally quite *wrong*—sentimental, subjective, possibly superstitious, anyway unprofessional. And to avoid such vices, they begin to write in a style best exemplified by an instance that John Cottingham cites in his excellent article on 'What is Humane Philosophy and Why Is It at Risk?'). The author quotes from a recent book:

> Let us define what it is for a proposition to be [practically] realizable by A at t, [that is] realizable by means of A's intentional behaviour at t. To say a proposition p is practically realizable by A at t is to say that there is some way of behaving W such that there are possible worlds in which all the actual truths that are causally independent of whatever A might think or do at t hold, and A intentionally behaves in way W at t, and in all these worlds p is true. . .[1]

You mightn't think it, but this is part of an article about free will. And since its style ensures that nobody is going to read it except from academic motives, we can be sure that it is not written from any vulgar desire for fame. It simply expresses strict obedience to what the author takes to be the principles of his profession.

That moralistic attitude, impressed throughout philosophical Oxford by Austin's authority, was what drove many perfectly capable philosophers, for instance Iris Murdoch and Isaiah Berlin, to drop the subject altogether. At that time, of course, nobody had spread the message which Iain McGilchrist has since brought us, that this exaltation of formal exactness may be an unreal demand, resulting chiefly from an ill-controlled left hemisphere in somebody's brain.[2] Yet, even in the 1940s, it was already known that this kind of narrowness is a fault in philosophy. So I was determined to resist it in every possible way. And I therefore set about writing, as Ian James Kidd and Liz McKinnell correctly report in their Introduction to this book, about a range of topics that included 'animals, ecology, ethics, evolution, farming, feminism, the Gaia hypothesis, human nature, science, moral reason, myth and metaphor, personal identity, rationality, wickedness and the practice and purpose of philosophy', arguing always (as they have explained) that 'the big picture matters'.

This meant, of course, that I found myself on the losing side in a clash that was spreading far beyond the philosophical terrain—a conflict that affects every kind of academic study in our age: the clash between the specialization that divides disciplines into smaller and smaller segments and a resistant sense that perhaps we ought actually to try to look at life as a whole. This was the time when terms like *holism* became regarded as dirty words throughout the sciences. And, even among my most sympathetic colleagues, I found that any mention of unfamiliar topics—for instance the forces behind evolutionary change, or the Incarnation, or Nietzsche's view of the soul—merely produced a bewildered expression and the enquiry, 'But what would that have to do with philosophy?' And 'philosophy' meant, of course, the points presently being discussed in articles in the journals.

That, I think, was when I concluded that philosophy is not really a separate territory on its own, whose inhabitants need passports to visit any other. *It is itself the art of connecting things*—the art of standing back and looking at the world to see how items that seem separate are actually related—to find the map on which they both appear. Today, the accepted response to such unexpected gambits is often an apologetic, 'I'm afraid that that is not my area', as if we were a population of foxes dividing the wood up into our separate territories. And this, I think, is not just a passing social difficulty due to the mere increase in numbers of scholars with the expansion of knowledge. It comes from a seriously mistaken notion of priority, a policy of concentrating on the gaps that divide us first, before looking for the wider background that will surely always bring us together.

So I continued building bridges, or sometimes rafts, to connect the various islands in this distracted intellectual archipelago. And one of the gaps that I most often found lying beneath the surface misunderstandings was a very ancient one—the Cartesian division between mind and body.

Though this is often dismissed as a mere outdated piece of metaphysics, it still persists in shaping our thought today, because the reasons why it was first invented are as active now as they were earlier. This split was not devised just in order to accommodate God. It was made so as to leave room for the new, powerful, developing science of physics, without entangling it with current ideas about the spiritual life, which did indeed centre on theology but included also all speculation about humans' inner lives. By placing these two in radically separate realms, Descartes and his friends hoped to make it impossible for them to conflict.

What they actually achieved, however, was merely to slice that awkward item, the human being, straight down the middle, regardless of the position of its various organs. They left no intelligible connexion between minds and bodies, hearts and brains, thus making the whole idea of LIFE—which involves both departments—radically unintelligible.

In this way they disrupted the intellectual cosmos and made sure that one of these incompatible systems would, in the end, try to swallow the other. And the increasing dominance of physical science and technology in our lives ensured that it was the physical squadron that would insist on being the predator rather than the prey. Thus, as Jane Heal points out, analytic philosophers now go to ingenious lengths to make physicalism seem the only honest metaphysical option. And—as Ian Ground notes—in spite of Wittgenstein they still use the concept of a 'theory of mind' to preserve the Cartesian picture. So we arrive at a situation today where otherwise-reputable physical scientists claim to have proved—scientifically—that they themselves, as thinking subjects, simply do not exist. But since this makes no sense, and it is not actually possible for one half of an organism to cut off and devour the other, that claim is surely empty.

What, then, do we need to do now? I think it has been obvious for some time that we have to drop the arbitrary Cartesian division and go back to thinking about human beings in a more natural way, not as compounded of two independent items, but *as wholes*. When we concentrate on someone's mind, we are not considering it as a separate individual. We are looking at that person from one side, attending to certain aspects of their life. When we attend to their body we look at them from another side, concentrating on something quite different. This is all perfectly familiar. Whenever we deal with a psychosomatic illness—asthma, say, or indigestion, or depression—either in ourselves or in someone else, we know that both these ways of thinking are necessary, and that they don't stop each of us from being actually a whole person. Indeed, this is perhaps how we think about each other most of the time.

But, over the last century, the whole force of Western 'scientific' thinking has been brought in to block this balanced approach. Biological purists insist that we reduce each person to a collection of strictly physical objects—genes, brain cells, hormones. And this, of course, is part of a wider attempt to redescribe the whole of reality in these terms—to bring it all within the range of physics. That is a very strange enterprise. To do it we would have to get rid of the idea of purpose itself, since that is something which non-living, purely physical subjects do not have. And when we are talking about animals—including human beings—this manoeuvre is often quite difficult. As James Lovelock once pointed out, it is hard to make any sense of the way in which salmon swim inexhaustibly upstream without supposing that they are trying to do something. And the same may indeed be true of scholars arguing inexhaustibly for physicalism or behaviourism.

But the area where purpose is hardest to eliminate, and seems most mysterious, is surely evolution. Neo-Darwinists have tried to get rid of it there by crediting all animal behaviour to a single aim—gene-maximization. But, even if this explanation could be made convincing, it is hard to see why that aim would be any less objectionable—any less teleological, any less subjective or anthropomorphic—than any other. It is in the nature of aims that they have to appeal to an agent.

What, then, has actually been happening during the course of evolution? Who, if anyone, has been doing what? Something, it seems, undoubtedly has been happening. Where there were once only hot rocks, and then the simplest of bacteria-like organisms, there is now an ordered host of highly organized beings such as elephants, albatrosses, whales, redwoods and termite-nests, not to speak of human beings. The current explanation for all this change is simply chance, working through natural selection, And 'chance' is just a negative notion, meaning chiefly that nobody planned it. But how could chance lead to so much order?

As Simon Conway Morris has pointed out, this prolonged development has not only been huge, it has also been directional. All sorts of creatures have been steadily increasing their consciousness and perception, steadily developing their sensitive faculties. (To explain this by saying that that kind of change always improved reproductive prospects is mere speculation. How come the environment always demanded that particular kind of change? Nobody, after all, has ever found a convincing evolutionary use for our huge mathematical capacities.) The natural way of understanding all this—which, in today's biological background, is also the best-attested way—is to see it as something self-created; that is, the effect of persistent individual choices of behaviour. And this means that (as Aristotle said) the creatures must actually have liked perceiving and thinking.

I think the best way to convey this fairly recent shift in evolutionary ideas to people who haven't yet encountered it is simply to cite the summary of it, which Brian Goodwin gave in the introduction to his excellent book *How The Leopard Got Its Spots*.[3] As Goodwin says, this improved insight was a response—a delayed one because of an interlude of neo-Darwinism—to 'the towering achievement of D'Arcy Thompson, whose 1917 book *On Growth And Form* re-established the organism as the dynamic vehicle of biological emergence'. As he explains, with this new perspective:

> Organisms cease to be simply survival machines and assume intrinsic value, having worth in and of themselves, like works of art. Such a

realization arises from an altered understanding of the nature of organisms as centres of autonomous action and creativity, connected with a causal agency which cannot be described as mechanical . . . It is relational order between components that matters more than material composition in living processes, so that emergent qualities predominate over quantities . . . As a result, values enter fundamentally into the appreciation of the nature of life, and biology takes on the nature of a science of qualities . . .

[By contrast] Darwinism is a very incomplete and limited story, based upon an inadequate view of organisms.[4]

Conway Morris has helpfully shown how this process works in evolution by pointing out the frequency of convergence—the independent development of similar eyes, and other cognitive faculties, by quite unrelated animals.

When I first came across this suggestion I welcomed it heartily, and I have continued to do so. Conway Morris, however, doesn't like the terms in which I welcome it. (He apparently thinks I have published nothing since 1995, but I don't think this accounts for his response). He repeatedly accuses me of naturalism, a word that I deeply distrust. It ought to mean a profound belief in *nature* as the green-and-brown living world that actually surrounds us, and in the forces behind that world. But this word is more often used to mean something almost opposite to this—a stark, reductive, materialistic nothing-buttery, a conviction that nothing is real except the ultimate particles of chemicals.

This is so far from my own views that I can only deduce what's meant by seeing how often Conway Morris accuses me of *leaving out* something he considers central: 'Some vital ingredient seems to be lacking' (p. 157) and '[o]nly we, I suggest, actually know anything at all, but where this gift comes from remains unacknowledged' (159) This surely points to God as the ultimate donor.

I have no wish to deny God's role in this whole drama, but it wasn't the subject I was writing about. My main interest has always been to bring forward evidence for the solid contribution of *nature* itself to the things we value in the world—for its essential function as the direct channel through which these things reach us. That contribution has been so systematically undervalued that one can't emphasize it too often. And if this contribution too is eventually God's gift, our appreciation of it can scarcely be harmful to his worship.

Conway Morris gives an interesting sidelight on his own view of the meaning of evolution in the last chapter of his book *Life's Solution: Inevitable Humans in a Lonely Universe*.[5] Here he imagines some people sitting on the English South Coast waiting for a visit from extraterrestrials and finding, when these arrive, that they are simply people—humans like themselves. In fact, it emerges that *we*—more or less as we are now—are apparently the expected summit of evolution . . . This confident idea seems to be linked with his equally confident claim that 'neither the birds nor any other cognitively competent animals actually understand what they are doing. In this sense, they are not rational'.[6] (How does he know this? Has he been inside their minds?) This kind of human exceptionalism is, of course, linked with a particular Christian view of the Incarnation as a final settlement, but I don't think it has much force otherwise.

Apart from these minor issues, I still find his views extremely nutritious and I want to say—more generally—that I have very much enjoyed reading all the essays in this collection. I have found them remarkably helpful, and I very much hope that other people will do the same.

NOTES

1. In *Conceptions of Philosophy: Royal Institute of Philosophy Supplement 65*, edited by Anthony O'Hear (Cambridge: Cambridge University Press, 2009), 233–255.
2. Ian McGilchrist, *The Master and His Emissary: The Divided Brain and the Making of the Western World* (New Haven, CT: Yale University Press, 2009).
3. *How The Leopard Changed Its Spots* (London: Phoenix Giants, Weidenfeld and Nicolson, 1994).
4. *How The Leopard Changed Its Spots*, xiv.
5. Cambridge: Cambridge University Press, 2004.
6. *Life's Solution*, 157.

The Works of Mary Midgley, compiled by Ian James Kidd

It is a sobering experience to compile the writings of Mary Midgley, for two reasons. The first is the sheer quantity of her writings: over 280 items are detailed below. The second is the diversity of her outputs. Alongside her single and co-authored books and edited books, there are articles and essays for philosophy journals, scientific periodicals, newspapers, popular environmental and intellectual magazines, as well as pamphlets, prefaces, interviews, forewords, and, in more recent years, podcasts. Midgley speaks clearly and eloquently on many topics to many audiences—a good mark of a 'public intellectual'.

I have included single and co-authored and edited books, journal articles and book chapters, pamphlets, and forewords and prefaces. I also added some selected interviews, videos, and podcasts. I have not included translations, reprints, or reviews. My bibliographical efforts were made much easier by the 'Bibliography of the Works of Mary Midgley' in *The Essential Mary Midgley* and by the wonderful resource that is Google Books. Any additions or corrections will be gladly received. Asterixed items were published under the name Mary Scrutton.

BOOKS

Beast and Man: The Roots of Human Nature (London: Routledge, 1978).
Heart and Mind: The Varieties of Moral Experience (London: Routledge, 1981).
Animals and Why They Matter: A Journey Around the Species Barrier (Harmondsworth, Middlesex: Penguin, 1983).
Wickedness: A Philosophical Essay (London: Routledge, 1984).
(co-authored with Judith Hughes) *Women's Choices: Philosophical Problems Facing Feminism* (London: Weidenfeld and Nicolson, 1983).
Can't We Make Moral Judgements? (Bristol: The Bristol Press, 1989).
Wisdom, Information and Wonder: What Is Knowledge For? (London: Routledge, 1989).
Science as Salvation: A Modern Myth and Its Meaning (London: Routledge, 1992).
The Ethical Primate: Humans, Freedom and Morality (London: Routledge, 1994).

Beast and Man: The Roots of Human Nature, revised edition (London: Routledge, 1995).
Utopias, Dolphins and Computers: Problems of Philosophical Plumbing (London: Routledge, 1996).
Science and Poetry (London: Routledge, 2001).
Evolution as a Religion: Strange Hopes and Stranger Fears, with a new introduction (London: Routledge, 2002).
Myths We Live By (London: Routledge, 2003).
The Owl of Minerva: A Memoir (London: Routledge, 2005).
The Essential Mary Midgley, David Midgley (ed.) (London: Routledge, 2005).
The Solitary Self: Darwin and the Selfish Gene (Durham: Acumen, 2010).
Are You an Illusion? (Durham: Acumen, 2014).

EDITED VOLUMES

(ed.) *Intersubjectivity and John Ziman's Legacy*, edited with Joan Solomon, *Journal of Consciousness Studies* 13, no. 5 (2006).
(ed.) *Earthy Realism: The Meaning of Gaia* (Exeter: Imprint Academic, 2007).

PAMPHLETS

Biological and Cultural Evolution: Institute for Cultural Research Monograph Series, No. 20 (Tunbridge Wells: Institute for Cultural Research, 1984).
'The Value of "Useless" Research: Supporting Scholarship for the Long Run', *Report by the Council for Science and Society* (London: The Council for Science and Society, 1989).
Gaia: The Next Big Idea (London: Demos, 2001).
Impact Pamphlet 15: Intelligent Design and Other Ideological Problems (London: The Philosophy of Education Society of Great Britain, 2007).

ARTICLES, BOOK CHAPTERS, AND LETTERS

'An Intellectual Novelist', *The Listener* issue 1164 (1951), 993.*
'The Natural History of Contradictions', *The Listener* issue 1180 (1951), 589.*
'Paradoxography', *The Listener* issue 1183 (1951), 743.*
'The Woman's Point of View', *The Listener* issue 1204 (1952), 510.*
'The Emancipation of Women', *The Twentieth Century* CLII, no. 901 (1952), 217–25.*
'Bishop Butler: A Reply', *The Twentieth Century* CLII, no. 905 (1952), 56–62.*
'Bourgeois Cinderellas', *The Twentieth Century* CLV (1954), 351–63.*
'Newcastle: Comments on a Case-history', *The Twentieth Century* CLIX (1956), 159–68.*
'Addiction to Fiction', *The Twentieth Century* CLIX (1956), 567–68.*
'On Being Reformed', *The Listener* issue 1428 (1956), 196.*
'Ou Sont les Neiges de ma Tante', *The Twentieth Century* (1959), 168–79.*
'The Month', *The Twentieth Century* CLXV (1959), 505–10.*
'Is "Moral" a Dirty Word?', *Philosophy* 47, no. 181 (1972), 206–28.
'The Concept of Beastliness : Philosophy, Ethics, and Animal Behaviour', *Philosophy* 48, no. 184 (1973), 111–35.

'The Neutrality of the Moral Philosopher', *Supplementary Volume of the Aristotelian Society for 1974* (1974), 211–29.

'The Game Game', *Philosophy* 49, no. 189 (1974), 231–53.

'On Trying Out One's New Sword on a Chance Wayfarer', *The Listener*, 15 December 1977.

'The Objection to Systematic Humbug', *Philosophy* 53, no. 204 (1978), 147–69.

'More about Reason, Commitment and Social Anthropology', *Philosophy* 53, no. 205 (1978), 401–03.

'Freedom and Heredity, *The Listener*, 14 September 1978.

'Animal Experiments', *New Scientist* 77, no. 1087 (1978), 240.

'Animals', *New Scientist* 78, no. 1097 (1978), 42.

'Brutality and Sentimentality', *Philosophy* 54, no. 209, (1979), 385–89.

'Gene-Juggling', *Philosophy* 54, no. 210 (1979), 439–58.

'The All-Female Number', *Philosophy* 54, no. 210 (1979), 552–54.

'Selfish Genes', *New Scientist* 81, no. 1139 (1979), 278.

'Beast and Man', *The Listener*, no. 2624 (1979), 212.

'Coals To . . .', *New Scientist* 84, no. 1180 (1979), 464.

'The Absence of a Gap between Facts and Values', co-authored with Stephen R. L. Clark), *Supplementary Volume of the Aristotelian Society for 1980*, 207–223.

'Consequentialism and Common Sense', *The Hastings Center Report* 10, no. 5 (1980), 43–4.

'Reply to Mr. Pratt', *Philosophical Books* 21, no. 1 (1980), 6–9.

'Why Knowledge Matters', in David Sperlinger (ed.), *Animals in Research: New Perspectives in Animal Experimentation* (Oxford: John Wiley and Sons, 1981), 319–36.

'Towards a New Understanding of Human Nature: The Limits of Individualism', in Donald J. Ortner (ed.), *How Humans Adapt: A Biocultural Odyssey* (Washington DC: Smithsonian Press, 1983), 517–46.

'Human Ideals and Human Needs', *Philosophy* 58, no. 223 (1983), 89–94.

'Selfish Genes and Social Darwinian', *Philosophy* 58, no. 225 (1983), 365–77.

'Duties Concerning Islands', *Encounter* LX (February 1983), 36–43.

'Sneering At Philosophy', *New Scientist* 98, no. 1363 (1983), 887.

'De-Dramatizing Darwin', *The Monist* 67, no. 2 (1984), 200–15.

'Sociobiology', *Journal of Medical Ethics* 10 (1984), 158–60.

'On Being Terrestrial', in S.C. Brown (ed.), *Objectivity and Cultural Divergence: Royal Institute of Philosophy Lecture Series 17* (Cambridge: Cambridge University Press, 1984), 79–91.

'Reductivism, Fatalism, and Sociobiology', *Journal of Applied Philosophy* 1, no. 1 (1984), 107–14.

'Persons and Non-Persons', in Peter Singer (ed.), *In Defence of Animals* (Oxford: Blackwell, 1985), 52–62.

'Philosophising Out in the World', *Social Research* 52, no. 3 (1985), 447–70.

'Correspondence', with Anthony Flew, *Journal of Applied Philosophy* 2, no. 2 (1985), 293–94.

'Lorenz Maligned', *New Scientist* no. 1521 (1986), 53.

'Can Specialisation Damage Your Health?', *International Journal of Moral and Social Studies* 2, no. 1 (1987).

'Keeping Species on Ice', in Virginia MacKenna, Will Travers and Jonathan Wray (eds.), *Beyond the Bars: The Zoo Dilemma* (Wellingborough: Thorsons, 1987), 55–65.

'The Flight From Blame', *Philosophy* 62, no. 241 (1987), 271–91.

'Embarrassing Relatives: Changing Perceptions of Animals', *The Trumpeter* 4, no. 4 (1987), 17–19.

'Evolution as a Religion: A Comparison of Prophecies', *Zygon* 22, no. 22 (1987), 179–94.

'Scientific Whaling', *New Scientist* no. 1569 (1987), 73.

'Tribal Warfare', *New Scientist* no. 1583 (1987), 73.

'Beasts, Brutes, and Monsters', in Tim Ingold (ed.), *What Is an Animal?* (London: Unwin Hyman, 1988), 35–46.

'Teleological Theories of Morality', in G.H.R. Parkinson (ed.), *An Encyclopedia of Philosophy* (London: Routledge, 1988), 541–67.

'Open Letter', *Philosophy* 63, no. (1988), 1–2.

'On Not Being Afraid of Natural Sex Differences', in Morwenna Griffiths and Margaret Whitford (eds.), *Feminist Perspectives in Philosophy* (London: Macmillan, 1988), 29–41.

'Practical Solutions', *The Hastings Center Report* 19, no. 6 (1989), 44–5.

'Myths of Intellectual Isolation', *Proceedings of the Aristotelian Society*, LXXXIX, Part 1 (1988–89), 19–32.

'Are You an Animal?', in Gill Langley (ed.), *Animal Experimentation: The Consensus Changes* (New York: Chapman & Hall, 1989), 1–18.

'Why Smartness Is Not Enough', in Mary E. Clark and Sandra A. Wawritko (eds.), *Rethinking the Curriculum: Towards an Integrated, Interdisciplinary College Education* (New York: Greenwood Press, 1990), 39–52.

'Homunculus Trouble, or, What Is Applied Philosophy?', *Journal of Social Philosophy* 21, no. 1 (1990), 5–15.

'The Use and Uselessness of Learning', *European Journal of Education* 25, no. 3 (1990), 283–94.

'Rights Talk Will Not Sort Out Child Abuse: Comment on Archard on Parental Rights', *Journal of Applied Philosophy* 8, no. 1 (1991), 103–14.

'The Origin of Ethics', in Peter Singer (ed.), *A Companion to Ethics* (Oxford: Blackwell, 1991), 3–13.

'Is the Biosphere a Luxury?', *The Hastings Center Report* 22, no. 3 (1992), 7–12.

'Towards a More Humane View of the Beasts?', in David E. Cooper and Joy A. Palmer (eds.), *The Environment in Question* (London: Routledge, 1992), 28–36.

'The Significance of Species', in Steven Luper-Foy and Curtis Brown (eds.), *The Moral Life* (Harcourt Brace Jovanovich, 1992).

'Philosophical Plumbing', in A. Phillips Griffiths (ed.), *The Impulse to Philosophise: Royal Institute of Philosophy Supplement 33* (Cambridge: Cambridge University Press, 1992), 139–51.

'Reply to Marc Bekoff', *Environmental Values* 1, no. 3 (1992), 256.

'Strange Contest: Science versus Religion', in Hugh Montefiore (ed.), *The Gospel and Contemporary Culture* (London: Mowbray, 1992), 40–57.

'Beasts versus the Biosphere', *Environmental Values* 1, no. 1 (1992), 113–21.

'The Idea of Salvation Through Science', *New Blackfriars* 73, no. 860 (1992), 257–65.

'Can Science Save Its Soul? Some Scientists Have Begun To Talk Confidently About Understanding God And Creation. They Are Crediting Science With Power It Doesn't Possess', *New Scientist* 1832 (1992), 43–6.

'The Four-Leggeds, The Two-Leggeds and the Wingeds', *Society and Animals* 1, no. 1 (1993), 9–15.

'Must Good Causes Compete?', *Cambridge Quarterly of Healthcare Ethics* 2, no. 2 (1993), 133–42.

'Intelligence Strikes', *New Scientist* 138, no. 1870 (1993), 51.

'Visions, Secular and Sacred', *Milltown Studies* 34 (1994), 74–93.

'The End of Anthropocentrism?', in Robin Attfield and Andrew Belsey (eds.), *Philosophy and the Natural Environment: Royal Institute of Philosophy Supplement 36* (Cambridge: Cambridge University Press, 1994), 103–12.

'Darwinism and Ethics', in K. W. M. Fulford, Grant Gillett & Janet Martin Soskice (eds.), *Medicine and Moral Reasoning* (Cambridge: Cambridge University Press, 1994), 6–18.

'Bridge-Building at Last', in Aubrey Manning and James Serpell (eds.), *Animals and Human Society: Changing Perspectives* (London: Routledge, 1994), 188–94.

'Matter of Choice', *New Scientist* 141, no. 1912 (1994), 50.

'Zombies and the Turing Test', *Journal of Consciousness Studies* 2, no. 4 (1995), 351–2.

'Reductive Megalomania', in John Cornwell (ed.), *Nature's Imagination: The Frontiers of Scientific Vision* (Oxford: Oxford University Press, 1995), 133–47.

'Trouble with Families?', co-authored with Judith Hughes, in Brenda Almond (ed.), *Introducing Applied Ethics* (Oxford: Blackwell, 1995), 17–32.

'The Challenge of Science, Limited Knowledge, or a New High Priesthood?', in Alan Race and Roger Williamson (eds.), *True to this Earth: Global Challenges and Transforming Faith* (Oxford: Oneworld Publications, 1995).

'The Mixed Community', in James P. Sterba (ed.), *Earth Ethics, Environmental Ethics, Animal Rights and Practical Applications* (New Jersey: Prentice Hall, 1995), 80–90.

'Visions, Secular and Sacred', *The Hastings Center Report* 25, no. 5 (1995), 20–7.

'Darwin's Central Problems', *Science* 268, no. 5214 (1995), 1196–98.

'The Ethical Primate. Anthony Freeman in discussion with Mary Midgley', *Journal of Consciousness Studies* 2, no. 1 (1995), 67–75.

'Sustainability and Moral Pluralism', *Ethics and the Environment* 1, no. 1 (1996), 41–54.

'One World—But a Big One', *Journal of Consciousness Studies* 3, no. 5/6 (1996), 500–14.

'Earth Matters; Thinking about the Environment', in Sarah Dunant and Roy Porter (eds.), *The Age of Anxiety* (London: Virago, 1996), 59–62.

'The View from Britain: What Is Dissolving Families?', co-authored with Judith Hughes, *American Philosophical Association, Newsletter on Feminism and Philosophy* 96, no. 1 (1996).

'Can Education Be Moral?' *Res Publica* 2, no. 1 (1996), 77–85.

'Science in the World', *Science Studies* 9, no. 2 (1996), 49–58.

'Pi In the Sky', *Third Way* 19, no. 2 (1996), 11–14.

'Visions of Embattled Science', in Ralph Levinson and Jeff Thomas (eds.), *Science Today: Problem or Crisis?* (London: Routledge, 1997), 35–50.

'The Soul's Successors: Philosophy and the "Body"', in Sarah Coakley (ed.), *Religion and the Body* (Cambridge: Cambridge University Press, 1997), 53–70.

'Are Families Out of Date?', co-authored with Judith Hughes, in Hilde Lindemann (ed.), *Feminism and Families* (London: Routledge, 1997), 55–68.

'Skimpole Unmasked', *History of the Human Sciences* 10, no. 4 (1997), 92–6.

'Putting Ourselves Together Again', in John Cornwall (ed.), *Consciousness and Human Identity* (Oxford: Oxford University Press, 1998).

'The Problem of Humbug', in Matthew Kieran (ed.), *Media Ethics: A Philosophical Approach* (London: Routledge, 1998), 37–48.

'Dawkins Determinant', *New Scientist* 157, no. 2121 (1998), 51–52.

'The Myths We Live By', in Wes Williams (ed.), *The Values of Science: The Oxford Amnesty Lectures 1997* (New York: Westview Press, 1999).

'Being Scientific about Our Selves', *Journal of Consciousness Studies* 6, no. 4 (1999), 85–98.

'Should We Let Them Go?', in Francine L. Dolins (ed.), *Attitudes to Animals: Views in Animal Welfare* (Cambridge: Cambridge University Press, 1999), 152–63.

'Determinism, Omniscience, and the Multiplicity of Explanations', *Behavioral and Brain Sciences* 22, no. 5 (1999), 900–901.

'Towards an Ethic of Global Responsibility', inTim Dunne and Nicholas J. Wheeler (eds.), *Human Rights in Global Politics* (Cambridge: Cambridge University Press, 1999), 160–74.

'Midgley on Murdoch', *The Philosophers' Magazine* 7 (1999), 45–46.

'Descartes' Prisoners', *New Statesman*, 24 May 1999.

'Me And My Memes', *New Scientist* 161, no. 2179 (1999), 56.

'Just So Stories', *New Scientist* 163, no. 2205 (1999), 55.

'Brutal Kinship', *Nature* 399, no. 6736 (1999), 537.

'Monkey business. *The Origin of Species* changed man's conception of himself forever. So why, asks Mary Midgley, is Darwinism used to reinforce the arid individualism of our age?', *New Statesman*, 6 September 1999.

'The Origins of Don Giovanni', *Philosophy Now* 25 (1999–2000), 32.

'Alchemy Revived', *The Hastings Center Report* 30, no. 2 (2000), 41–3.

'Biotechnology and Monstrosity: Why We Should Pay Attention to the "Yuk Factor" ', *The Hastings Center Report* 30, no. 5 (2000), 7–15.

'Sorting Out the Zeigeist', *Changing English: Studies in Culture and Education* 7, no. 1 (2000), 89–92.

'Both Nice and Nasty', *New Statesman*, 13 March 2000.

'Earth Song', *New Statesman*, 2 October 2000.

'The Need for Wonder', in Russell Stannard (ed.), *God for the 21st Century* (Radnot: Templeton Foundation Press, 2000), 186–88.

'Individualism and the Concept of Gaia', *Review of International Studies* 26 (2000), 29–44.

'Consciousness, Fatalism and Science', in Niels Hendrik Gregerson, Willem B. Drees and Ulf Gorman (eds.), *The Human Person in Science and Theology* (Edinburgh, T&T Clark, 2000), 21–40.

'Human Nature, Human Variety, Human Freedom', Neil Roughley (ed.), *Being Humans: Anthropological Universality and Particularity in Transdisciplinary Perspectives* (Berlin: Walter De Gruyter, 2000), 47–63.

'Why Memes?', in Hilary Rose and Steven Rose (eds.), *Alas, Poor Darwin: Arguments Against Evolutionary Psychology* (London: Jonathan Cape Rosenthal, 2000), 67–84.

'Individualism and the Concept of Gaia', in Ken Booth, Tim Dunne, and Michael Cox (eds.), *How Might We Live? Global Ethics in a New Century* (Cambridge: Cambridge University Press, 2001), 29–44.

'Homage to Gaia: The Life of an Independent Scientist', *Environmental Values* 10, no. 1 (2001), 141–42.

'The Problem of Living With Wildness', in Virginia A. Sharpe, Bryan Norton and Strachan Donelley (eds.), *Wolves and Human Communities, Biology, Politics and Ethics* (Washington: Island Press 2001), 179–90.

'Walk on the Dark Side', *The Philosophers' Magazine* 14 (2001), 23–5.

'Being Objective: The Idea of Scientists As Impartial Observers Is Hard To Shake, But Is Complete Detachment Justified?', *Nature* 410, no. 753 (2001), 753.

'The bankers' vision is limited', *The Guardian*, 24 August 2001.

'The bankers' abstract vision of the globe is limited', *The Guardian*, 4 October 2001.

'The Refractory: Vision', *The Lancet* 357, no. 9266 (2001), 1455.

'Animal Thoughts', *New Scientist* 171, no. 2301 (2001), 71.

'Heaven and Earth, an Awkward History', *Philosophy Now* 34 (2001–2002), 18.

'Does the Earth Concern Us?', *Gaia Circular* (2001–2002), 4–9.

'Choosing the Selectors', in Michael Wheeler, John Ziman and Margaret A. Boden (eds.), *The Evolution of Cultural Entities: Proceedings of the British Academy 112* (Oxford: Oxford University Press, 2002), 119–33.

'Reply to Target Article: "Inventing the Subject; the Renewal of 'Psychological' Psychology" ', *Journal of Anthropological Psychology* 11 (2002), 44–45.

'Pluralism: The Many Maps Model', *Philosophy Now* 35 (2002), 10–11.

'How Real Are You?', *Think* 1, no. 2 (2002), 35–46.

'Enough is never enough', *The Guardian*, 28 November 2002.

'It's all in the mind', *The Guardian*, 21 September 2002.

'Understanding the "War on Terrorism"', *openDemocracy*, 24 October 2002.

'The Problem of Natural Evil', in Charles Talliaferro and Paul J. Griffiths (eds.), *Philosophy of Religion: An Anthology* (Oxford: Blackwell, 2003), 361–7.

'Fate by fluke', *The Guardian*, 1 March 2003.

'Curiouser and Curiouser', *The Guardian*, 27 September 2003.

'Science and Poetry', *Situation Analysis* 2 (2003), 29–31.

'Great Thinkers—James Lovelock', *New Statesman*, 14 July 2003.

'Criticising the Cosmos', in Willem B. Drees (ed.), *Is Nature Ever Evil? Religion, Science and Value* (London: Routledge, 2003), 11–26, with replies by Silvia Volker and Hans Radder.

'Mind and Body: The End of Apartheid', in David Lorimer (ed.), *Science, Consciousness and Ultimate Reality* (Exeter: Imprint Academic, 2004), 173–97.

'Science and Poetry', John Haldane (ed.), *Values, Education, and the Human World* (Exeter: Imprint Academic, 2004), 219–33.

'Atoms, Memes, and Individuals', in John Haldane (ed.), *Values, Education, and the Human World* (Exeter: Imprint Academic, 2004), 234–49.

'Do We Even Act?', in Dai A. Rees and Steven Rose (eds.), *The New Brain Sciences: Perils and Prospects* (Cambridge: Cambridge University Press, 2004), 17–33.

'Why Clones?', *Network Review* (The Scientific and Medical Network) 84 (2004).

'Zombies Can't Concentrate', *Philosophy Now* 44 (2004), 13–14.

'Counting the Cost of Revenge', *The Guardian*, 5 June 2004.

'Us and Them', *New Statesman*, 13 September 2004.

'Souls, Minds, Bodies, and Planets (part 1)', *Philosophy Now* 47 (2004).

'Souls, Minds, Bodies, and Planets (part 2)', *Philosophy Now* 48 (2004).

'On the Origin of Creationism', *New Scientist*, no. 2479 (2004), 29.

'Souls, Minds, Bodies, and Planets', in Anthony O'Hear (ed.), *Philosophy, Biology, and Life: Royal Institute of Philosophy Supplement* 56 (Cambridge: Cambridge University Press, 2005), 83–104.

'Mixed Antitheses', in James E. Huchingson (ed.), *Religion and the Natural Sciences: The Range of Engagement* (Eugene, OR: Wipf and Stock, 2005), 6–39.

'Visions and Values', *Resurgence* 228 (2005), 18.

'Designs on Darwinism', *The Guardian*, 6 September 2005.

'Proud not to be a doctor', *The Guardian* 3 October 2005.

'Mapping Science: In Memory of John Ziman', *Interdisciplinary Science Reviews* 30, no. 3 (2005), 195–7.

'Imagine There's No Heaven', *New Scientist* 192, no. 2572 (2006), 50–51.

'Ways of Seeing', *New Scientist* 192, no. 2578 (2006), 25.

'Rethinking Sex and the Selfish Gene: Why We Do It', *Heredity* 93, no. 3 (2006), 271–2.

'Dover Beach Revisited', *Think* 4, no. 12 (2006), 69–74.

'Dover Beach Revisited', in Philip Clayton and Zachary Simpson (eds.), *The Oxford Handbook of Religion and Science* (Oxford: Oxford University Press, 2006), 962–78.

'Dover Beach: Understanding the Pains of Bereavement', *Philosophy* 81, no. 2 (2006), 209–30.

'Editorial Introduction', *Journal of Consciousness Studies* 13, no. 5 (2006), 8–16.

'Introduction: The Not-So-Simple Earth', in Mary Midgley (ed.), *Earthy Realism: The Meaning of Gaia* (Exeter: Imprint Academic, 2007), 3–9.

'What Do We Mean By Security?', *Philosophy Now* 61 (2007), 12–15.

'A Plague on Both Their Houses', *Philosophy Now* 64 (2007), 26–27.

'The Flawed Frontier', *New Scientist* 195, no. 2623 (2007), 22.

'Elementary, Watson', *New Scientist* 196, no. 2630 (2007), 23.

'Crimes Beyond Religion', *The Guardian*, 30 September 2006.

'Mary Midgley on Dawkins', *Interlog: Exploring Buddhist-Christian Christian-Buddhist Themes*, 10 August 2007.

'Why Farm Animals Matter', in M. Dawkins and R. Bonney (eds.), *The Future of Animal Farming: Renewing the Ancient Contract* (Oxford: Blackwell, 2008), 21–32.

'Does Science Make Belief in God Obsolete? Of Course Not', *John Templeton Foundation* (2008), http://www.templeton.org/belief/essays/midgley.pdf.

'Love and Its Disappointment', *Philosophy Now* 75 (2008), 42.

'Proud Not to Be a doctor', *The Guardian*, 3 October 2008.

'Cold Wars and Grand Conclusions', *The Guardian*, 28 October 2008.

'All Too Human', *The Guardian*, 19 December 2008.

'Reason's Just Another Faith', *New Scientist* 199, no. 2666 (2008), 50–51.

'Thinking Matter', *New Scientist* 201, no. 2688 (2008), 16.

'Mary Midgley', in Mick Gordon and Chris Wilkinson (eds.), *Conversations on Truth* (London: Continuum, 2009), 142–54.

'Purpose, Meaning and Darwinism', *Philosophy Now* 71 (2009), 16–19.

'Selectionism Can Only Take Us So Far', *The Guardian*, 9 February 2009.

'Hobbes' *Leviathan*, part 1: Strange Selves', *The Guardian*, 6 April 2009.

'Hobbes' *Leviathan*, part 2: Freedom and Desolation', *The Guardian*, 13 April 2009.

'Hobbes' *Leviathan*, part 3: What Is Selfishness?', *The Guardian*, 20 April 2009.

'Hobbes' *Leviathan*, part 4: Selling Total Freedom', *The Guardian*, 27 April 2009.

'Hobbes' *Leviathan*, part 5: The End of Individualism', *The Guardian*, 4 May 2009.

'Hobbes' *Leviathan*, part 6: Responses to Readers', *The Guardian*, 11 May 2009.

'Hobbes' *Leviathan*, part 7: His Idea of War', *The Guardian*, 18 May 2009.

'Hobbes' *Leviathan*, part 8: Can We Ride the Leviathan?', *The Guardian*, 25 May 2009.

'Formulas Built in Myth', *The Guardian*, 15 August 2009.

'Religious Agenda', *New Scientist* 201, no. 2700 (2009), 22–23.

'Darwinism, Purpose and Meaning', in Anthony O'Hear (ed.), *Philosophy and Religion: Royal Institute of Philosophy Supplement 68* (Cambridge: Cambridge University Press, 2010), 193–201.

'What Darwin Got Wrong', *The Guardian*, 6 February 2010.

'The Abuses of Science', *The Guardian*, 12 June 2010.

'Metaphysics and the Limits of Science', *The Guardian*, 28 August 2010.

'There Are Truths Far Too Big to Be Conveyed in One Go', *The Guardian* 27 December 2010.

'Moral Brains', *New Scientist* 208, no. 2788 (2010), 29.

'Why the Idea of Purpose Won't Go Away', *Philosophy* 86 (2011), 545–61.

'The Mythology of Selfishness', *The Philosophers' Magazine* 53 (2011), 35–45.

'Lost in Space', *New Scientist* 211, no. 2823 (2011), 28.

'Age Is a Continuum—Not Two Tribes to Be Made Equal', *The Guardian* 14 November 2011.

'The Selfish Metaphor: Conceits of Evolution', *New Scientist* 209, no. 2797 (2011), 26–27.

'Existential Issues', with Peter Hacker, Jane Heal, and Anthony O'Hear, *New Scientist* 211, no. 2829 (2011), 32.

'On Being an Anthrozoon: How Unique Are We?', *Minding Nature: A Journal of the Center for Humans and Nature*, 5, no. 2 (2012), 11–16.

'Choose Free Will', *New Scientist* 215, no. 2880 (2012), 30.

'Getting Real', *New Scientist* 216, no. 2887 (2012), 30.

'Death and the Human Animal', *Philosophy Now* 89 (2012).

'Two Become One', *New Scientist* 217, no. 2909 (2013), 30.
'Art of Psychiatry', *New Scientist* 218, no. 2916 (2013), 30–31.
'Does Philosophy Get Out of Date?', *Philosophy Now* 103 (2014).
'Scientism and Free-market Jihad', *openDemocracy*, 19 November 2014, https://www.opendemocracy.net/mary-midgley/scientism-and-free market-jihad.

UNDATED WRITINGS

'On Not Needing Omnipotence: What Does It Mean to Be Human Today?', *Mary Midgley Website*, https://marymidgley.wordpress.com/on-not-needing-omnipotence-mary-midgley/, no date.
'Death and the Human Animal', *Mary Midgley Website*, https://marymidgley.wordpress.com/death-and-the-human-animal/, no date.

FOREWORDS

'Foreword' to Georg Breuer, *Sociobiology and the Human Dimension* (Cambridge: Cambridge University Press, 1983), ix–xii.
'Foreword' to Eric Walter Frederick Tomlin, *Psyche, Culture, and the New Science; The Role of PN* (London: Routledge and Kegan Paul, 1985), viii.
'Foreword' to Alex Bentley (ed.), *The Edge of Reason? Science and Religion in Modern Society* (London: Continuum, 2008), xvii–xxiv.
'Foreword' to Iris Murdoch, *The Sovereignty of Good* (London: Routledge, 2014), x–xvi.
'Foreword', to M. O'Brien, *Dialogue and the Discursive Character of the Academic Discipline: Rethinking Widening Participation from the 'Inside-out'* (Liverpool: University of Liverpool, 2008).
'Foreword' to Rebekah Humphreys and Sophie Vlacos (eds.), *Creation, Environment and Ethics* (Newcastle upon Tyne: Cambridge Scholars Publishing, 2010), vii–viii.
'Foreword' to Michael Bavidge, *Mad or Bad?* (Bristol: Bristol Classical Press, 1989).
'Foreword' to Mark Thornton, *Do We Have Free Will?* ((Bristol: Bristol Classical Press, 1989).

UNSOURCED WRITINGS

'What Gaia Means', *The Guardian*, 2001.

SELECTED INTERVIEWS AND PODCASTS

Andrew Brown, 'Mary, Mary, Quite Contrary', *The Guardian*, 13 January 2001.
Horatio Morpugo, 'Books By and An Interview With: Mary Midgley', *Three Monkeys* blog, 1 February 2007, http://www.threemonkeysonline.com/books-by-and-an-interview-with-mary-midgley/.

Sheila Heti, 'Mary Midgley', *Believer*, February 2008, http://www.believermag.com/issues/200802/?read=interview_midgley; a full version of the interview is here http://bysheilaheti.blogspot.co.uk/2010/06/interview-with-mary-midgley.html.

'Discussing Darwin: An Extended Interview With Mary Midgley', *Theos*, 2009, http://www.theosthinktank.co.uk/files/files/Reports/DiscussingDarwin.pdf.

David Cayley, 'How to Think About Science: part 21', November 2009, https://beta.prx.org/stories/41041.

'Meeting Mary Midgley', *Remembering* blog, 27 October 2010, http://pattern-whichconnects.com/blog/meeting-mary-midgley/.

'The Solitary Self', *The Royal Society of Arts*, 21 September 2010, https://www.youtube.com/watch?v=qSFEr2zV5Oo.

Matthew Reisz, 'Mary Midgley: More Than a Sum of Parts', *Times Higher Education*, 3 April 2014.

'Midgley on Philosophy', *Only a Game* blog, 26 October 2010, http://onlyagame.typepad.com/only_a_game/2010/10/midgley-on-philosophy.html.

'Interview: Philosopher Mary Midgley', *The Journal* (Newcastle-on-Tyne), 24 August 2011.

'Does Science Know the Meaning of Life', debate with Peter Atkins, *BBC Radio 4*, 17 March 2011.

Peter Aspden, 'Lunch with the *FT*: Mary Midgley', *Financial Times*, 4 April 2014.

Andrew Anthony, 'Mary Midgley: A Late Stand for a Philosopher With a Soul', *The Guardian*, 23 March 2014, http://www.theguardian.com/books/2014/mar/23/mary-midgley-philosopher-soul-human-consciousness.

'Understanding the Self: Mary Midgley, Jonathan Rée, Raymond Tallis', *Philosophy@LSE*, 28 February 2014.

Tom Wakeford, 'Podcast 3: Gaia—Thinking About the Whole', *Centre for Agroecology, Water and Resilience*, 2014, http://coventryuniversity.podbean.com/e/podcast-3-gaia-thinking-about-the-whole/.

Tom Wakeford, 'Podcast 2: Selfish Genes and Other Myths', *Centre for Agroecology, Water and Resilience*, 2014, http://coventryuniversity.podbean.com/e/podcast-2-selfish-genes-and-other-myths/.

Tom Wakeford, 'Podcast 1: Science and the Imagination', *Centre for Agroecology, Water and Resilience*, 2014, http://coventryuniversity.podbean.com/e/podcast-1-science-and-the-imagination/.

Timandra Harkness, 'Blaspheming Against the Prophets of Scientism', *Spiked Online Review of Books*, 16 May 2014, http://www.spiked-online.com/review_of_books/article/blaspheming-against-the-prophets-of-scientism/14990#.VMunDaFFDGI.

David Cayley, *How to Think About Science*, CBS, http://www.cbc.ca/ideas/episodes/2009/01/02/how-to-think-about-science-part-1–24-listen/#episode11.

Mary Midgley, 'Are Selves Unreal?', *IAI TV*, http://iai.tv/video/are-selves-unreal.

'Poetic Theories: Can Scientists Learn from Poets?', panel with Ruth Padel, Ken Binmore, and Mary Midgley, *IAI TV*, http://iai.tv/video/poetic-theories.

'The Solitary Self—Darwin and the Selfish Gene', *IAI TV*, http://iai.tv/video/the-solitary-self-darwin-and-the-selfish-gene.

'Philosophy Bites Back: Has Physics Made Philosophy Obsolete?', panel discussion with Lawrence Krauss, Mary Midgley, and Angie Hobbs, *IAI TV*, http://iai.tv/video/philosophy-bites-back.

Contributors

Ian James Kidd is an Addison Wheeler Fellow in Philosophy at the University of Durham. His work ranges over epistemology, philosophy of medicine, philosophy of religion, and philosophy of science and includes a number of papers on the cognitive and cultural authority of science, intellectual virtues, and the nature of a religious life.

Liz McKinnell is a Teaching Fellow in Philosophy at the University of Durham. She works on areas in applied ethics and political philosophy, including environmental ethics, the moral status of animals and intergenerational justice. She has published on moral obligations to the dead and on connections between environmental ethics and the philosophy of cognition and biology.

Andrew Brown is the editor of the Belief section of *The Guardian's* 'Comment is Free' website and was formerly religious affairs correspondent for *The Independent*. He is particularly interested in the relationship between religion and science. His book *The Darwin Wars: The Scientific Battle for the Soul of Man* (2000) explores the relevance of evolutionary theory to culture and belief.

Stephen R.L. Clark is Emeritus Professor of Philosophy at the University of Liverpool. His work includes a number of influential books on animal ethics, including *The Moral Status of Animals* (1977), *Animals and their Moral Standing* (1997) and *Biology and Christian Ethics* (2000).

Simon Conway Morris is Professor of Evolutionary Palaeobiology in the Department of Earth Sciences at Cambridge. Morris is extremely active in promoting the public understanding of science and delivered the *Royal Institution Christmas Lectures* in 2006. A practicing Christian, Morris is involved in the public debate about the apparent 'conflict' between science and religion and makes the case that a worldview informed by modern science does not commit us to a vision of a Godless universe.

David E. Cooper is Emeritus Professor of Philosophy at the University of Durham. His many distinguished publications include a number of works on environmental philosophy and animal ethics. Recent publications include *The Measure of Things* (2002), *Meaning* (2003), *A Philosophy of Gardens* (2006) and *Convergence with Nature: A Daoist Perspective* (2012).

Ian Ground is Teaching Fellow in Fine Art at Newcastle University and is Secretary of the British Wittgenstein Society. His research interests include aesthetics, animal minds, philosophy of education, and the life and thought of Ludwig Wittgenstein. His books include *Art or Bunk?* (1991), *Can We Understand Animal Minds* (1994), and *Portraits of Wittgenstein* (2015).

Jane Heal is Emeritus Professor of Philosophy at the University of Cambridge and a Fellow of St John's College. She has written on Quine and Wittgenstein (*Fact and Meaning*, 1989) and a collection of her essays on philosophy of mind, *Mind, Reason and Imagination*, was published in 2003.

Benjamin Lipscomb is Professor of Philosophy at Houghton College. He specialises in ethics and the history of modern philosophy. He has edited a collection on Kant and has published articles on Kantian ethics, early modern natural law theories, and the American agrarian tradition.

Gregory S. McElwain is Assistant Professor of Philosophy and Religious Studies at The College of Idaho. His research interests include environmental philosophy, religion and animal ethics. He is especially concerned with Midgley's thought and conceptions of environmental ethics in relation to human nature.

Rupert Sheldrake is a biologist and author of more than 80 papers in scientific journals. His work explores plant development, animal behaviour, perception and cognition, and his books include *A New Science of Life* (1981), *Seven Experiments That Could Change the World* (1995), *Dogs That Know When Their Owners Are Coming Home* (1999) and *The Science Delusion* (2012).

Raymond Tallis trained as a doctor, and combines scientific insights with work in philosophy, poetry, and cultural criticism. His many books range from novels to works on anthropology, literary criticism and art theory. Recent publications include *Aping Mankind: Neuromania, Darwinitis and the Misrepresentation of Humanity* (2011), The Kingdom of Infinite Space (2008), *Hunger* (2008), and *The Black Mirror: Fragments of an Obituary for Life* (2015).

Baroness Mary Warnock is a moral philosopher and cross-bench peer in the House of Lords. Much of her political and philosophical work has focused on education, existentialism the environment, and biomedical ethics, including *Nature and Mortality* (2004) and *Easeful Death* (2008).

Françoise Wemelsfelder is a biologist and senior animal welfare scientist at Scotland's Rural College in Edinburgh. She leads a research program on the qualitative assessment of animal expressivity, and lectures on topics such as animal emotion and consciousness, with a particular interest in crossing and opening-up disciplinary boundaries.

Index